Concepts in American History

Concepts in American History

History

Robert Asher
University of Connecticut

Concepts in American History by Robert Asher.

Copyright © 1996 HarperCollins College Publishers

HarperCollins® and ▣® are registered trademarks of HarperCollins Publishers Inc.

ISBN: 0-06-501483-9

96 97 98 99 9 8 7 6 5 4 3 2 1

For Carol

Contents

Preface

Acknowledgments

Preface

I have written this book because I believe students are interested in analyzing the historical evolution of important concepts. I have selected concepts that I think are central to an understanding of the history of the United States. Each concept is discussed for a time span of approximately four hundred years, from the time of the first sustained European contacts with the peoples of the North American continent to the present.

To facilitate the student's understanding of each concept, I have often cited primary sources that indicate how men and women of the past thought about concepts. I have paid particular attention to the texts of the Declaration of Independence and the Constitution of the United States of America.

Concepts exist only in the minds of human beings. As a species, *homo sapiens'* most important difference from other animals is the ability to understand concepts (abstractions). Humans often use concepts to guide or justify their actions. Of course, concepts are never static. Concepts change, although they rarely are totally transformed. Five hundred years ago, hardly anyone in the world believed in democracy and capitalism existed in only a few places. The only thing we can predict with certainty about the future is that the basic concepts people have about government, social groups, and economic institutions will change. Analyzing the character of these changes will keep future generations of historians busy, and hopefully, fully employed.

Acknowledgments

I would like to thank my partner, Carol June Williams, who supported this project from its inception, critiqued every chapter, and stressed the importance of encouraging readers, whenever possible, to think about key concepts in the context of their own lives. Sam Arenson offered sagacious and inspirational reactions to several chapters. Tanya Arenson's expertise refined the discussion of race and genetics. Stephen Merlino's thoughtful reactions to the entire manuscript led to many additions to the narrative. Jessica Bayne's deft editorial queries and skillful prose editing greatly improved the book. Jonathan Michaels made innumerable suggestions that improved the quality of the narrative. Paul Steinberg's knowledge of natural resource science saved me from several errors. R. Kent Newmyer's views about the centrality of the concept of constitutionalism in American history influenced me greatly. Carmen Cid's encouragement and candid reactions to the manuscript greatly improved its structure. Allen Ward tried to save me from oversimplifying Greek and Roman history. Ann Higginbotham corrected my misinterpretations of English history. Amy Kesselman's advice greatly improved the chapter on women's rights. Wendy St. Jean's critiques were helpful, as were the materials she (and Michael Robinson) provided on Native-American history. Rebecca Mlynarczyk and Kevin Boyle offered suggestions that helped me refine the argument of several chapters. Jasper Williams gave the manuscript his sanction. Robert Engstrom eliminated one redundant President from the narrative. Bruce Borland's faith in the project was essential. The author is solely responsible for all interpretations and any errors of fact in this book.

CHAPTER 1

Liberty and Civil Liberties

I

Liberty is freedom. The Latin word for liberty, *liber*, means free. It comes from the same source as the Greek word for free, which was used to describe the condition of people who were free people *rather than being slaves.* It is no accident that liberty was defined as the opposite of slavery. Slavery was, in theory, a complete deprivation of freedom, since slaves were subject to the authority of their masters and mistresses for twenty-four hours a day and had no right to choose the type of work they would perform, their hours of sleep, or even the persons they would marry. In ancient Greece, many people began their lives as slaves, while large numbers of free people became slaves when they were captured in battle or when their city-states were conquered by the military forces of Persia or other Greek city-states.

Virtually all the people who read this essay will be free people—free people who may take for granted the freedom they enjoy. Yet Abraham Lincoln did not make any such assumption. In 1863, in the Gettysburg Address, the most important and eloquent speech in the history of the United States, Lincoln described the way our forebearers

> brought forth on this continent, a new nation, conceived in Liberty and dedicated to the proposition that all men are created equal.

1

Lincoln indicated that the aim of the Union side in the Civil War was to preserve such a nation, and keep intact the liberty and equality its people enjoyed. He believed the expected victory of the Union forces would produce major benefits for the country and predicted

> that this nation, under God, shall have a *new birth of freedom*, and that government of the people, by the people and for the people shall not perish from the earth. [emphasis added]

Lincoln assumed that the Union victory would guarantee the death of slavery. Lincoln was convinced that the end of slavery was *essential* to the maintenance of liberty and democracy in the United States. He could not imagine that freedom could exist securely in a society in which free men and women had to compete for work with unfree people—slaves.

As a concept, liberty is closely linked to the concept of *equality* of rights, both natural and constitutional. (see Chapter 4) Note the way Lincoln mentioned both liberty and equality in the first sentence of the Gettysburg Address. Historically, elites who wanted to challenge the power of monarchies asserted the right to different types of liberty and other rights, contending that there were God-given basic rights and liberties that *past* kings and queens had given to *all* subjects. In practice, elites sought to guarantee only their own liberties. Eventually, non-elites used the ideas and rhetoric developed by elites to demand a truly equal distribution of the liberties that elites had claimed were due to all free citizens.

From the time of the earliest settlements, the English who came to the Atlantic colonies emphasized that they were *free*born *English* people who were entitled to "have and enjoy all liberties and Immunities of free and naturall Subjects." What were the liberties allegedly available to all individuals in England? To understand the meaning of rights and liberties to the English colonists, we will need to begin with an overview of English history between 1215 and 1689.

Englishmen believed in the right to a trial by a jury of one's peers. A person accused of a crime was only protected against the possible tyranny of a judge, sheriff, mayor, or monarch if he was guaranteed a jury trial. A closely related liberty was the freedom from being charged twice for the same crime (double jeopardy). These rights had first been given to nobles in the Magna Carta of 1215. After 1215, Parliamentary laws and the common law of England broadened these rights to apply to *all* freemen.* (Of course, people too poor to hire a lawyer could not take advantage of their rights.)

Another right that preserved the freedom of arrested persons was the right to be *charged* with a *specific* crime. To protect this right, lawyers for an arrested person could go to court where they were entitled to a writ of *habeas corpus*, which required that the person be brought to court and charged with a crime, or released. Without this right, a monarch or judge could arrest economic or political rivals and keep them in jail indefinitely.

One of the most important liberties claimed by the English settlers in North America was the right to government by *consent of the governed*. In 1215, this liberty was first granted, *on a very limited basis,* to the richest men in England. Threatening to make war on King John I, the nobles forced him to accept the Magna Carta, which included a clause specifying that non-feudal taxation† had to have the *consent of the governed*, as expressed through a council of the wealthiest landowners (including bishops and abbots) of England. This right was reaffirmed in 1297, when protesting nobles held a parliament (assembly) that forced King Edward I to issue a charter that stated that except for

---

*The reader will note that key phrases from the Declaration of Independence and other statements on liberty refer to the rights and conditions of *men*. While women did enjoy many of the basic civil liberties discussed here, they did not have the right to vote. Since almost all the writers on the theory of rights and liberties were men reared in patriarchal cultures, they generally referred to free adult citizens as freemen.

† The Magna Carta allowed the English monarch to levy feudal taxes on the nobles who were the feudal vassals of the monarch. These vassals were nobles to whom the monarch had given the right to rule and farm royal lands in return for their promise to provide the monarch (their feudal lord) with military forces and to pay a variety of feudal taxes. Most of these feudal taxes were abolished in 1660.

"ancient aids and prises [taxes] due and accustomed," the monarch would not levy any taxes "except by the common assent of the whole kingdom." Thereafter, the elites of English society would assume that their Parliament was the legislative body that would have to consent to taxation on behalf of the whole kingdom.

By 1600, the English Parliament had changed considerably. Two houses of Parliament had developed. The House of Lords was composed of nobles who were hereditary peers and bishops of the Church of England. An elected house of Parliament—the House of Commons—was chosen by about 20 percent of adult English men, most of whom who were moderate or substantial property owners. By 1600, many members of Parliament, especially members of the House of Commons, believed that since the kings and queens who reigned after 1297 had not violated the 1297 charter, a *tradition* had been established that required a monarch to secure the consent of Parliament—the House of Commons *and* the House of Lords—to *any* taxes to be collected by the monarch.

The English referred to the right to consent to taxation as a *liberty*. Why? They believed that *without such a right, no man could be at liberty*, i.e., free. To the English settlers in North America and to the people of England, taxation was not just a device used by government to raise revenue; *taxation was seen as an action that took some of their property*, either in the form of animals, animal products, crops, or money. When a government taxed the public it was acting to "take away by *force* and *power* the properties" [emphasis added] of the taxed. Thus if property was to be taken from a person by government, the settlers believed that the taking had to be authorized by the *consent* of a body chosen by the subjects of the government. English and colonial freemen recognized the need for government, but they feared government officials might spend money on activities that the freemen did not want—war, luxurious buildings, or land speculation. Freemen believed that their freedom would be lost if their property could be taken without the consent of a legislative governing body elected by free property owners. Without property, a freeman would lose his freedom and become economically *dependent* on others. Such dependency was seen as a step on the road to slavery, the direct opposite of freedom.

In the ancient Roman Empire, the Caesars claimed that *their* integrity and power guaranteed the liberties of the average citizen against abuses by judges, the Roman Senate, and rich citizens. Unlike the Romans, the English colonists thought that *all government officials were potential tyrants* who might assault the liberties of freemen. The first generation of English North American colonists had watched many members of Parliament charge that King Charles had violated the English constitution in the late 1620s by *demanding* repeated loans* of unprecedented amounts from his rich subjects. Charles I jailed and denied the right of *habeas corpus* to prominent men who challenged the forced loans, claiming that the loans were non-feudal taxes requiring the consent of Parliament. Many Englishmen and colonists were alarmed by Charles I's manipulation of the English courts to prevent these tax resisters from gaining their freedom. (In 1627, Charles also ordered his judges to refuse to rule on challenges to the legality of the forced loans.)

On several occasions between 1626 and 1642, when Charles I was angered by the actions and criticisms of members of the House of Lords and the House of Commons, he had particular critics, including Lords, arrested. Parliamentary protests often led Charles I to exercise the monarch's customary right to dismiss Parliament, for both short and long periods. In 1629 Charles suspended Parliament when it would not authorize the taxes he wanted. Charles did not allow Parliament to meet again until

---

*By English custom, when a king or queen began their reign, Parliament granted the monarch the right to collect taxes (tonnage and poundage) on imports for the rest of their lives. Because the House of Commons in 1626 was uneasy about Charles I's marriage to a Catholic French woman and was suspicious of his desire to go to war with Spain, it voted to approve the King's collection of tonnage and poundage for only one year. The House of Lords wanted to give the King lifetime authority to collect these. With Parliament stalemated, Charles decided to resort to forced loans to raise money.

1640. Members of Parliament were uneasy over the frequency with which Charles I exercised this traditional right and claimed that he did not or should not have the right to interfere with the meeting of Parliament.

Running out of money in 1637, Charles I tried to turn a traditional right of the monarch—to collect "ship money" from the residents of port cities *during emergencies*, money that would be used to finance the British navy's protection of merchant ships on the high seas—into a broad-based, annual tax. Attempting to triple the funds raised from such collections, Charles ordered *inland* cities to provide "ship money." As Charles continued to collect "ship money" each year, resistance mounted, as many affluent Englishmen claimed the "ship money" was a tax requiring Parliament's approval. By 1640 hardly any "ship money" was coming in.

Most Protestants in England were alarmed by the religious policies of William Laud, whom King Charles had appointed Archbishop of Canterbury (1633), the chief officer of the government church, the Church of England (also known as the Anglican Church). Archbishop Laud's theological ideas— especially his belief in the importance of many sacraments— appeared to many Protestants to be much closer to Catholicism than to Protestantism. Laud attempted to limit preaching by Protestant ministers to one sermon a week. He arrested and cut off the ears of preachers who were not ordained and of non-Anglican Protestants who published pamphlets on religious subjects. Although largely ineffective, Laud's attempts to force all Protestants in England and Scotland to adopt Anglican prayers and ceremonies alarmed many Protestants, who concluded that the archbishop was plotting to establish the authority of the Pope (the head of the Catholic Church) over the Church of England. Militant Protestants (in England and on the European continent) believed that the Catholic Church represented the work of the Antichrist, the Devil. (Catholics held similar views of Protestants.) In the mid-1630s, militant Protestants were outraged when Charles I, influenced by his Catholic wife, allowed agents of the Pope to attend the King's court and to convert noblemen and noblewomen to Catholicism. Many Protestants—especially Calvinists—were alarmed by the King's assault on their religious liberties, which had generally been respected by Queen Elizabeth I and King James I, Charles I's predecessors. (Elizabeth and James had been much less tolerant of Catholics, barring them from holding public religious services.) Many Protestant Englishmen concluded that only Parliament, not the monarchy, was capable of protecting the religious and economic liberties of Protestants.

Between 1640 and 1642, the English government was challenged on two fronts: Scottish troops, enraged by Charles's insistence that Presbyterian Scots use an Anglican prayer book for their religious services, invaded northern England; and Irish Catholics launched a military rebellion to free Ireland from English rule. Parliament and King Charles strongly disagreed over the way to deal with these threats. These disagreements were intensified by bitter memories of past disputes over Parliamentary authority and by the continued fear of many English Protestants that the Pope and Catholics in England were plotting to seize power. Unwilling to offer a compromise over Parliamentary authority acceptable to a majority of the House of Commons and many members of the House of Lords, King Charles dissolved Parliament in 1642 and tried to rule without any legislative consent. Civil war began. By 1649, the Parliamentary armies led by the devout Puritan, Oliver Cromwell, defeated and executed Charles I. Cromwell's rule reflected the domination of the Puritan religious sects, who banned the practice of Catholicism and made the Anglican Church illegal.

In the 1640s and 1650s, as different groups struggled for power in England, some English farmers, generally small landowners, who called themselves Levellers, demanded that liberties, including free religious worship (for Protestants, not Catholics), equality before the law, and government by consent, *actually be given to all free Englishmen*. They claimed that " 'tis the first principle of a people's liberty that they shall not be bound but by their own consent." By this the Levellers meant that they should be given the right to vote.

Fed up with the Puritan dictatorship, opposition groups restored the English monarchy in 1660, placing King Charles II on the throne. During its struggles with Charles I in 1641 and 1642, Parliament had passed bills that strengthened its civil liberties and powers by prohibiting the monarch from dismissing Parliament, by requiring calling a Parliament every three years, and by strengthening the right of *habeas corpus*. Under English custom, unless the monarch assented (by affixing the royal seal) to bills passed by Parliament, they were not laws. Charles I had refused to assent to these bills. But when his son, Charles II, was placed on the throne he assented to these laws, reaffirmed the exclusive right of Parliament to levy taxes, and agreed that the monarch did not have authority to legislate by issuing proclamations.

In 1679 Charles II violated the law against dismissing Parliament. But he backed down when the predominantly Anglican Parliament challenged his authority to issue *many* special dispensations (exemptions from laws) that would have allowed non-Anglican Protestants and Catholics to worship freely. While Parliament admitted the monarch's power to issue limited numbers of dispensations, it argued that widespread exemptions constituted new legislation, which only Parliament could enact. In 1679, Parliament passed and Charles II signed a new Habeas Corpus Act, which reduced the amount of time between the issuance of a writ of *habeas corpus* and the court hearing that would require the charges against the arrested person to be presented.

The political crisis precipitated by the Catholic James II's accession to the throne in 1685 led to a settlement that included legislation, known as the Bill of Rights (1689), which reaffirmed the right of Parliament to consent before any taxes were levied and prevented the monarch from suspending laws without the consent of Parliament. The Bill of Rights also protected the civil liberties of members of Parliament by stipulating that Parliamentary elections were to be "free," and that "parliament ought to be held frequently." The freedom of speech of *members of Parliament* was to be protected, and debates in Parliament were "not to be impeached or questioned in any court or place out of parliament." These rights strengthened the power of Parliament, making it impossible to arrest members of Parliament for speaking their minds. The Bill of Rights extended only one right to *all* people: "the right of the subjects to petition the king."

For members of Parliament, freedom of speech meant that they could not be imprisoned for their speeches and votes. Historically, a civil liberty or civil right helped people preserve their condition as *free* persons, avoiding jail or enslavement. Without such guarantees of freedom for its members, the power of Parliament or any legislature to consent or not to consent to taxation or other legislation proposed by the monarch would have been weakened. Clearly, the threat of being deprived of their freedom for expressing views contrary to those of monarchs (or non-hereditary executives) would make legislators reluctant to refuse to consent to policies proposed by the executive.

One of the main points of contention during the English Civil War and the next forty years of political turmoil in England was the right of different Protestant denominations and Catholics to worship freely. The settlement reached in 1689 recognized the diversity of religious beliefs in England, but did not provide religious liberty to all; and it limited the political rights of people who were not members of the *established* Anglican Church, whose doctrine had been altered to remove the most extreme practices that Archbishop Laud had introduced in the years before 1642. An established church is one that is, by government order, supported by taxation on all adults. Thus all adults in England and Scotland, including those who were not members of the Church of England, *had to pay church taxes to support only the Church of England*. All people who were not members of the Church of England also had to pay *penalties* for not attending Anglican services. Members of the other Protestant denominations—Congregationalists, Presbyterians, Baptists, and Methodists—were allowed to worship freely, but were initially barred from holding government office. Catholics were technically not allowed to worship according to their conscience, but were given this liberty in practice. Until 1829, Catholics were barred from voting and were ineligible to run for election to Parliament.

II

In the English North American colonies, the early settlers found themselves far removed from England and the authority of King and Parliament. Most of the early colonies had received some type of charter from the King. The royal charters generally allowed the colonists to use their judgment in establishing most of the structures of their own governments, and the colonists, drawing on their heritage as Englishmen, did just that. They wrote covenants (agreements witnessed by God) and compacts (agreements witnessed by the signers) by which they agreed to join particular communities. These agreements, entered into by means of *voluntary consent*, established the rules of government for the communities they formed. Many covenants and compacts asserted the *rights* of the settlers as *freeborn Englishmen*. Thus the Pilgrims approved the Plymouth Agreement (1630), which asserted that "as freeborn subjects of the state of England we hither came endowed with all and singular the privileges belonging to such being assembled." Moreover, the Plymouth Agreement claimed that no

> act[,] imposition [,] law [,] or ordinance be made or imposed upon us
> at present, or come but such as shall be imposed by Consent of the
> body of associates or their representatives legally assembled,
> according to the *free liberties of England.* [emphasis added].

Similar claims were made in the Virginia Charter (1606), and the charters of the Massachusetts Bay Colony (1629), Maryland (1632), Maine (1639), Connecticut (1662), Rhode Island (1663), and Carolina (1663) (see Chapter 3).

The key principle underlying the authority of the governments established by the colonies was that rules and laws were based on the consent of some body of citizens. When towns governed by town meetings joined with other towns to form *colonial* governments, legislatures were established to pass laws. And because the principle *of government by consent of the governed* was carried over to the creation of the legislatures, at least one house of the legislature was *elected*. (When the colonial legislatures had only one house, it was elected.)

As time passed, the elected members of the colonial legislatures came to think of themselves as colonial Parliaments. Logically, the colonial legislators applied the traditions of the English constitution to their colonial political systems. The most important right claimed by colonial legislatures was the right to *consent to the enactment of taxes*, a right the English Parliament also claimed. The colonial legislatures asserted that like the monarch of England, a colonial governor, whether elected or appointed by the English monarch, *could not raise taxes without legislative approval*. Of course, by exercising the power of the purse, legislatures could deny governors their salaries, since the English government had decided that royal governors would not be paid by the English monarchy but by the colonies to which they had been sent by the monarch.

During the first half century of settlement, the English colonists gained a great deal of experience with government by consent of an elected legislature. When Charles II came to the throne in 1660, he attempted to void many of the colonial charters. In New England, Charles tried to impose a new government, a confederation ruled by Sir Edmund Andros, who did not think much of the rights of legislatures. The settlement of the English Civil War in 1688 and 1689, which brought a new hereditary line of monarchs to England and which guaranteed the legislative supremacy of Parliament, reassured the colonists that their elected legislatures would be preserved.

Between 1689 and 1763, educated colonists reflected on the meaning of the threats to the liberties of Parliament and English taxpayers that had occurred from 1626 to the settlement of 1688–

1689. They read the writings of English political theorists who supported the settlement, men like Algernon Sidney, John Locke, and William Blackstone. At the core of the colonists' theories about government and liberties after 1689 was Locke's concept of *natural rights*. Colonial natural rights theorists began with the assumption that men without any government were living in a *state of nature*, in which the natural liberties (rights) they enjoyed were given to them *by God*. The reference to God's will was important. By claiming that God had given basic, natural rights to people, the colonists could argue that it was *contrary to the will of God to deprive anyone of their natural rights*. Not even a monarch, who was acknowledged to be God's lieutenant on earth, could legitimately deprive people of liberties granted to them by God. Colonial political thinkers claimed that in a state of nature, all *equally enjoyed the basic rights* (liberties) that God had given them. As Theophilus Parsons, a Massachusetts lawyer put it, God "at our births, disperses his favors, not only with a liberal, but with an equal hand."

Colonial political theorists argued that people often decided that they *needed to form a government* to advance their overall interests and to protect the natural liberties of members of a community. This decision was to be one that involved the *free consent* of the people deciding to be subject to the rule of a government. Like John Locke, the colonists believed that because government helped protect people's liberties, people were *freer in a civil state*, where they enjoyed civil liberties, than they were in a state of nature. They also believed that it was wrong for any body of people to consent to laws that violated their natural liberties or rights.

Natural rights theory maintained that when people went from a state of nature to a civil society, they *did not give up certain natural rights*. These were *unalienable* natural rights. As Thomas Jefferson wrote in the Declaration of Independence, men were

> endowed by their Creator with certain unalienable rights; that among these rights are life, liberty, and the pursuit of happiness; that, to secure these rights, governments are instituted among men, deriving their just powers from the consent of the governed.

No government could take those rights away without fair procedures, which were called *due process*. A jury trial was necessary to decide if persons accused of a crime were guilty. The right to earn a living and enjoy the property acquired in that pursuit could not be infringed upon without the *consent* of the governed. (As Chapter 2 explains, the colonists who were property holders believed that men who did not own property should not be allowed to vote, which deprived them of the right to consent to being governed.)

However, during the first century of settlement, most English colonists in North America did not believe in a natural right to freedom of religious worship. Many colonists were persecuted for their religious convictions. Protestants frequently persecuted Catholics, and at times persecuted other Protestants. Thus the Puritans who controlled the Massachusetts colony punished Anne Hutchinson and Roger Williams, who had developed very different interpretations of the Bible from the Puritans.

By the time of the American Revolution, religious freedom had developed *more broadly in the colonies than it had in England*, largely because the power of the English Anglican Church was remote—an ocean away. The Anglican Church became the established church in five southern colonies and four counties of New York, but with the exception of South Carolina, it never attracted a large membership and often lacked the power to tax non-Anglicans directly. While the Congregationalist church was the established church in Massachusetts and Connecticut, Quakers and Baptists in Massachusetts used their connections in Parliament to force the Massachusetts legislature (in the 1730s) to exempt them from the taxes that supported the Congregational Church. There were many different religious denominations—Congregationalists, Presbyterians, Baptists, Methodists, and Quakers—in the colonies. After 1688, *no colony had limited the right to vote to members of any particular Protestant church*. (Maryland denied Catholics, about one-fourth of the population, the right to vote.) Because the members of nonestablished Protestant denominations could vote, they often pressured legislatures to exempt them and members of other

Protestant denominations from paying taxes to support the established church.

The members of the nonestablished denominations protested bitterly against being taxed to support an established church. They feared that if a government, even an elected one, could decide which denominations to tax, it could also, at some point, refuse to tolerate the very existence of any denomination besides the established, government-financed church. Moreover, the tolerated but taxed denominations pointed out that "religious liberty is so blended with civil [liberty] that if one falls it is not to be expected that the other will continue." That was the general way many people in the newly created United States thought about their natural rights and liberties: an assault that weakened one right would create a dangerous precedent that might encourage government officials to restrict other rights.

After 1763, Parliament and King George III agreed that for the first time since the founding of the colonies, direct taxes should be levied on the North American colonies. Many colonists protested that the taxes were illegal. The colonists elected no members of the House of Commons, and no one living in the colonies was a peer in the House of Lords. The colonists argued that Parliament had no right to tax them, since *an unrepresented people could obviously not give their consent* to taxation. They believed that as subjects of England they were entitled to the basic liberties of Englishmen, including the right to consent to taxation.

In 1759, the Anglican Church began to pressure Parliament to authorize the Church to create an American bishop and to collect taxes in all the colonies to support the Church. The colonists protested bitterly that their liberties were being threatened. They were concerned that a more powerful established church would interfere with the power of non-Anglican established churches in the colonies and with the basic freedom of worship of nonestablished churches in each colony. Moreover, the colonists saw in the English plan a threat to their right to *consent* to taxation. *Establishing the Anglican Church would require Parliamentary authorization of taxation to finance the Church*, and since the colonists were not represented in Parliament, they objected.

About a third of the colonists actively protested British policies. Their resistance to the authority of Parliament led that body to suspend most of the elected government of Massachusetts in 1774, replacing elected officials with royal appointees. Large numbers of British troops were dispatched to the colonies. Fearing for their liberties, those colonists who were strongly anti-British declared their independence. These colonists believed that British policies did not give them the truly "equal degree of freedom" that they thought all men should enjoy. The colonists also claimed that King George III and Parliament had broken an assumed agreement to give all colonial subjects equal rights to their British counterparts. The Declaration of Independence (1776) claimed that the King of England was planning to establish an "absolute despotism" over the colonists. It was the duty of the colonists to "throw off such government." Having declared independence from England, the pro-independence forces believed that the former colonies were *in a state of nature*. The Declaration of Independence asserted the right "to provide new guards for" the public's "future security." Voters in the new United States of America chose to form new state governments and a national government that were not subject to the authority of the English King or Parliament.

The colonists who favored independence would insist that the new governments they formed to take them out of a state of nature be based on the consent of the governed. Hence their reliance on elected legislatures or constitutional conventions to draft new constitutions and their insistence that the new constitutions be *ratified by special elections of the voters*, a process by which the voters *consented* to be governed under the rules written down in the constitutions (see Chapter 3).

III

By the time the United States Constitution was written (1787), most people in the United States had concluded that legislative power, like executive power, had to be prevented from infringing on the basic liberties of citizens. The state constitutions included clauses limiting legislative and executive powers (and sometimes contained separate bills of rights). Following its ratification, the U. S. Constitution would be quickly expanded by the ratification of ten amendments, often called the Bill of Rights (1791). But even without those amendments, it is clear that the Constitution guaranteed one of the most important natural rights valued by Americans: the right to government by consent of the governed.*
It did so by specifying that the House of Representatives was to be elected, that the President was to be chosen by *elected* electors chosen (either by state legislatures or directly by the voters), and that the Senate was to be chosen by state legislatures. Everyone knew that the state legislatures *were elected*, and were likely to remain so, since all the states had adopted constitutions specifying that their legislatures were to be based on the sovereignty of the voters, and would be chosen only by consent of the voters.

But Americans were faced with a dilemma: they agreed they needed government to protect their liberties, yet they feared that if government, especially the national government, were too strong (See Chapter 5), it could trample on the liberties of freemen. Thus, the overwhelming majority of Americans eligible to vote (about two-thirds of the adult, white males) insisted on more guarantees of the "natural rights and liberties of the people" than the Constitution had provided. Speedily ratified by 1791, the Bill of Rights spoke to the desire of most voters to limit

---

*To be more precise, we should say that sovereignty rested on the consent of the voters. The United States did not become a true democracy until 1975, by which time the 1965 Voting Rights Act had enabled African Americans living in the south to register and vote freely. Between 1920, when all women were enfranchised, and 1975, the government of the United States rested on the consent of most, but not all, of the governed adults.

specifically *government* power, and especially the power of the national government. The ten amendments in the Bill of Rights offered all *free* citizens of the nation more protection of their basic liberties than existed anywhere else in the world.

The First Amendment barred Congress and only Congress from passing any "law respecting an establishment of religion." This meant that Congress could not designate any church as an official, established church that would have been supported by taxes levied on all religious groups. Yet several state governments still supported established churches. The First Amendment allowed this kind of inequality to continue because it would not have been ratified if it had drastically altered existing conditions. It is clear that in 1789 the members of established churches had no objection to forcing others to pay taxes to support a particular established church. What the members of the *different* established churches in particular states feared was national legislation that would make a denomination other than theirs the official established church of the entire country. Those who believed that state governments should not limit religious liberty in any way, including allowing established churches, succeeded by 1833 in amending all state constitutions to eliminate all government-financed churches.

The First Amendment also appeared to guarantee freedom of speech and freedom of the press against Congressional action, and especially against censorship before people spoke or published their views. Unlike the English Bill of Rights, *these freedoms protected by the First Amendment were not limited to members of the legislature.* They applied, equally, to everyone. Yet hardly anyone believed such liberties were absolute. Why? Because there was one exception that a government based on the consent of the governed would not tolerate: advocacy of the overthrow of the government itself.

During the administrations of John Adams (1797–1801) and Thomas Jefferson (1801–1809), Federalists and Democratic Republicans were bitterly critical of each others' policies. Democratic Republicans feared that Federalists wanted to establish a monarchy in the United States or ally the United

States with England, a country that still had a powerful monarchy. Federalists feared that Democratic Republicans wanted to ally the nation with France and bring the class warfare and property redistribution of the French Revolution to the United States. With both sides believing they were engaged in a high-stakes struggle over the basic values of government structure and the sanctity of the rights of property, neither side was very tolerant of criticisms made in the newspapers of their opponents. Hence Adams and Jefferson each had their attorneys general bring sedition charges against opposition newspaper editors. (Sedition is speech or writing that is believed to stir up opposition against an established government. Treason involves actual planning and acting to overthrow a government by the use of force.)

By 1820, sedition prosecutions of newspaper editors had ceased. A national *consensus* had emerged that the United States should be a *democratic republic* and that government should not radically redistribute wealth from the affluent to the poorer groups in society (see Chapters 2 and 4). Hence partisan political criticism of the national government was not seen as threatening the very *form* of that government. During World War I, Congress passed sedition laws barring publication of materials that contained criticism of the war and the military draft. Civil libertarians maintained that the sedition laws violated the First Amendment, but the majority of the Supreme Court allowed *wartime* sedition prosecutions.

The Fourth Amendment was a direct reflection of the experience of the colonists with the British crackdown on the colonies in 1774 and thereafter. Unlike the First Amendment, the Fourth Amendment applied to both the national government and all the state governments. It said that

The right of the people to be secure in their houses, papers, and effects, against unreasonable searches and seizures shall not be violated.

The Fourth Amendment dealt with the question of being literally at liberty. It also banned arrest warrants unless they specified the person to be arrested and the probable cause for the arrest.

The Sixth Amendment required speedy and public jury trials when a government charged a person with a crime. The Sixth Amendment also guaranteed the right of *habeas corpus* to arrested persons. It gave the accused a right to cross-examine the witnesses who testified that he or she had committed a crime. It also allowed the accused to get a court order (a subpoena) to require testimony of the witnesses who, according to the accused, could provide evidence to refute the charges against him or her. The Sixth Amendment also guaranteed the right of the accused to be represented by a lawyer. The Eighth Amendment added a ban on excessive bail. The Seventh Amendment guaranteed a jury trial to a person sued in a civil suit, an action taken by a person who was not a government official who charged another private person with harmful actions that caused financial or psychological damage.

During periods of social crisis, the federal and state courts often looked the other way when the Fourth Amendment rights of alleged radicals, and especially immigrant radicals, were being violated. During the rebellion of debt-ridden farmers in Massachusetts in 1786 (Shays's Rebellion), the state government suspended the writ of *habeas corpus*. President Abraham Lincoln did the same during the Civil War, since he believed there were numerous Confederate sympathizers living in the nonseceding states. In 1919 and early 1920, U.S. Justice Department agents and local police cooperated in the unconstitutional arrest of thousands of foreign-born blue-collar workers. Fourth Amendment requirements for specific warrants were ignored. Why did this happen? A wave of socialist revolutions in Europe had created a panic in the United States. Many public officials feared that radicalism was being carried to the United States by immigrant agitators. In reality, there were hardly any violent revolutionaries, native or foreign-born, in the country.

The Fifth Amendment provided additional protections to persons accused of crimes. It barred double jeopardy, preventing a government from harassing a person by trying them a second time for an alleged crime, when they had been acquitted in their first trial. A grand jury indictment was required to try a person for a major crime. People charged with a crime could not be forced to testify against themselves. Equally important, the Fifth Amendment required that "due process of law" be used when any branch of government acted to deprive a person of their life, liberty, or property. *Due process* referred to the procedural safeguards of rights that were specified in the first eight amendments to the Constitution. (Lawyers and judges would debate—and still debate—whether or not the Fifth Amendment limited the powers of the state governments.)

Today we take such rights for granted. But at the time the Constitution was written, many of these rights were not available to *ordinary* people. This was especially true in England, where the affluent men elected to Parliament had their rights protected, but then passed laws limiting the freedom of speech of common people (including limiting even their right to petition the government) and refused to pass legislation establishing the kinds of protections given by the Fourth, Fifth, Sixth, and Eighth Amendments to secure the liberties of the citizen accused of a crime.

IV

The protections offered in the U. S. Bill of Rights are limitations on the power of *government*. Protections of natural rights applied to constitutional law and criminal prosecutions. These protections (except for the right to a jury trial in civil suits for $20 or more) did not apply to *civil* law, which dealt with the relationships between people who were not acting as government officials. When a nongovernment official, like an employer, denied an employee a natural right, the employee had limited protection from the law, *unless a state or federal law had been passed that provided such protection*. Consequently, throughout most of the nineteenth century, wage earners were often denied their basic civil liberties when they were at work.

Consider the following examples of such denials. Coal miners who complained about broken ventilation fans, which meant that the air they were breathing was low in oxygen content and filled with explosive gasses, were often dismissed for exercising their free speech rights. Likewise, workers who simply joined a union were often fired. Until the 1880s, state courts *assumed* that a worker who had been hired by an employer had agreed to work for a specific time period, not a single day. If a worker left work or was fired before the assumed (or agreed upon) time period was over, the courts denied the worker the right to collect *any* back pay that was owed. State courts almost always accepted an employer's justification for firing a worker, even if the employer *had not given the worker any reason for her or his dismissal at the time the worker was fired*. The courts also looked the other way when an employer goaded a worker into quitting, which enabled the employer to avoid paying the worker's back wages. These judicial biases allowed unscrupulous employers to take a worker's wages without due process of law. Many workers thought that this process, which took money they had already earned, was robbery. Throughout our nation's history, there has been a wide gap between the Constitution's safeguards against *government* denial of an individual's civil liberties and the degree of protection the courts and legislatures have given individuals against the denial of their liberties by other private persons, including business corporations, which had the same legal status as private individuals* (see pp. 79-82).

One group of workers—slaves—were deprived of most of their civil liberties by their owners and were also denied their basic constitutional civil liberties when charged with crimes, since they were not allowed to be tried by juries of their peers

---

* State legislation and court decisions made business corporations legal individuals. This status gave corporations the same legal protections against deprivation of life, liberty, and property that the Constitution gave to individuals.

and were not allowed to bring suit in court against any law enforcement officer who violated their civil rights. But, the reader may ask, didn't the Constitution prohibit the enslavement of individuals, the most drastic denial of liberty short of murder? The answer is "No." Slaves were owned by private individuals. The courts ruled that slaves were to be categorized as private property, not as free humans. Hence the Constitutional guarantees that prevented a free individual from having her or his liberty diminished *by government* through imprisonment or execution did not apply to the relationship between a slaveowner and an owned slave. In fact, the owner of a slave was protected by the Fifth Amendment against any confiscation of his or her slave property without due process of law.

By the 1830s, severe criticisms of slavery were being made in the nonslave states. One important argument was that wherever slavery existed, slaveowners were so afraid of slave rebellions and slave escapes that they pressured legislatures to pass laws restricting the free speech of critics of slavery. Another concern that became especially intense during the 1850s was that slaveowners wanted to bring slavery to states that had been legally designated as nonslave, or free states by the Northwest Ordinance (1787), the Missouri Compromise (1820), and the Compromise of 1850. White *farmers*, as well as workers in industry and commerce, used the term *free* labor to describe themselves. They feared having to compete with unfree, slave labor. Why? Because slave laborers were usually forced to work for lower rewards than were rural and urban free laborers. Competition with farmers who used slave labor would undercut the earnings of farmers who were free persons and employed free labor on their farms. Competition with slave labor also *lowered the wages employers were willing to pay to free laborers, both rural and urban*. Moreover, free whites believed that their social status was degraded by having to work with and compete with people of color.

In 1858, in *Dred Scott* v. *Sanford*, the Supreme Court held that the Constitution had not made slaves citizens of the United States. Therefore, slaves did not have the civil liberties accorded to citizens. The Court ruled that the Constitution defined slaves as property, and that a slaveholder could take his slaves into any state—even a free state whose constitution banned slavery—without fear of having his slave property confiscated. The Dred Scott decision thus invalidated two previous political compromises between the slave states and the free states—the Missouri Compromise (1820) and the Compromise of 1850—which had more or less evenly divided the western territories (and the states formed from them) into areas that would allow slavery and areas that would prohibit slavery. The Dred Scott decision meant that it was legal for slaveowners to bring slaves into any state in the country and use the labor of their slaves to compete with the labor of free women and men.

This controversial decision stimulated the rapid growth of the Republican Party, which captured the presidency with a demand to ban slavery in *all* the territories. When Abraham Lincoln took office, most of the slave states left the union, and the Civil War began. When the Civil War ended in 1865 with a Union victory that forced the seceding states to rejoin the United States, Congress attempted to prevent the reappearance of slavery and possible secessionist movements by passing three Constitutional Amendments that expanded the rights and liberties of African Americans. The Thirteenth Amendment abolished slavery. The Fourteenth Amendment was intended to guarantee the rights and liberties of the former slaves. It did this by barring *state* governments from taking life, liberty, and property without due process of law. The Fourteenth Amendment also barred any state government from denying to any person the "equal protection of the law." The Fifteenth Amendment banned the national government and any state government from using the grounds of "race, color, or previous condition of servitude" to deny or limit the right of any citizen to vote.

During Reconstruction, the active voting of African Americans in the South helped to elect judges and legislatures that respected the constitutional civil liberties of black women and men. By 1870, African Americans were allowed to vote in the northern and western states. After Reconstruction ended in

1877, most of the southern states began to limit the voting rights of African Americans. Social segregation in public places—trains, schools, parks, hotels, sports arenas, and theaters—would become required by law in southern states. Such segregation deprived people of color of their basic liberty to move and assemble freely in public places. By 1900 hardly any African Americans voted in the South. It would take half a century of social change, during which concepts of basic rights would expand and modern science would demonstrate that no "race" was superior to another, before African Americans organized large-scale, public protests against racial inequality. These protests were designed to pressure the national government and state governments to enforce the Fifteenth Amendment and the guarantees of the Fourteenth Amendment against taking life, liberty, and property without due process of law (see Chapter 4).

Besides African Americans, women were also denied the full protection of the rights and liberties supposedly guaranteed in the Constitution (see Chapter 8). And the courts have never been willing to extend to elementary and high school students the protections the Constitution and state constitutions give to the civil liberties of adults. While a few states have passed legislation guaranteeing the privacy rights and civil liberties of gay men and lesbian women, the Supreme Court has refused to void the many state and city laws restricting the employment, marriage, and adoption rights of gays and lesbians.

Courts in the United States took the initiative in limiting some of the basic Constitutional rights of wage earners, especially in the nineteenth century and for the first third of the twentieth century. Until 1842, the "right of the people peaceably to assemble," guaranteed in the First Amendment, was denied to manual workers who formed labor unions. In New York and Philadelphia, city officials prosecuted shoemakers who joined unions, charging that by organizing they were engaged in illegal conspiracies. While the courts did not actually dissolve the unions involved, their members were fined for exercising their First Amendment rights. After 1842, the courts legalized unions. But when unionized workers went on strike, their free speech rights were often severely restricted by court orders known as *injunctions*. Judges often ordered workers to cease picketing in front of the business they were striking. Some injunctions aimed to stop strikes by banning communication between union officials in different cities.

Most of these court injunctions were issued by judges after the employer being struck appeared in court and asked for action to stop the strike. But the workers who were the object of the court injunctions *were not given a chance to present their arguments against the issuance of an injunction at the hearing held by the judge who issued the anti-strike order.* Such court injunctions were known as *ex parte* injunctions. While judicial injunction hearings were not trials of people formally charged with a crime, the process by which an *ex parte* injunction was issued violated the spirit of the Sixth Amendment, which guaranteed persons accused of improper behavior the right to cross-examine accusers.

Determining the civil liberties that should be allowed to strikers—especially their free speech rights to picket—is much more complicated that it might seem at first glance. In addition to the striking workers, a strike often involved two other groups of workers: (1) nonstriking workers who had been employed at the particular business being struck, and (2) strikebreakers who were looking for work. Animosity and violence during strikes usually were caused by confrontations between strikers and workers who wished to work. Sometimes strikers verbally intimidated and attacked strikebreakers who tried to cross picket lines. At other times, strikebreakers were the aggressors. Sometimes the strikebreakers were people who had been excluded—because of their race or nationality—from working at the business being struck because the regularly employed workers had pressured employers not to hire them. And at other times the strikebreakers were criminals who had been recruited by employers to initiate violence, because it was easier to obtain a court injunction halting a strike if there had been fighting between strikers and strikebreakers.

While an "objective" judge—if anyone can truly be objective—might have had trouble balancing the civil liberties of strikers against the civil liberties of nonstrikers, most nineteenth- and early twentieth-century judges were biased against striking wage earners. Judges' biases reflected the class differences between affluent, well-educated, judges and wage earners who were manual workers. Many judges were also biased against immigrant workers. And many judges believed that in the United States, individuals did not need to combine in groups (unions) to advance economically. These judges thought that in a nation that guaranteed *individual* rights, the idea of using *collective* bodies—unions—to advance economically was a radical, un-American notion that was embraced only by foreigners who emigrated from Europe. Most judges thought that any sensible American, who understood the rights of citizens in a republic, could not possibly endorse unions. Hence, most judges concluded that unions were "un-American."

The first law limiting the use of injunctions against striking workers, thereby protecting the liberties of workers who wanted to strike, was the Norris-LaGuardia Act, passed by Congress in 1932. In 1935, the National Labor Relations Act made it a civil offense, punishable by the award of lost wages, to fire, demote, fine, or penalize an individual worker for asserting her or his First Amendment rights to join a union and participate in its activities. In 1940, the Supreme Court ruled that picketing was a form of free speech protected by the First Amendment.

V

By the late 1930s and thereafter, an increasing number of judges were influenced by the views of former Supreme Court Justice Oliver Wendell Holmes, Jr., who had argued that legal doctrines had to be flexible, adjusting to the economic and social changes that accompanied the rise of industrial society. Holmes believed that the economic and political vitality of democratic societies was enhanced by tolerating a diversity of conflicting ideas, freely debated in public speech and writing. In 1919 he wrote that

> the ultimate good [for society] is better reached by free trade in ideas. . . . the best test of truth is the power of the thought to get itself accepted in the competition of the market [of ideas].

Holmes viewed society, and law, as part of an evolutionary process, and believed that ideas that were unpopular at one point in time might eventually become accepted and important to the well-being of the nation.

Between 1935 and 1981, the judges of the Supreme Court expanded many of the civil liberties of Americans, providing the individual with an unprecedented level of protection against limitation of his or her freedom by employers and governments. The same court that had moved decisively against racial discrimination in 1954 (see Chapter 4) would expand First Amendment protections of freedom of speech. In 1940, Congress had passed the Smith Act, a law banning membership in the Communist Party and the advocacy of the overthrow of the government. At first the courts upheld Smith Act prosecutions. But in 1957, after the Korean War against Communist China had ended, the Supreme Court ruled that the First Amendment allowed *abstract, theoretical* statements about the desirability of the eventual overthrow of the government. Actual planning to overthrow the government—stockpiling weapons and organizing a physical attack on government property and officials—was still treason.

In the 1930s, the Supreme Court began for the first time actually to hold states accountable to the due process protections of civil liberties written into the Fourteenth Amendment. In 1932, the Court held that in some situations an arrested person had to be provided with a lawyer if she or he could not afford one. After 1937, the majority of the Supreme Court judges considered freedom of expression and assembly a crucial right that could not be denied to a person unless exceptional circumstances (especially war) justified limiting that right.

In the 1960s, the Supreme Court ruled that all criminal defendants had not just a right to hire an attorney to represent them, but actually *had to be represented* by an attorney. If a defendant was too poor to hire a lawyer, the city, state, or county government in whose court the arrested person was to be tried was required to pay for an attorney to represent the defendant.[*] The Court also ruled that if law enforcement officials did not have a proper search warrant, the evidence they seized from a person could not be used against that person. This decision let some criminals go free, but protected the liberties of innocent people. In its most controversial criminal procedures decisions, the Supreme Court held that detained and arrested people could not be forced to answer questions unless they had been told they had a right to say nothing and to have an attorney present. Here the Court could find no exact language in the Constitution to back up its decision, since the Constitution only specifically barred *forced* statements by suspected criminals. But the majority of the judges, whose broad aim was to enhance the spirit of democratic government by giving civil liberties very strong protections, argued that the constitutionally guaranteed rights against self-incrimination and the right to be represented by an attorney were useless unless an accused person was reminded of such rights and given an attorney before they were questioned by law-enforcement authorities.

In effect, the Supreme Court was *legislating*, since it was interpreting the Constitution and laws passed by Congress by establishing procedures for guaranteeing the rights mentioned in the Constitution and Congressional and state legislation. Put another way, the Supreme Court was now often ruling that government *had to* take action to make sure that individuals had

---

[*] In 1974, Congress founded the Legal Services Corporation, a national government agency whose lawyers provided free legal representation to poor people and also brought lawsuits against city, state, and national governments to increase the ability of poor people to obtain welfare state benefits due to them by law.

the financial resources necessary to take advantage of their Constitutional rights.

In 1965, the Supreme Court asserted that the Constitution, although not mentioning privacy, could be read to suggest that all citizens were entitled to a *right* to privacy. The Court ruled that no state government could limit the decision of adults to obtain contraceptives. Eight years later, in 1973, the Court again referred to the right to privacy, holding in *Roe* v. *Wade*, that women had a right to control their bodies (see also Chapter 8). The judges concluded that a mother had the right to end a pregnancy that was affecting her body and her economic and psychological well-being. But the Court held that this right *was not an absolute right*. Hence the Court allowed state governments to restrict a mother's abortion rights during the last three months (trimester) of a pregnancy, since by this point the fetus had become a person that had a chance of being kept alive outside the uterus. The debate about the appropriateness of abortion during the third trimester is a good example of the difficulty of securing agreement when *two competing rights* are directly opposed to each other, since protecting the rights of the mother will infringe upon the rights of the fetus, and vice versa. Public opinion polls show that a large majority of women want the *Roe* v. *Wade* decision to stand, since they believe it greatly expands their rights.

Between 1968 and 1975, the Supreme Court also expanded the rights of persons receiving income-maintenance benefits like disability payments and aid to families with dependent children. These persons were especially protected against any state, county, or city administrator who tried to cut off welfare benefits without holding a formal hearing. The Court also made it easier to qualify for welfare state benefit programs that were established by law. In the 1970s, the Supreme Court also expanded the rights of disabled people to receive adequate educational services. However, the justices of the Supreme Court refused to break with tradition in one important area of social custom. In 1982, they upheld a state law banning sex between men. The judges refused to extend to homosexuals the right of privacy given to heterosexual couples and to pregnant women. In this case, the Court's majority decided that it was more important to maintain a particular, long-established, majority-endorsed custom than it was to protect the personal liberties of a minority.

Throughout the half century beginning in 1935, Congress and the Supreme Court took many actions that enhanced the civil liberties of groups whose liberties had not previously been specifically protected by the government. The result has been increased racial conflict, gender conflict, and conflict over different religious interpretations of human rights, as an *expanding number of different social and economic groups* have made competing claims to the right to exercise their liberties.

Between 1981 and 1992, presidents Reagan and Bush, who both thought that the Supreme Court had overreached its constitutional role, appointed new justices who believed that court rulings should be based solely on the wording of the Constitution. These judges argued that if a right or liberty was not specifically mentioned in the Constitution, it was not guaranteed to Americans. Their influence led the Supreme Court to modify many of its earlier rulings on the rights and liberties of the nation's people. Against a background of rising social anxiety about crime, doubts about the ability of our economy to create enough good jobs, racial conflict, disagreements about issues like reproductive freedom, and disputes about the civil liberties of criminals, Americans have focused an increasing amount of media and public attention on Supreme Court decisions and presidential nominations of Supreme Court justices. Controversy over the appropriate degree of civil liberties that should be available to different groups in American society is not likely to decrease in the foreseeable future.

The next chapter will discuss the emergence of the idea that the liberties of adults would be strengthened by allowing a large segment of adults to vote (democracy) and by creating a republican form of government, in which all government power would be derived solely from voters, and not automatically assigned on the basis of heredity or wealth.

CHAPTER 2

Democracy

I

Democracy comes from a Greek word (*demokratia*) that means sovereignty (rule) of the people. It was first used in 462 B.C. to refer to the authority given to a jury court—whose members were drawn by lot from *all* free males in the city-state of Athens—to limit the power of the council of the wellborn. As Athenian "democracy" developed, the most important institution in the city-state's government was the Assembly, which was composed of all free male citizens. When the Assembly voted, each citizen cast one vote. Pericles, the great Greek orator and archon (top executive) of Athens, proudly exclaimed that the Athenian government's "administration favours the many instead of the few; that is why it is called a democracy." The development of democracy in the modern world would eventually change the size of the group allowed to participate in government (mainly by voting for government officials) from the "*many*" to *most* adults, and then to *all* adults.

The Athenian political system excluded free women and slaves from voting or serving on government bodies. Participation in the Assembly's permanent executive committee was limited to only those citizens who had residences in Athens and a rural district. Since a relatively small number of wealthy Athenians had such residences, the executive committee was a restricted, elite institution. By modern standards, Athens clearly was not a democracy. Our concept of democracy stresses the necessity of *equal* political rights—to vote and to run for office—of *all* adult citizens. Yet, until the founding of the United States, Athenian democracy was the most democratic government to rule over a large number of people.

The Europeans who conquered North America in the seventeenth and eighteenth centuries believed that democracy was a dangerous, unstable form of government. In 1600, England had what contemporaries called a "mixed constitution." Sovereignty (the authority to rule) came from three sources: the monarchy, the aristocracy, and the voters. (Only 20 percent of adult men in England were allowed to vote in 1600. This is why it would be misleading to say that at this time that sovereignty came from the *people*, since this term implies all the adult citizens of a society.) The English elites believed that England's system of sovereignty promoted *order and stability* in society.

Affluent Englishmen believed that a hereditary monarchy and the House of Lords (whose members inherited their membership or were appointed by the King or the Archbishop of Canterbury, the head of the established Anglican Church) were institutions that protected their property rights and promoted respect for authority. English kings, queens, and aristocrats generally believed that monarchs, governors, and judges were God's representatives on Earth. The authority of government was believed to be backed by the will of God. Government officials were to be obeyed because they spoke for God. It was also assumed that the existing *form* of government—the "constitution" of government—was ordered by God. When the English referred to their constitution, they meant either the entire structure of their government or all the past royal decrees and Parliamentary laws that determined the different branches of government and the powers of each branch (see Chapter 3). The English thought of their governmental system as a *mixed government* that blended three elements: the monarchical, the aristocratic (in the House of Lords), and the democratic (in the elected House of Commons).

But there was nothing common about the members of the House of Commons. They had to be wealthy men. Members of the House of Commons received no pay and electioneering expenses could be very high. Only wealthy men could afford to run and serve in the House of Commons. Wealth requirements to vote in elections of members of the House of Commons in the eighteenth century qualified only about one-fifth of the English adult male population to vote. Yet members of the House of Commons argued that they represented the only part of the English constitution that spoke for the English "people."

In the years before 1800, most affluent Englishmen believed that the majority of the people in their nation—small farmers and landless agricultural workers, artisans, and common laborers who worked in towns and cities—did not have enough of an economic *stake in society* to be trusted to vote in elections of representatives to the House of Commons.* Large and middle-rank property owners in England feared that if the vote was given to the poor, the poor would want to raise taxes on property holders or, in some cases, confiscate the land and other wealth of the rich and distribute it to the poor. Sir Thomas More, the learned counselor to Henry VIII, was very concerned about radical writers who suggested to the poor that "lordes [rich people's] landes and all honest mens goodes" should be "pulled from them by force and distributed among beggers." It was also believed that only those voters who had enough wealth to be economically independent would be able to resist the manipulation of wealthy tyrants.

Between 1600 and 1689, different groups of Englishmen disagreed bitterly about the amount of authority the monarchy should exercise, the amount of power that the House of Commons should have, and the government's policy toward

---

*In the "democracy" of ancient Athens, the philosopher Aristotle worried about trustworthiness of those who owned little or no property. He proposed that when the Athenian Assembly voted on laws, the total property owned by the advocates of a law would be calculated, as would the total property of the opponents. The Assembly would adopt the position favored by the *majority of property*, not the majority of voters.

religion. During the civil war that raged in England between 1642 and 1649, small numbers of radical ministers, farmers, and artisans demanded abolition of the English monarchy and the House of Lords. Some but not all of these radicals favored giving the vote to any free man, irrespective of his wealth. This was not the same as universal manhood suffrage. Groups like the Levellers did not believe that servants should be allowed to vote, since they were under the authority of their employers during the time period they had contracted to be servants. (Large numbers of Englishmen hired out as servants at this time.) The Levellers thought that servants would not be independent voters and would most likely be told how to vote by their masters. None of the radical groups in England in the seventeenth century proposed allowing women to vote.

In 1689 and 1690, Parliament passed a series of laws that changed the English government's structure significantly. The new monarchs, King William and Queen Mary, agreed to these changes. Above all, the power of the monarchy was reduced. (1) The monarch could no longer suspend laws that had previously been passed by Parliament and accepted by the monarch. (2) The monarch could not issue decrees that had the force of law. Only bills passed by Parliament could become laws—if they received the royal assent. (3) Taxes could not be levied unless they had been voted by Parliament. (4) The monarch could not create a standing army without the approval of Parliament.

To justify these changes, English political theorists made a major break with past thinking. They rejected the notion that the authority of government was based *only* on the will of God. The most influential English theorist of the late 1600s, John Locke, insisted that God had given men *natural rights* when he created humans. But thereafter, Locke argued, God did not determine the character of government in human society. Rather, *governments were formed by the people* for their own protection. Only a strong government could protect each man's basic natural rights against the attacks of wrongheaded men. *However*, when Locke talked about "the people" he meant *only those men who owned a substantial amount of property*. Affluent men like Locke trembled at the thought of giving to poor people the right to vote, by which voters transferred the authority to govern to elected representatives.

Generally, the English elites and the elites that would emerge in the English North American colonies believed that their domination of the poor was necessary because the poor were supposedly lazy, stupid, ignorant, violent, and vulgar. Sixteenth-century English political theorists argued that those not deserving of the vote, including most laborers, poor farmers, and artisans, should "have no voice nor authoritie in our common wealth, and no account is made of them but onelie to be ruled." All the colonies established property requirements for voting *and* for running for office. The higher the office, the larger the amount of wealth that was required to vote and stand for the office.

In most colonies only the colonial legislature and local justices of the peace were elected. The common, "middling" farmers and craftsmen usually elected more affluent men than themselves to the legislature. The average voter did not directly elect the men who filled the most powerful government posts. Colonial governors were either elected or were royal governors appointed by the English king. The governors appointed wealthy men to councils that acted in both executive roles and sometimes as the equivalent of a second house of the colonial legislature. *This was not a democratic form of government.* It was a form of mixed government, combining elements of monarchy and nondemocratic representative government (legislatures), as was the English system.

In the colonies, as time passed, political ideas began to evolve. The ideas of John Locke greatly influenced the colonists. Thus, in 1691 Congregational ministers such as Increase and Cotton Mather would criticize the new government charter imposed on Massachusetts by the English Parliament because the charter made the governor an appointee of the King. Upset that this change made civil government "more *Monarchical* and less *Democratical* than in former times" the Mathers took solace in the fact that "the People have a Negative upon all the Executive Part of the Civil government, as well as the Legislative." This statement indicates acceptance of the concept of the sovereignty of the people over government. As the Reverend Samuel Willard explained, "A People are not made for Rulers, but Rulers for a People." Of course, since these elite theorists believed in the "stake in society" theory of government, they did not believe that people at the bottom of the social ladder should be allowed to vote.

But in the colonies the electorate *was never as small a fraction of the free population as it was in England.* In England, an average of about 20 percent of adult males qualified to vote at the start of the eighteenth century. This number declined somewhat by the time of the American Revolution. By 1763, about 66 percent of all free, white men could vote in the colonies that would become the United States. Why was this so? Throughout the colonies, the overall scarcity of labor meant that agricultural workers and craftsmen received higher payment for their labor (and the products of their labor) than did English artisans. There was a huge supply of cheap land for sale. Many colonial governments attracted immigrants by offering them land. And soldiers who fought Native Americans were often rewarded with a grant of land. Consequently, *a much higher percentage of colonists owned land than did the English who remained in England.*

Until the 1770s, affluent colonists were not too concerned about the large percentage of white men who voted. Economic elites and solid middle-class colonists felt that their form of mixed government would protect their particular interests against any confiscatory impulses. The vote was denied to the very poorest people—especially day laborers and slaves—many of whom could not imagine themselves advancing economically without directly attacking the men who paid them low wages. Upper-class and solid middle-class groups knew that proposals that would attack their property would be resisted by many in the middling group of property-owning voters, because *these small holders hoped to acquire more wealth* and would not want to think that their gains might then be taken from them. The affluent also expected that if the middling sort ever united to attack the economic interests of the wealthy, the latter could rely on the protection of the governors and the appointed upper houses of the legislatures, because the men chosen for these offices (by the monarch and by the governors chosen by the monarch) were always rich men.

Until 1763, the middling farmers and craftsmen almost always voted for candidates who came from the middle and upper groups of colonial society. These middling voters *deferred* to the education, experience, and alleged devotion to the public interest of the more affluent. The more affluent generally believed that they truly had virtue and were looking out for the best interests of all social groups, both of nonvoters and less affluent voters. This notion was closely connected to the concept of *virtual representation* that the English had advanced to justify excluding *all* the colonists, even the elites, from any representation in the House of Commons. Those who believed in virtual representation argued that every member of the House of Commons represented the interests of all the Englishmen in England—in every electoral district—and all the Englishmen in the colonies.

Between 1763 and 1776, many of the colonists engaged in disputes with England over the right of Parliament, which had no members from the colonies, to levy taxes on the colonists. Most of the colonists who wrote pamphlets and broadsides criticizing Parliamentary taxes were affluent men. They used powerful slogans like "no taxation without representation," and language like that of the Declaration of Independence, which proclaimed that "all men are created equal" and were "endowed by their Creator with certain unalienable rights," including "life, liberty, and the pursuit of happiness" (see Chapter 4). Many colonists who thought that a monarch should protect the basic rights of "the people," and especially the ownership of *private property*, now believed that King George III had become a true tyrant and was conspiring with wealthy Englishmen (including his appointees in the colonies) to plunder the property of the vast majority of the colonists, including the middle ranks and some of the most affluent colonists.

In resisting England, the bulk of the middle level and affluent colonists did not abandon their belief in mixed government. But middling and low-status groups were no longer willing to defer to the leadership of their social superiors. Artisans who did not trust all merchants on nonimportation committees to enforce regulations against buying British goods insisted that *artisans* be included on the committees as an *interest* (today we would use the term interest group). The artisans believed that *only artisans* understood and were committed to the interests of artisans, whose specific needs and interests were different from those of more affluent urban voters. Small farmers also concluded that their interests were very different from the large landowners who they had previously elected. Why? First, many of the large farmers were Tories, who backed the royal governors and the English king. Second, many of the large farmers were creditors who had loaned money to the smaller farmers. As the wild swings of the North American economy and changes in the value of currency during the Revolutionary War often made it impossible for smaller farmers to repay their debts, tensions between large farmers and their middling debtor neighbors created a belief that the two groups had very different interests. Small and middle-sized farmers concluded that they had to elect farmers similar to themselves. As the Revolutionary War continued, voters elected more and more modest farmers and artisans to the legislatures of the newly independent states.

During the Revolutionary War, these arguments also motivated soldiers. In Philadelphia, enlisted militiamen voted for their own kind to be their officers. (During the nineteenth century, advocates of equal political rights for women would use the same arguments that had been used by male artisans, farmers and militiamen: Virtual representation was a sham; and only the vote and the election of women would allow the interests of women to be represented in government.)

After the break with England in 1776, the state constitutions that were drafted by state legislatures or special conventions rarely reduced property-owning requirements for the vote. State governors were now elected, but stiff property-owning requirements to run for governor (and sometimes extra property requirements to vote for governor) allowed only the very wealthy to be elected to high office. The new states had upper houses of their legislatures, with higher amounts of property needed to run for these bodies than for the "lower" houses. What Americans rejected was the notion that was prevalent in England but had never been implemented in English colonies: the right of a hereditary aristocracy to hold executive (the monarchy) and legislative/judicial (the House of Lords) government positions. But the political system in the newly independent states was still constructed to give superior political power automatically to the owners of property, and especially substantial owners of property, allowing them more opportunity to advance and protect their interests.

The experiences and rhetoric of the revolutionary age also convinced many of those who had been denied the vote that in a world of very specific individual needs and natural rights, they too deserved to be given the vote as a basic right. Put another way, the nonvoters claimed that while men might differ in their ability to farm or do business or learn a profession, *all men had the same capacity to choose to give their consent to be governed.* Thus it was believed that all free men were and should be *equal* in one important way: their ability to exercise a basic political liberty—the giving and withholding of *consent to govern.*

II

Between 1787 and the late 1820s, the suffrage expanded by fits and starts. Nonvoters became more assertive and elites became less afraid that giving the vote to the landless would create social conflict. The size of the new nation expanded, as millions of acres of fertile farmland were acquired. Prosperous manufacturing was emerging in New England and the Mid-Atlantic states. Abundance appeared to make it less likely that the poor would demand radical government policies, since they could expect improvements in their condition by virtue of their own labor. State constitutional conventions in Massachusetts (1820–1821), New York (1821), and Virginia (1830) eliminated all landowning, taxpaying, and personal wealth requirements for the suffrage, establishing political democracy for white males. Connecticut and Louisiana followed suit in 1845, as did Ohio (1851) and Rhode Island (1887). By contrast, England gradually extended the right to vote, beginning in 1832 when middle-class men were enfranchised, and ending in 1918 when all men finally were given the right to vote. English women were enfranchised by 1928.

What were the arguments that helped convince delegates to the state constitutional conventions that white manhood suffrage was desirable? Certainly theoretical arguments about no taxation without representation (consent of those taxed by government) were important:

> the only reasonable scheme [is] that those who are to be affected by the acts of government, should be annually entitled to vote for those who administer it.

Practical warnings about the consequences of *not extending the suffrage* were very influential too. In 1821, a delegate to the Massachusetts constitutional convention noted that

> By refusing to give this right [the vote] to them, you array them against the laws; but give them the rights of citizens—mix them with the good part of society, and you disarm them.

A delegate to the 1821 New York constitutional convention pointed out that in town meetings, where universal white manhood suffrage was practiced, the results offered the "highest proof of the virtue and intelligence" of a body politic composed of propertied and unpropertied voters. Another delegate to the same convention noted that requiring property ownership for the vote discriminated against farmers who rented their land by means of long-term leases and who often earned more income than voters who owned small farms. He further claimed that experience had shown that the New York State Senate, which was elected by landowners only, had not behaved in a more principled manner than had the assembly, which had been elected by universal white manhood suffrage.

In 1829, Virginia still had a landowning requirement for the suffrage—a law that disenfranchised about half of free adult white men. Some of these men owned valuable personal property—like the tools of artisans—but because they did not own land, they could not vote. Some landless people were very poor and worked as agricultural laborers. When the Virginia constitutional convention met in 1829 and 1830, the landless demanded the right to vote, arguing that by supporting the war for independence from Britain and in their loyalty to the new republic, they and their forefathers had proven their devotion to the public interest. Hence they deserved to be included in the definition of "the people":

> Attachment to property . . . is not to be confounded with the sacred flame of patriotism. The love of country . . . is engrafted in our nature. It exists in all climates, among all classes, under every possible form of Government. Riches oftener impair it than poverty. . . . To ascribe to a landed possession, moral or intellectual [superiority] . . . would be truly regarded as ludicrous.

The nonvoters hinted that if they were denied the right to the vote, they might resist government authority, as so many colonists had done in the previous century:

> It was not the oppressive weight of the taxes imposed by England on America: it was the assertion of a right to impose any . . . [burdens] whatever upon those who were not represented; to bind by laws those who had no share, personal or delegated, in their enactment, that roused this continent to arms.

These arguments carried the day. All free white men were granted the vote in the 1830 Virginia constitution.

With the elimination of landowning and personal wealth requirements for voting, the political system of the United States had become more democratic. The enfranchised white male citizens called the system in which they now all participated as legal equals a "democracy" or a "democratic republic." A republic was a government that had no monarch or aristocracy legally entitled to hold government positions (see Chapters 3 and 4).

The non-landowning men in Virginia (and elsewhere) who had argued so eloquently for suffrage for themselves also maintained that "for obvious reasons, by almost universal consent, women and children, aliens and slaves, are excluded [from the suffrage]." Slaves were in no position to openly contest this view, although free African Americans like Frederick Douglass did. In 1848 a group of Northeastern women held a women's rights convention at Seneca Falls, New York. Drawing on the language of natural rights used in the Declaration of Independence, they asserted that

> woman is man's equal—was intended to be so by the Creator, and the highest good of the race demands that she should be recognized as such.

As the equal of men, women deserved the vote. Men who opposed women's suffrage argued that women were represented by male voters, a rehash of the virtual representation argument. Men also contended that women were generally economically dependent on men and therefore were not proper voters for a republican form of government. The 1851 national women's rights convention countered that only the vote could give "woman" the power to "place her in a position to protect herself."

The Civil War brought important advances in American democracy. In the aftermath of the war, the nation adopted constitutional amendments abolishing slavery and guaranteeing the vote to African-American men. The reasoning underlying the grant of the suffrage included the desire of leaders of the Republican Party to strengthen their position in the South, where most African Americans lived. But a majority in Congress also believed that free men deserved the vote. Otherwise they would not truly be able to keep the civil rights the Constitution gave them. And one of the main aims of the Northern coalition that had fought the Civil War was to make sure that slavery was abolished and replaced by free labor. Free laborers could not protect their economic rights unless they could vote.

In 1869, as Congress debated the Fifteenth Amendment, proponents of women's suffrage demanded that all adults, regardless of sex, be given the same political rights. Elizabeth Cady Stanton, the foremost feminist orator of the nineteenth century, based her case for women's suffrage on the natural rights argument:

> [The] fundamental principle of our government [is] the equality of all the citizens of the Republic. . . . Hence we apeal to the party now in power. . . . to end this protracted debate on suffrage, and declare it the inalienable right of every citizen who is amenable to the laws of the land, who pays taxes and [is subject] to the penalty of crime.

Stanton also warned that a republic that excluded any large social group would be *unstable*:

> Thus far, all nations have been built on caste* and [have] failed. . . . If serfdom, peasantry, and slavery have shattered kingdoms, deluged continents with blood, scattered republics like dust before the wind, and rent our own Union asunder, what kind of a government, think you American statesmen, you can build, with the mothers of the race crouching at your feet.

Congress rejected the women's suffrage arguments. The women's suffrage movement continued, but did not begin to gather steam again until the first decade of twentieth century.

III

In the 1890s, many people in the United States became alarmed at the emergence of the large corporation, which used its money to buy political influence. Another concern, held especially by middle-class citizens, was the influence of political party organizations on the political process. Critics of both corporate

---

*Caste originally meant race or breed. Stanton understood caste to mean a system of social stratification based on sex, race, religion, or income.

and political organization influence called for reforms that established *direct* democracy (see pages 229-230).

In the meantime, racial and class conflict in the South had led the dominant landowning and industrial forces in the South to try to limit the voting participation of all blacks and of poor white farmers and laborers. Many southern whites favored using force to prevent blacks from voting. One of the major activities of the Ku Klux Klan was attacking and murdering blacks who were active voters and whites who helped organize black voters. When the withdrawal of U.S. Army troops from the South was completed in 1877, white vigilantes were free to intimidate black men who voted. Slowly, the black vote in the South began to decline.

In the 1880s and 1890s, the poorest white groups in the South were increasingly active in politics, trying to elect candidates who favored lower taxes on the poor and raising taxes on the rich, who backed more spending on schools and schoolbooks for poor whites, and who would allow more local (county) officials to be elected, instead of being appointed by the legislature, which seemed to favor the most affluent men in each county. At times these efforts were successful. Counterattacking, the prosperous white groups elected legislators who passed poll tax laws, which made voting too expensive for many poor men.

When struggling white farmers allied with black farmers in the Populist movement in the 1890s, the prosperous white groups countered by bribing many black voters to vote for conservative Democrats. The establishment Democrats also race-baited the Populists, charging that if the voters elected them to the legislatures, they would pass laws promoting the social equality of blacks with whites. These tactics were very successful. Ironically, when groups representing white agrarian protestors captured control of many southern legislatures in the early twentieth century, they passed laws that banned virtually all blacks from voting. Only in this way, argued the reformers, could the white establishment be prevented from using the black vote against democratic groups.

There were similar developments in many northern states in the first decade of the new century. Republican legislators in New Jersey passed a voter registration law that ostensibly reduced the influence of corrupt Democratic political machines that illegally registered immigrant voters. But the law made registration so much more difficult that it led to a significant decline in the legitimate voting of immigrant and black voters. In many cities, elite groups backed new rules for electing city councilmen, hoping that they could reduce the influence of lower-income voters. Most cities had relatively small districts for electing councilmen. A poor candidate or a candidate of modest means could walk around the district and make contact with most voters. By enlarging the size of election districts, which favored more affluent candidates who had the funds (and access to newspaper support) to reach large numbers of voters, elite groups hoped to reduce the influence of lower-income voters. This tactic succeeded in many medium-sized cities. Fewer blue-collar workers and Socialists were elected to positions in these city governments.

Despite these limitations, Americans taking stock of their nation's democracy at the time World War I started could be proud that they had one of the most democratic governments on earth. England still had a hereditary monarch and a House of Lords. Although their power had been drastically reduced, especially between 1900 and 1911, these elite institutions still had an impact on government policy. In Germany, not only was a hereditary monarch in place, but in Prussia, the largest German state, the votes of the wealthy and the middle classes were given much more weight in elections for the Prussian legislature than were the votes of the poorest 60 percent of the German population. Among the major industrial powers of Europe, only France was a true republic.

President Wilson and Congress enthusiastically endorsed the nation's entry into World War I, promising that our armed forces would help to make the world safe for democracy. Proponents of women's suffrage seized on this rhetoric to try to embarrass the president and Congress into supporting women's right to participate directly in the democratic political system of their nation. A combination of militant picketing of the White House, vigorous congressional lobbying, and opposition to the reelection of senators and congressmen who were opposed to women's suffrage finally carried the day. The Nineteenth Amendment was ratified and women in every state voted in the 1920 elections.

However, the nation's democracy was still flawed. African Americans living in the South were denied their Constitutional right to vote. But blacks living outside the South could vote, and did so with increasing effectiveness, especially after 1910, when a 60-year period of intense black migration from the South to the North began. By the end of World War II, the growing influence of those blacks who could vote pressured democratic presidents to expand the civil rights of blacks. Thus, in 1948 President Truman ordered the desegregation of the armed forces.

The civil rights movement that began in 1955 used sit-ins and public marches to pressure the local and state governments to abandon racial discrimination in public places and on public transportation. Nationally, the 1964 Civil Rights Act contained some provisions designed to increase the black vote in the South. But these provisions were not tough enough to overcome southern resistance. Mass marches of blacks who demanded to be registered to vote were organized by the Southern Christian Leadership Conference. These demonstrations pressured President Johnson and Congress into action. The 1965 Voting Rights Act provided for special federal marshals and voting registrars to put southern black men and women on the voting rolls. Ten years later, black voter registration in the South was virtually equal to white registration. By 1975 the American electorate was truly all-inclusive. All adults in the nation now were political equals in an important sense[*]: they all had obtained the most basic democratic right, the right to vote.

---

[*]This conclusion is carefully worded to avoid implying that total political equality had been attained by all citizens by the mid-1970s. In 1964 the Supreme Court ordered that all legislative districts have roughly equal numbers of voters. But it has not enforced this decision strictly. Moreover, the

The next chapter will explain why people living in the United States believed that the liberties of free adults and the republican form of government would not be secure unless they were specified in written constitutions that could not be changed without the approval of voters.

---

drafters of the Constitution had deliberately created an unequal apportionment scheme for the United States Senate. Since each state was given two senators, states with small populations have much more proportional power in the Senate than states with larger than average populations. The drafters of the Constitution deliberately adopted this inequality in representation because they wanted to protect the rights of the states that individually had small populations. As a group, these small population states would be in the minority in the House of Representatives. By giving the smaller states equal representation to the more populous states in the Senate, their position as a minority was given protection against being dominated by the majority states. At the time this arrangement—the famous Connecticut Compromise—was adopted, the states that were in the minority were the states with few slaves, while most of the larger states were the slave states of the South. After 1820 immigration from Europe rapidly increased the population of the nonslave states. Only the unequal representation of smaller population states in the Senate allowed the southern slave states to resist the pressure from the national majority to curb the expansion of slavery.

CHAPTER 3

Constitutional Government

I

All societies have laws. Imagine the confusion and damage that would result if small groups and large societies did not have any rules of conduct for both business dealings and relationships between people. *Constitutions are the laws that determine the structure of the government of an organization, a state, or a nation and the way government officials are to be selected.* When people living in the United States hear the term constitution, they think of a *single*, written document that specifies the powers of an organization. But before 1776, most societies had constitutions that combined the decisions of different sources of authority: (a) orders issued by a monarch; (b) agreements signed by a monarch; (c) customs not written down in documents; and (d) the sum total of the laws, passed by legislative bodies at different times, that specified the powers of legislative bodies, judicial bodies, and monarchs.

The English constitution established the system of government that the North American colonists knew best and most admired. Parts of the English constitution, like the Magna Carta (1215), were issued by monarchs, like King John, whose nobility waged war against him to limit his powers. In 1297, the threat of a rebellion had forced Edward I to issue a charter that required the agreement of Parliament before any non-feudal tax could be authorized. For the next three centuries English monarchs honored this part of the English constitution. But in 1626, King Charles I tried to turn a traditional right of the king— to deal with emergency threats to national security by demanding loans from rich men—into an annual obligation to loan money to the king. Many members of Parliament accused him of violating the constitution, since they regarded the regular loans as a tax. Parliament and Charles never resolved the basic issue of whether or not the English constitution should, as Charles wanted, be changed to allow the monarch to impose taxes unilaterally. Other conflicts followed, and in 1642 a civil war started in England. When Oliver Cromwell and the Puritans emerged victorious, Cromwell drafted (1653) the first distinct constitution in English history, the Instrument of Government. This constitution lapsed when the monarchy was restored in 1660.

In 1688 and 1689, a settlement was finally reached on the main issues that had led to civil war in England. Parliament passed a series of laws—the Bill of Rights, an Act of Settlement, and the Toleration Act—that altered the English constitution considerably. These laws guaranteed that the monarch could not suspend laws passed by Parliament; granted the House of Commons the sole authority to originate tax legislation; specified that the monarch could not be a Catholic and could not marry a Catholic; and allowed all Protestants to worship at the church of their choice. Parliamentary authority had been increased, while the power of the monarch had been reduced (but hardly eliminated).[*]

Before 1776, the English colony of Rhode Island had a royal charter (1644) that authorized the inhabitants to write their own basic constitution. Two other colonies, Connecticut (1662) and

---

[*]The customary right of the monarch to veto laws enacted by Parliament by refusing to give the royal assent was not revoked by Parliament. Yet Queen Anne (1707) was the last monarch to withhold the royal assent to Parliamentary legislation. If the present English monarch were to refuse the royal assent to a law passed by Parliament, the English would claim that the action was unconstitutional. Since the *custom* of not withholding the royal assent has existed for over 250 years the English assume that the custom *has become part of the English constitution.*

Massachusetts (1691), had royal charters that were constitutions, since they *established* the form of government in each colony. The constitution of Pennsylvania was the Charter of Liberties issued in 1701 by the colony's proprietor, William Penn, who had been given the power to govern Pennsylvania by Charles II in 1681. In 1669, the proprietors of the Carolinas drafted and proclaimed the Fundamental Constitutions, which were revised in later years, but were not accepted as lawful by the elected colonial assembly. For two periods, 1632–1654 and 1715–1776, Maryland's government structure was based on a charter issued by Charles I that stipulated that the laws written by the governor had to receive the consent of the freemen of the colony. With the exception of Rhode Island, the voters of the colonies did not exercise *full* sovereignty (the power to rule) over the constitution of their governments, since *only the proprietors or the English monarch could alter their constitutions.*

Throughout the nearly two centuries before the colonies broke away from England, the British government had been so busy with European wars and with its successful campaign to take over the French colonies in the Western Hemisphere, that it had allowed the English colonists to exercise a great deal of self-government in many aspects of their lives. The form of such self-government that appealed to the colonists was based on the notion that groups of people should constitute themselves by adopting written group agreements—covenants or compacts or charters—that signified their membership in a church, a town, or a club. These agreements all were based on the *consent* of the signers. The first political compact to establish a government was signed in 1637 at Providence, Rhode Island. It read:

> We whose names are hereunder, desirous to inhabit in the town of Providence, do promise to subject ourselves in active and passive obedience to all such orders and agreements as shall be made for the public good of the body. . . . by the *major consent* of the present inhabitants, masters of families, incorporated together into a Towne fellowship, and others whom they shall admit unto them only *in civil things* [emphasis added.]

The government constituted by this compact was based on majority rule (hence the term "major consent"). The sovereign people in the community were the "masters of families," a term understood to mean men who headed families. And the compact anticipated the likelihood that *men* might move into the town who might not want to join the church of the town founders or who might be excluded from this church. The compact allowed the original sovereign signers to choose to admit such persons into the civil society of the town, which meant allowing them to vote at the town assembly.

Covenants and compacts were signed *voluntarily* by all the members of the group. The signing indicated their acceptance of the rules and regulations of the charter and of the decision-making bodies established by the charter. This tradition inclined the colonists to the idea that *constitutions should be ratified by those who would be governed by the constitutions*.

In 1776, most of England's North American colonies (Canada was the notable exception) rebelled against British rule. Declaring their independence, the majority of the colonists insisted that they could not be governed, and especially taxed, without direct representation in the English Parliament. The voters in the newly independent states logically applied this principle to the constitutions that each state adopted. The former colonists believed that *only a government body that was elected by the voters could write a basic set of laws that established the structure and power of the new state governments*. (About two-thirds of white, adult men were eligible to vote in 1776.) Moreover, the people in the new states wanted *written* constitutions that gave detailed descriptions of the power of each part of government.

Between 1763 and 1776, the English Parliament, the King, and the royal governors appointed by the King had *ordered many changes in the powers of the colonial legislatures and courts*, changes that reduced their authority. This kind of *arbitrary* exercise of authority scared the colonists, since they worried that their basic natural rights—to control the property they owned, to travel, to be secure against unfair arrest, and to have a jury trial when accused of a crime—could not be protected if the constitution of their government, the rules of the game so to speak, could be *changed at the whim of the officials of a single branch of their government.* The colonists' notion of natural rights reflected the views of the influential English political theorist, John Locke, who had argued in the 1680s and 1690s that people made a compact with their government, giving it power to rule, but not to violate their basic, natural rights (see pages 12, 13, 34).

Turmoil and war raged in the United States in 1776 and 1777. Under these conditions, it was hard to hold special constitutional drafting and ratifying conventions. This is why most of the first state constitutions were written by state legislatures instead of by specially elected constitutional conventions. But some colonists, strongly committed to republicanism, believed this was a great a mistake. The first group to issue such a criticism was the town meeting of Concord, Massachusetts. In October 1776, Concord's inhabitants noted that the goal of a constitution should be to create a form of government that protected the rights of the subjects of the government "against any encroachment of the governing part." The colonists, of course, had had their fill of tyrannical actions by government officials *who had not been elected by the colonists*: royal governors, Parliament, and King George III. Sensitive to the danger of governmental officials abusing their authority, the residents of Concord argued that if their own elected legislature, which was "the governing Part" of their society, had the power to write and then alter a constitution, it left the citizens with "no Security." (Indeed, fear of too much concentrated government authority was the biggest concern of most of the citizens of the new nation.) Voters in Massachusetts turned down the 1778 constitution drafted by the legislature; in 1779, they approved a constitution written by an elected constitutional convention.

But even those state legislatures that chose to write a state constitution accepted the notion that the constitution should be *ratified by the voters.* The consensus on the *exclusive sovereignty of the voters*, the fundamental principle of *republicanism*, was widespread. In a republic, the power to rule, or sovereignty, must originate with the voters. Officials elected by voters can appoint other government officials. Most people in the newly independent United States of America wanted no element of monarchy in their governments, preferring pure republics to mixed government. The voters in the new, republican states also believed that *only the voters had the sovereignty to approve the constitutions that established the basic structures of the governments* that would be run by elected officials. By 1787 most state constitutions had been ratified by a special election or referendum. The Articles of Confederation, the first constitution of the United States, were ratified by the state legislatures.

Seeking stability and predictability in government by means of written constitutions, the voters of the new states also determined that *super*-majorities were necessary to ratify basic constitutions and any new amendments to these constitutions. Two-thirds or three-quarters majorities of representatives or voters were required to approve the new constitutions and their subsequent amendments.

II

In 1787, a group of state delegates gathered in Philadelphia to consider amending the Articles of Confederation. These men believed that the power of the national government under the Articles of Confederation was so weak—lacking the authority to raise enough money through taxes to maintain an effective army and navy—that only a new constitution could remedy the problem (see Chapter 5). The delegates wrote such a document, the draft of the Constitution of the United States of America. The delegates at the Philadelphia convention disagreed about many aspects of the structure of the new national government, and the relationship of that national government to the state governments. But the delegates *did not dispute the need to ask the sovereign voters of each state to ratify this new written constitution.* Thus, Article VII of the Constitution stated that "the ratification of the conventions of nine states shall be sufficient for the establishment of this Constitution between the States so ratifying the same." This meant, as James Madison eloquently observed, that the Constitution was a "dead letter, until life and validity were breathed into it by the voice of the people, speaking through the several State Conventions."

When the delegates to the Philadelphia convention discussed the method of amending the constitution, an overwhelming majority of them agreed that the goal of *stability* of government required that amending the constitution be a difficult—but not impossible—procedure. They reasoned that since a substantial majority of the states (9 of 13) was required to ratify the constitution in the first place, that a similar ratio, three-fourths, should be applied to the number of state ratifying conventions or state legislatures whose agreement would be needed to approve an amendment. (Such an amendment could be sent to the states by either a two-thirds vote of each house of Congress or by a convention called by two-thirds of the states.) Thus there were two steps necessary to amend the Constitution, and each step required that a proposed amendment be approved by a *substantial* majority.

There were some dissenters, however. The best known was Thomas Jefferson, who believed that Americans should hold constitutional conventions whenever there were basic controversies about the wisdom or meaning of any of the provisions of the existing Constitution. Because he believed that "the earth belongs always to the living," Jefferson thought that at a minimum there should be a constitutional convention for each generation (every 19 years). Jefferson also insisted that only conventions chosen by the sovereign voters should be allowed to alter the meaning of the Constitution. Therefore he opposed as inappropriate Supreme Court decisions that he believed altered the Constitution.

One unique feature of the new state constitutions and the Constitution of 1787 was that they were the first whole written constitutions in the modern world to be drafted and adopted by means of a process that *excluded hereditary nobles and monarchs*. In the new United States, the state constitutions were drafted and approved directly by the voters or by government bodies—either state legislatures or elected constitutional conventions—that were chosen by the voters. Neither the state constitutions, the Articles of Confederation, nor the Constitution of 1787 assigned any government office or the right to vote because a person was a member (by birth or by monarchical appointment) of the aristocracy. The rejection of the legitimacy of a legal aristocracy was a central part of the political philosophy of most of the voters in the United States, who believed that their nation should be a *republic*. As James Madison would explain in 1788, the people (those authorized to vote) were "the only legitimate foundation of [government] power." Therefore, in a republic all the power of government was delegated to elected officials by the *sovereign voters* and by no one else. *No hereditary rights to hold office* were allowed in a republic. As the Constitution of 1787 specified,

> No title of nobility shall be granted. . . . and no person holding any office . . . shall, without the consent of Congress, accept of any present, emolument, office, or title, of any kind whatever, from any king, prince, or foreign state.

Moreover, the Constitution held that the national government of the United States, "shall guarantee to every State in this Union a republican form of government." This ensured that in the future, existing or new states would have a republican form of government.[*]

---

[*]In the nineteenth century, Germany and Italy had mixed systems of government, while France had a short-lived republic (1848–1852), establishing a permanent republic in only 1871. England is still not a republic. The hereditary House of Lords has the power to refuse for three years to pass a bill approved each year by the House of Commons. It has not done so since 1911, although the House of Lords has refused to pass particular bills in a given year. The House of Lords agreed to this limitation on its power in 1911

The Constitution created three branches of the national government: the executive (the president), the legislative (Congress), and the Judiciary (the Supreme Court). The Constitution described the powers of the executive and the legislative branches in great detail. Article III specifically empowered the Supreme Court to decide disputes between different states. It also gave the Court the authority to decide all cases "arising under this Constitution, the laws of the United States, and treaties made . . . [and] controversies to which the United States shall be a party." It was not until the *Marbury* v. *Madison* case (1802) that the Supreme Court, led by Chief Justice John Marshall, asserted that this language allowed it to void a law passed by Congress if the Court believed the law violated the Constitution. (In 1793 the Court had already asserted its obvious power to rule on the constitutionality of state laws.) We call the power of the Supreme Court to determine the constitutionality of congressional legislation the power of *judicial review*. This power generally was viewed by conservative property holders as a source of security for property against demands for higher taxation or regulation of the freedom of action of property holders. Knowing that the Supreme Court had this power made many property holders defenders of the Constitution.

III

For a relatively brief time, a small minority of politicians in the United States favored modifying the republican form of government, either by establishing a monarchy or by giving the president a life-time term in office. But by 1812 the republican majority had defeated the anti-republican minority in one election after another. The Federalist party, which had been the home of the anti-republican groups (although many Federalists,

---

because increasing resentment against its veto of social legislation was threatening to create a very unstable social and political situation in England.

and especially President John Adams, were committed to a republic), collapsed. After 1812 all politicians, no matter what faction or party they joined, agreed that the United States must remain a republic.

During the four decades following the Constitution's ratification (1789), the government structure established by the Constitution was accepted by the overwhelming majority of the voters of all the states. But as the existence of slavery in the southern and southwestern states created more and more tension and anger between the slave states and the nonslave states, a new theory of the foundation of the power of the national government and its relationship to the state governments was developed by Vice President John Calhoun in 1828. Representing the slave state of South Carolina, which did not want to be bound by the national tariff law enacted in 1828, Calhoun wrote a pamphlet that asserted that the legislature of South Carolina could nullify the application of any national law to the state of South Carolina. Calhoun claimed that when each state had ratified the Constitution each state had kept sovereignty within its borders. He believed that neither Congress, nor the Supreme Court, nor the President could order a state to take actions against its will.

But Calhoun's challenge to the sovereignty of the national government under the Constitution went further. He argued that a state that disliked a law passed by Congress could withdraw from the union of states under the Constitution. Calhoun proposed a complex procedure for doing this: if a state nullified a national law; and if one-fourth of the state legislatures agreed, the law would be a dead letter unless three-fourths of the states passed a Constitutional amendment incorporating the text of the nullified law. If the states overruled the nullifying state, it could either accept the new Constitutional amendment or could *withdraw from the Union.*

Calhoun's approach would have given unusual power to a minority of one-fourth of the states. They could act to veto the enforcement of a law passed by Congress. Remember, it was much easier to get a one-quarter *minority* of the state legislatures to act to block the enforcement of a law than it was to get a *majority* of three-quarters of the legislatures to affirm the law. Moreover, the power of the national legislature, Congress, was undermined if the will of a majority in the Congress could not be enforced unless a three-quarters majority of the *state* legislatures approved the law. Calhoun's proposal would have meant that the effectiveness of every law passed by a majority in Congress would be in doubt unless the simple majority was certain that a *three-fourths majority* of the state legislatures would approve the law if it was challenged.

The notion that basic *legislation* had to be approved by a *three-fourths* majority was unusual. No state constitution applied such a large majority requirement for enacting state laws. The Constitution required a two-thirds Senate majority for the ratification of treaties. To overcome a presidential veto Congress needed to muster a two-thirds majority. To remove a federal officer charged with criminal actions, a two-thirds majority of the members present in the Senate had to vote for removal. The "cloture" rule passed in 1917 by the United States Senate required a two-thirds plus one majority to end debate on a bill (i.e., to stop a filibuster). In the United States the three-fourths majority requirement was required only to add amendments to the Constitution. If *legislation* were to have been subjected to the same drastic requirement, the national Congress would have been paralyzed, and a huge amount of its power would have been transferred to the states.

James Madison maintained that Calhoun's theory of nullification was contrary to the essential principle of a republic's government: the sovereignty of a *majority* of voters. As Madison put it, Calhoun's scheme allowed

> the ascendancy of a minority over a large majority, in a Republican System, the characteristic rule of which is that the major [majority] will is the ruling will.

Madison also challenged Calhoun's scheme with a second argument. The Articles of Confederation had been ratified by the state legislatures. But the state constitutions in force by 1787 had been ratified by special elections of all voters. And the

Constitution of 1787 had been ratified by specially elected state constitutional conventions. Thus, said Madison, in each state the *voters*, not elected legislatures, had ratified both the U.S. Constitution and the state constitutions. Therefore, Madison concluded that the state constitutions and the national Constitution rested equally on the sovereignty of the voters, and not the state legislatures.

Furthermore, maintained Madison, the process of ratifying the Constitution of 1787 represented an agreement by the sovereign voters of all the ratifying states to come together not as people in separate states, but as "*one people* for certain purposes [emphasis added]." The purpose was to create a national government with specified powers. We can appreciate Madison's position by comparing the wording of the Articles of Confederation, which describes the government it created as a "perpetual Union between the States," with the preamble of the Constitution of 1787. The preamble *does not mention the states*. Rather, it mentions "the people." The preamble proclaims, "We the people of the United States . . . do ordain and establish this Constitution of the United States of America." As Madison saw it, since the Constitution was a compact that formed the people of all the states into one union, it was illogical to allow any state either to nullify national laws or to withdraw from the union.

But how was a dispute over a power claimed by two equally authorized governments, a state government and the national government, to be resolved? Nationalists like James Madison had a simple answer. They argued that the Constitution clearly empowered the judicial branch of the *national* government (ultimately the Supreme Court) to resolve such disagreements. Article III, Section 2, of the Constitution stated that the judicial power of the national government extended "to controversies to which the United States shall be a party." In 1819, the first such case to come before the Supreme Court, *McCulloch* v. *Maryland*, involved the constitutionality of a law passed by the state of Maryland. The law taxed the notes of the Bank of the United States, which had been chartered by the national government. In a majority opinion that declared the Maryland tax unconstitutional, Chief Justice John Marshall asserted that *national power was superior to state power when the national power was authorized by the Constitution.* Marshall argued that the national government "was the government of all; its powers are delegated by all; it represents all, and acts for all."

Of course, logic and historical precedent do not always determine actions. In 1861, seven southern states seceded from the Union and formed the Confederate States of America. Convinced that their interests were threatened by remaining in a nation whose newly elected President (Abraham Lincoln) and his party (the Republican party) were committed to excluding slavery from the Western territories, many defenders of slavery wanted to leave the Union. Because they believed in the concept of constitutionalism, in each slave state the proponents of secession called for a special convention, composed of elected delegates, to consider whether or not to secede from the United States. Eventually 11 slave states seceded, while four stayed in the United States.

The Confederacy was defeated in the Civil War that followed, and the seceding states were occupied by the U.S. Army. The Union states ratified the Thirteenth Amendment (1865) to the Constitution, abolishing slavery. The authority of the national government over all the states that had joined the Union was confirmed so decisively that since 1865, no state government has challenged that power by extrajudicial means, such as secession.

After the Civil War, Congress debated the terms for readmitting the seceding states into the Union. Obviously the states would have to agree to accept the authority of the Constitution. But the readmission of the states that had seceded was complicated by the desire of a majority in Congress to guarantee that the groups that had led the secession movement in the South, at best a slim majority, did not reclaim political power. Congress refused—as was its right under the Constitution—to recognize the state governments formed under the guidelines suggested by Presidents Lincoln and Johnson. It believed that these governments were inclined to restore many elements of slavery, would challenge the authority of the national government, and might even secede again. To prevent this, the majority in Congress first drafted the Fourteenth Amendment, which protected the freed slaves against *state* government action that deprived them of "life, liberty or property without due process of law." States that denied the right to vote to any *male* inhabitant would have their representation in the House of Representatives reduced.

The Fourteenth Amendment was the first Constitutional amendment that applied only to the actions of state governments. Initially, all southern legislatures except that of Tennessee refused to ratify the Fourteenth Amendment. (Tennessee was readmitted to the Union in 1866.) To force the other seceding states to recognize national sovereignty, in 1867 Congress passed several reconstruction laws that set up a series of readmission requirements for the former Confederate states. Each state had to hold a special election for a constitutional convention that would write a new state constitution. If Congress did not approve the new state constitution, it would simply refuse to vote for readmission. The legislatures elected under these new constitutions also were required to ratify the Fourteenth Amendment before their states could be readmitted to the Union. In 1868 six of the remaining ten states outside the Union were readmitted according to this procedure.

Despite the Fourteenth Amendment, violations of the civil rights of African Americans in the South, especially violence directed against black voters, continued. Meanwhile, between 1867 and 1869, voters in nine northern states defeated referenda that would have given blacks the right to vote. To protect the black vote, which the Republican leaders in Congress believed to be essential to their political success in the northern states and in the South, Congress was persuaded in 1869 to pass the Fifteenth Amendment, which banned denying to any man the right to vote on the basis of his race, color, or previous condition of servitude.

The Republican majority in Congress insisted that the four southern states remaining outside the Union also ratify the Fifteenth Amendment as a condition of readmission, which they did by the end of 1870. There was substantial opposition to the Fifteenth Amendment in many northern states, since racial prejudice against African Americans was strong. Without the votes of the remaining four southern states that still had not been readmitted to the union, the Fifteenth Amendment would not have been ratified.

Like the Fourteenth Amendment, the Fifteenth Amendment *restricted state sovereignty*, overriding the clause of the original Constitution that made the states the sole judges of the qualifications of voters. But in 1876, the Supreme Court ruled that Congressional legislation had given the national government excessive power to *enforce* the Fifteenth Amendment, power that was not mentioned in the amendment and that violated the protections of the First Amendment (*U.S.* v. *Reese*). The Court also ruled (*U.S.* v. *Cruikshank*) that the Fourteenth Amendment did not provide any protection when *individuals*, rather than state governments, interfered with the liberties of people of color. These Court decisions weakened significantly the protections of the Fourteenth and Fifteenth Amendments gave to the civil liberties of African Americans. (The ruling in *U.S.* v. *Cruikshank* was consistent with the refusal of the courts to protect the civil liberties of workers when employers infringed upon them.) (see pages 20-21,79-82).

After the Civil War, the authority of the Constitution was challenged by some states. John Peter Altgeld, the governor of Illinois, verbally protested the 1894 decision of President Grover Cleveland to send federal troops into Illinois to suppress the Pullman Strike. Altgeld maintained that there was no disorder and that the Constitution did not authorize the president to dispatch federal troops to a state without a request from the governor. However, while Altgeld protested the dispatch of the federal troops, he did not order the Illinois state militia to try to prevent the federal troops from carrying out their mission. About 70 years later, in 1963, George C. Wallace, the governor of Alabama, seemed willing to challenge U.S. marshalls who, in accordance with a federal court order, were escorting the first black students to break the color line at the University of

Alabama. But at the last minute Wallace stepped aside, deciding not to defy the authority of the national government.

In 1973, a small group of Native Americans, organized in the American Indian Movement (AIM), armed themselves, took hostages, and resisted national government authority on the Pine Ridge Reservation in South Dakota. Arguing that throughout most of the history of the United States they had not been allowed to vote in U.S. elections, and that their own elected tribal councils had been improperly influenced by the U.S. government, they contended that the treaty concessions these councils had made to the U.S. government to allow the economic development of Native American reservation lands were illegal. The theoretical position of the American Indian Movement was not a repudiation of the principle of constitutional government, but was rather an assertion that Native Americans were being governed *without their consent*.

Most Americans continue to believe that when the laws and actions of the national government are in conformity with the Constitution there can be no legitimate obstruction of the authority of the national government. The logic of a constitutional, all-inclusive democratic republican form of government is that legal, peaceful means are available to change the Constitution and government policy. Using their sovereign power, voters can elect representatives who will draft constitutional amendments and new laws.

By the 1830s, people living in the United States had reached a consensus on the need for civil liberties, republican government, constitutional government, and a democracy for free white adult males. The next chapter will analyze the conflicting ideas Americans had about equality. Many Americans defined equality in a restrictive way, which limited the number of people who enjoyed equal rights.

CHAPTER 4

Equality

I

> We hold these truths to be self-evident: That all men are created
> equal; that they are endowed by their Creator with certain
> unalienable rights; that among these are life, liberty, and the pursuit
> of happiness.

These are among the most famous phrases in the Declaration of
Independence. They tell us a great deal about the meaning of the
concept of *equality* to the leaders of rebellion against English
colonial rule and to succeeding generations of Americans.

How much equality was there in the world in 1776? Today
there are many democratic republics in which all citizens have
equal political rights. In 1776 there were none. Today none of the
major nations of the world allows slavery. In 1776 slavery was
legal everywhere. Today women in the United States have the
same rights to own property as do men. In 1776 most married
women could not make contracts and had no control over the
property of their households. Today laws prescribe equal
penalties for men and women who commit the same crimes. In
colonial times, married women who committed adultery were
often punished more severely than were married men.

So what did Jefferson mean when he used the word "equal"?
Note that he modified "equal" with the word *created*. Jefferson
clearly did not mean that everyone should *end up* equal in *every*
respect. Rather, he was advancing the theory that all white men

were born with equal natural *rights or liberties*. Some of these
rights were so important that they were considered to be
inalienable rights; this is, they *could not be taken away*.
Following John Locke's ideas and English customs, thinkers like
Jefferson and James Madison believed that when men chose to
leave the state of nature and form a Civil Society, they could be
asked by the government they formed to give up some rights; but
Jefferson and other natural rights theorists believed that men
always *retained their unalienable natural rights*. The 1776
Virginia Declaration of Rights, written by George Mason,
explained that

> all men are by nature equally free and independent, and have certain
> inherent rights, of which, when they enter into a state of society
> [Civil Society], they cannot, by any compact, deprive or divest their
> posterity [succeeding generations].

James Madison believed that at the time men entered Civil
Society, each man was *equal* to all other men *in the natural
rights that he kept and the natural rights that he gave up*.

Chapter 1 discussed the basic liberties, or civil rights, of
individuals that the people of the newly formed United States of
America wanted protected against the authority exercised by
governments. To protect these liberties, the principle of the legal
equality of each individual white male in dealing with
government power was stressed. This chapter will analyze the
historical demands made by *groups* of people to be given *equal*
political rights and *equal* economic rights.

The origin of the general idea of equality before the law can
be traced to England and the Magna Carta (1215). For the first
time in history a monarch agreed that some free subjects, the
nobility, could not be imprisoned without a trial and would be
tried in accordance with "the law of the land." This meant that
the monarch *was limited by the laws* that had previously been
enacted. Thus one aspect of the power of the monarch had been
put on an plane of *equality* with that of other hereditary
aristocrats.

By the seventeenth century, many English people insisted that the monarch and free subjects were equally bound by the same laws in all circumstances. Beginning in 1626, the House of Commons struggled with King Charles I to force him to agree to honor the 1297 charter issued by Edward I that required parliamentary consent to levy *general* taxes. (The Magna Carta had limited the monarch's right to tax members of the nobility.) During the debates in the House of Commons regarding Charles' stand, one member, John Glanville, clearly stated the principle of equality before the *law*: "Our law says that the King's command contrary to the law is void." Glanville meant that even a king, who everyone at the time agreed was God's lieutenant on earth, was bound by the law. Hence all people in England, including the monarch, were equal before the law.

Once the principle of this kind of equality was established beyond a shadow of a doubt in England (and it took a civil war to settle the point) it became a crucial part of the political thinking of the English and of the mainly English settlers of the English colonies in North America. But belief in another type of equality was also developing in the colonies in a way it did not develop in Great Britain.

Richard Bland was a Virginian who wrote many pamphlets asserting the right of affluent colonists to enjoy rights equal to those of affluent Englishmen. In 1766 he wrote that "*rights* imply *equality* in the instances to which they belong and must be treated without respect to the dignity [social standing] of the persons concerned in them." But ordinary people in the newly independent United States would insist that the kind of argument Bland made be carried to its logical conclusion. Equal rights were due to free men, irrespective of their wealth and social status.

By the end of the Revolutionary War, most of the people in the newly independent states believed in *republican equality*. By this they meant that in a modern republic, a form of government that allowed no one to have a right to public office by virtue of heredity, all *voters* should have *equal political rights:* the right to vote and the right to run for public office. (Remember, this is not the same idea as democracy, which we defined as the notion that *all adults* should be *voters*, and would have equal political rights.) People who advocated republican equality applied their belief in voter equality to voting for representatives to constitutional conventions, to referenda on constitutional amendments, and to elections for government offices. Anyone who voted should be able to vote for the candidates running for *all* elected offices. In 1776, many states had *extra* property requirements for voting for the state's governor or for the upper house (senate) of the state legislature. This meant that poorer voters only voted for members of the lower house of the state legislature.

In Virginia, George Mason, a wealthy planter, proposed that his state's first constitution create a legislature with an upper house whose members would have to own *inherited* lands worth at least two thousand pounds, which would make newly wealthy men ineligible to serve in the legislature. Why didn't affluent advocates of a republican form of government in the new United States believe in political equality? They wanted *substantial property holders to have extra political rights*. Otherwise, believed republicans like James Madison, the natural rights of substantial property holders would be threatened by laws passed by representatives of small property holders and propertyless men. The lower economic orders might push for higher taxes on the rich or for laws that made it difficult for prosperous moneylenders to collect on the debts owed to them by the lower orders.

Madison did not change his views. He thought that state senates elected by the more prosperous would be more competent and less radical than the lower legislative houses elected by all voters. But Madison understood that the special privilege given to affluent voters would "offend the sense of equality which reigns in a free Country." It did. As Chapter 2 explained, by the 1830s, in most states the pressure of the less affluent voters, who called themselves *democratic* republicans, convinced the legislatures to abolish all property qualifications for voting and for running for office. Now equal suffrage rights were available to all free, adult white males. From this point on white men in the United States referred to their nation as a democracy. But true political equality was still lacking, and would not be attained fully until 1975, by which time the 1965 Voting Rights Act had been in force long enough to allow African Americans living in the South to register and vote.

People sometimes believe that political equality means that each voter, in addition to casting a single vote like all other voters, has *influence* equal to that exercised by each other voter. But *the U.S. Constitution did not fully apply the notion of equality to the question of how much influence the voters in each state exerted in the election of the House of Representatives and the Senate*. Compromises made at the Constitutional Convention deliberately *over-represented* some voters and *underrepresented others*. The Constitution used a population formula to assign seats in the House of Representatives. In theory, this meant that each voter voted for one representative and that since each congressional district would have the same number of voters, the influence of the voter in any particular congressional district would be equal to the influence of any voter in any other congressional district. But at the Constitutional Convention, pressure from the slave states forced a departure from the principle of equal voter influence. Slaves, *none of whom voted*, would be counted as three-fifths of a person. This meant that in a slave state the number of *potential voters* who could vote to elect a congressman was *less* than the number of potential voters in a congressional district in a nonslave state. In short, the individual voter in a slave state had more clout than the individual voter in a non-slave state.

The Constitution provided that Congress would use the results of the census of population to allocate seats in the House of Representatives to each state. The number of representatives would be proportional to the population of each state (subject to the rule that the population total for each state would count each slave as three-fifths of a person). Each state legislature was left to determine the actual geographical boundaries of each congressional district. Some state legislatures chose to create congressional districts very *unequal* in size. This meant that voters in congressional districts with lower than average populations were *overrepresented* in Congress. Likewise, voters in larger than average districts were *underrepresented* in Congress.

As these inequalities in congressional district population developed after 1788, the clearest pattern that emerged was the overrepresentation of *rural* areas of states and the underrepresentation of *cities*. The same disparity existed in the districts created by state legislatures for election to the lower and upper houses of the legislatures. Why did this happen? Originally, the nation had few cities. Rural interests naturally controlled the legislatures, since most voters were farmers who lived in rural areas. But as the economy grew, and urbanization created larger towns and cities, especially in industrial regions, *rural legislators did not want to give up power to the expanding urban areas in their states*. It was not until 1964 that the U.S. Supreme Court would rule that legislative districts had to be *approximately* equal in population. This meant that for about a century, cities, where the majority of industrial workers had been concentrated, had been significantly underrepresented in state legislatures and the House of Representatives.

Under the Constitution, the people of small population states elected two U.S. senators, and the people of large population states also elected two senators. Each *state*, large or small, was given equal political influence in the Senate. But this equal influence was based on the state as a basic political unit. *Those who believed the voter should be the basic political unit, and that equality meant that all voters should be equally represented, were very critical of this arrangement.* From this point of view, it is clear that the *voters in the large population states were underrepresented* in the Senate, while the *voters in the small population states were overrepresented.*

The structure of the House and the Senate resulted from a series of compromises adopted at the Philadelphia convention. Without these deals, there would have been no United States. These compromises show that *all people do not always want*

complete equality in political rights, especially if they represent a
minority. In 1787, the smaller, less populous states were too
fearful of being outvoted in Congress to accept a Senate, as well
as a House of Representatives, based on equal representation of
the population of each state. They saw the inequality of
representation in the Senate as a protection of their interests and
basic rights. And the slave states simply refused to join a nation
that did not give their voters extra influence.

As our national legislature developed, each house of
Congress established its own rules of operation. By the years
after the Civil War, the House of Representatives and the Senate
had both established *seniority* (i.e., number of years of service in
each house), as the basis for the right to be a committee
chairman. Committee chairmen exercised more power than the
ordinary senator or congressman. The seniority system meant
that at any given session of Congress, all elected members did
not have *equal access* to the most important positions of power.
Rather, those who had served longer terms in Congress had a
special advantage. Of course, it could be argued that experience
usually makes people more effective legislators and
administrators. Thus many people believe that pure equality is
not always a desired policy.

As we have seen, equality is *not the operational principle of
our national legislature.* (When votes of the full Senate and
House of Representatives are taken, of course, each congressman
has only one vote.) Probably the most intriguing example of a
legislative procedure that gave disproportionate power to a
minority group was the adoption in the U.S. Senate in 1917 of
the *cloture* rule. The Senate had always had a tradition of
unlimited debate. In theory, this meant that a senator could talk
as much as he wanted about a particular piece of legislation. In
the years before the Civil War there were a few situations in
which the Senate had come close to voting to prevent a senator
from exercising the right to unlimited debate in a way that
prevented a vote on a bill. This kind of "talking to death" tactic is
called a filibuster. In each of these early cases, the senator was
convinced to stop his speechmaking. In 1917 a handful of

senators, led by Robert La Follette, the famous Wisconsin reformer, were filibustering to prevent a vote on a resolution to declare war on Germany. To enable the majority to quickly overcome a filibuster in an emergency situation, the Senate adopted a cloture rule. A majority of two-thirds plus one senators could vote to end debate. This meant the Senate could immediately vote on the bill being filibustered. The purpose of the 1917 rule change was to prevent a small minority from obstructing the majority. Ironically, the bill created a situation in which a *large* minority could *block the will of the majority*. If one-third plus one of the Senators, a sizable minority, voted against cloture, there could be no vote on the bill being debated. This meant that in the Senate, unlike the House of Representatives, *it actually took more than a majority vote to pass a bill.*

In the years following the enactment of the cloture rule, senators from southern states used the threat of a filibuster or an actual filibuster to fight civil rights legislation. Even in the 1960s, as the civil rights movement was peaking, the filibuster was an effective weapon, since it forced backers of civil rights legislation to make deals with senators whose votes were needed to invoke the cloture of debate. While only a majority vote, 50 votes, was needed to pass the 1964 Civil Rights Act, 17 extra votes were needed to shut off debate so that a vote could be taken. Many of the senators who supplied those 17 extra votes did not back civil rights legislation as strong as that desired by dedicated supporters of civil rights. Consequently, major compromises had to be made to get moderate senators to provide the votes necessary to get a vote on the Civil Rights bill. Clearly, the cloture rule gave a minority of senators *disproportionate power* compared to the majority.

In 1973 the Senate voted to require only 60 votes to invoke cloture. This made it somewhat less difficult to stop a filibuster. However, in an era when many votes in the Senate are very close, the existence of the cloture rule makes the threat of a filibuster by a minority a very powerful weapon, one that can be used to block legislation opposed by the minority or to force revisions in the terms of bills disliked by the *very small* minority of senators whose votes are needed to defeat the filibuster.

II

Let us now consider the topic of *economic* equality. Historically, in the United States and in many European countries, some people have believed that all adults should end up in an *equal economic condition*. This is a very different view of equality from the one held by the drafters of the Declaration of Independence and the Constitution. Since all existing societies that allow private ownership of property have significant differences in wealth and income, reaching a condition of equality of condition requires *redistributing* wealth and income.

The first group in the modern world to publicly advance this view of equality was a small sect of English farmers, who called themselves the Diggers. Convinced that God had intended all people to farm God's land in small groups, with all sharing the product of their labor, the Diggers demanded (1649) the confiscation of large estates, with the land being parceled out to groups of the landless and those with too little land to make a living. The Diggers believed that "the earth is made by our creator [God] to be a common treasury of livelihood to one equal with another, without respect of persons." By persons, the Diggers meant social rank. The Diggers also claimed that Parliament owed them land as a reward for their military service in fighting and deposing King Charles I.[*]

Two hundred years later, Thomas Skidmore, a New York City machinist, wrote a book advocating using tax policy to *redistribute* property. He wanted to guarantee that all people in the nation owned enough land to make a decent living. Skidmore

---

[*]In 1381 English peasants revolted against what they regarded as unjust taxation and the restrictions of the freedom of serfs. Through their spokesman, Wat Tyler, the peasants demanded that the large landholdings of the Catholic church be "divided among the people of the parish." We do not know if this was a demand for equal distribution.

was more individualistic than the Diggers, since he did not believe in group ownership of land. But his aim was similar: all men were equally entitled to own at least enough land to make a decent living. Skidmore would have allowed for some to own more land than others, as long as everyone had enough land to support themselves.

Skidmore also argued that the equality before the law that Thomas Jefferson had endorsed in the Declaration of Independence was not enough to ensure a *condition* of life, liberty, and happiness for all:

> Do we not every day, see multitudes, in order to acquire property in the very pursuit of that happiness which Mr. Jefferson classes among the unalienable rights of man, obliged to sacrifice both liberty and health and often ultimately life. . . . If then property be so essential and indispensable in the pursuit of happiness . . . how can it be said, that I am created with an equal right to this happiness—with another [who already owns large amounts of property], when I must purchase property of him, with labor and suffering—and when he is under no necessity to purchase the like of me at the same costly price?

Public opinion polls indicate that most—but not all—citizens of the United States today *do not* believe that all adults should be on an approximate plane of equality of wealth and income. The majority of the public is more comfortable with the view of equality that calls for all adults to have equal rights, or, as some put it, *equal opportunity* to compete with others in the economic, political, and social spheres of life.

The views of people in the United States on equal economic opportunity cannot be understood without examining the history of their ideas about the structure of economic opportunity and the relationship between the way different economic groups influence government decisions. The English colonists and newly independent Americans were familiar with the history of pure monarchies and governments like England's, which gave almost all political power to hereditary aristocrats and a limited number of nonhereditary economic elites. In the past, under such governments, *public office* (i.e., a government position) *was almost always used by the officeholder to increase his or her wealth.* This meant that a person's economic standing—their income and wealth—would depend greatly on their political position. (And of course, wealthy people could gain a tremendous amount of political influence, including royal appointments, in return for using their wealth to do favors for those who offered them political power.) Political position in a nonrepublican government was often gained by *hereditary* claims to a particular government office (in England a position in the House of Lords) or when government positions could be filled *only by members of a hereditary group,* like the monarchy. This meant that hereditary elites had special economic opportunities, chances that were not available to other citizens.

In North America, many of the English colonists—the royal appointees and their political friends—benefited greatly from holding office. Their government posts often had substantial salaries or allowed the officeholder to earn income by charging fees for services provided—like issuing legal papers to allow imported goods to enter the colony. Royal governors could make lucrative land grants to friends and relatives. Most of the royal governors and the men connected to them by the exchange of political support and economic favors became Tories, who sided with England against the rest of the colonists who demanded independence.

The men who drafted the Virginia Declaration of Rights in 1776 were all large planters. *But they were not members of the small circle of planters who had supported the colony's royal governor.* The Declaration of Rights began with a statement of natural rights and then asserted the two basic parts of the concept of republicanism:

> That all power is vested in, and consequently derived from the people. . . . [and] That no man, or set of men, are entitled to exclusive . . . emoluments [pay] or privileges from the community, but in consideration of public services; which, *not being descendible,* *neither ought* the offices of magistrate, legislator, or judge *to be hereditary.*

These affluent Virginians were seeking to prevent any *small* elite from obtaining special political or economic advantages over all the other groups—including the other economic elites—in their society.

When the Constitution was ratified, and the new national government of the United States was elected, one group of economic elites, led by Alexander Hamilton, and members of the Federalist "party," attempted to get the national government to adopt policies that would favor a small group of wealthy men. The rest of the nation's economic elites banded together, under the leadership of Thomas Jefferson and James Madison, to block most of these policies. Generally, the Federalists represented the oldest, most established, and wealthiest men in any given state. The Jeffersonians, who at first called themselves Republicans (and later Democratic Republicans), included merchants, lawyers, bankers, and planters who were often much younger and less established than the Federalists. By 1812 the Republicans had won such a great political victory that the Federalist group dissolved.

In power on both the national and state levels, the Republicans insisted that national economic policies encourage the development of all sections of the nation. Jefferson arranged the Louisiana Purchase, adding millions of acres of farmland to the nation. Thereafter, the national government kept the prices of government land relatively low, which allowed many people to buy farm land and establish themselves as independent entrepreneurs.

Jefferson and most Democratic Republicans believed that if most citizens of the republic owned enough land to be economically independent, the *political stability* of the republic would be assured. This was a form of the policy Aristotle had proposed in his classical study of politics:

> Poverty is the cause of the defects of democracy. That is why measures should be taken to ensure a permanent level of prosperity. This is in the interest of all classes, including the prosperous themselves.

Aristotle wanted to attain this level of prosperity by means of periodic

> grants to the poor [from the Athenian treasury]. The ideal method of distribution, if a sufficient fund can be accumulated, is to make such grants sufficient for the purchase of a plot of land: failing that, they should be large enough to start men in commerce or agriculture.

In the United States, the national and state governments owned so much land, and the price of land was so low, that they could promote the goal that Aristotle described, ensuring "a permanent level of prosperity," by selling or giving land away (see pages 197, 224-225), rather than by distributing actual government monies.

When the Civil War ended, the newly freed African Americans demanded land (their slogan was "40 acres and a mule") as compensation for having been exploited as slaves. The former slaves wanted the land of their former owners to be redistributed to the men and women who had been enslaved. But the overwhelming majority of the U.S. Congress would not consider such reparations. They did not want to allow large amounts of private property to be *confiscated* and distributed by the government to the humans who had been exploited by their former masters. To do so would have set a precedent for compensating *free workers* for unfair treatment by their employers.

In early nineteenth-century United States, most non-farm businessmen were small scale entrepreneurs. There were no laws that gave one *small* entrepreneur an advantage over another. But many businessmen began to complain that some affluent businessmen were given a special privilege—the right to form a limited liability corporation (see Chapter 10). Charters of incorporation could only be acquired by getting a state legislature to pass a special law that incorporated the single business that was seeking incorporation. Critics argued that this process favored entrepreneurs with special business connections, and businessmen who had the money to bribe legislators. The solution, adopted first in New York State in 1838, was "free" incorporation. Thereafter *any* group of investors could incorporate by paying a modest fee and filing papers of incorporation with the state government.

By the 1830s, most middle- and upper-class white people in the United States believed that their nation offered its citizens historically unprecedented opportunities to compete for the income and wealth that would allow them to enjoy a comfortable standard of living. There were no special legal privileges awarded to an aristocracy. Adult white male citizens had attained civic equality, since they could vote. The phrase "republican equality" was often used to describe these forms of equality. Abundant natural resources were available to most whites (see Chapter 9). Eight years of free public education was offered to the young in most states. Assuming that true equality of economic opportunity existed, many Americans concluded that when inequalities of economic *condition* existed in their society, the inequalities were *justified*, since the competition for advancement had been fair, with all competitors *equal* before the law. The comfortable and the affluent believed that they had earned their position by means of hard labor, saving, and moral behavior. Conversely, the groups that were "making it" economically in American society believed that those stuck in poverty were lazy, stupid, and immoral, and thus *deserved* their condition. James Fenimore Cooper summed up this viewpoint in a passage from his 1838 book, *The American Democrat*:

> All men have essentially the same rights, an equality which, so far from establishing that "one man is as good as another," in a social sense, is the very means of producing the inequality of condition that actually exists.

But was society in the United States as open and equitable as the more affluent, and many of the native-born white men and women of modest means, believed? A negative answer to this question would point to the race and sex-based prejudices that severely limited the economic opportunities available to people of color, to members of many non-English immigrant groups, and to women (see Chapters 6, 7, and 8). It is also clear that while low-income children received a minimal basic education, their schools were vastly inferior to the public and private schools attended by middle- and upper-class children. Hardly any low-income male children attended high school until after World War I, especially because their parents needed to send their children to work to supplement low family incomes. Without advanced education, it was almost impossible to qualify for the best nonmanual professional and managerial jobs.

Inequalities of *legal* power, based on class, also limited the liberties and earnings of lower-income wage earners. Most manual workers were too poor to hire an attorney if their supervisor or employer cheated them out of the wages they had earned, a common occurrence. Workers had no legal recourse when they were unfairly fined by a supervisor, and those who protested against policies they believed were unjust were often fired. Beginning in 1843, prosperous judges invented legal rules (the common law doctrines of industrial torts) that made it virtually impossible for wage earners to recover damages when an employer's carelessness caused industrial accidents that hurt workers physically and mentally, resulting in medical bills, lost wages, death, and disabilities that caused a permanent loss of earnings. The legal defenses judges thought up to help employers were used to prevent sympathetic juries from deciding lawsuits brought by injured workers. Applying these defenses, the judges simply dismissed many lawsuits brought by injured workers. The defense of contributory negligence held that even if a worker was slightly negligent and the worker's employer had been grossly negligent, with an injury to the worker resulting, the worker could not recover *any* damages from the employer for the employer's carelessness. Under the doctrine assumption of risk, the *courts assumed* that when a worker was hired she or he had agreed, *despite the absence of a written release*, to give up the right to sue an employer for his careless actions, including the failure to guard machinery, as long as other employers in the same industry were similarly careless. When a worker actually complained to a business owner or manager about an unusual hazard, the employer was held harmless for an injury caused by the hazard, since the courts reasoned that the worker had freely chosen to stay at work after having clearly identified the hazard. Underlying the actions of these judges was a belief that railroads and factories were the instruments of economic progress. Therefore, judges thought that in the early period of industrialization the owners of enterprises that promised plenty for the nation should be *shielded from high business costs*, like the cost of paying for the medical expenses and lost earning power of workers injured through the negligence of their employers.

The nation's courts enforced the contracts businesses made with each other, and prevented state governments from invalidating such contracts after they were made. (*Fletcher* v. *Peck*, 1810) In 1819 the Supreme Court held (*Dartmouth College* v. *Woodward*) that after a state government gave a corporation a legislative charter, the charter was to be treated like a contract and could not be altered, making it illegal to decide subsequently to regulate the corporation. Nonetheless, until 1923, no court in the United States would enforce against an employer the terms of a contract that the employer had signed with a labor union representing his employees.

Between 1885 and 1900, many federal court judges, including the judges of the U.S. Supreme Court, became alarmed by the increasing number of strikes by workers and by state and national legislation that protected the health and civil liberties of workers by limiting the number of hours men and women could work, requiring obedience to workplace safety codes, and preventing employers from forcing workers to sign contracts promising they would not join unions or go on strike. The majority of federal judges concluded that they had to protect private property against popular reform proposals that the judges believed would lead to socialism. To protect the property rights of businessmen, the judges developed a new way of looking at property rights. They began to define property rights, which were protected by both the Fifth and Fourteenth Amendments, in a *dynamic* manner. This meant that they would block actions—like strikes and labor legislation—that limited the freedom of the employer to use his or her property to do business. Thus, strikes were often ended by court injunctions that held that the strikes prevented a factory owner or railroad company from operating. Laws protecting the civil liberties and the bodies of workers, which were, for the worker, the equivalent of the productive capital of the businessperson, were ruled unconstitutional on the grounds that they interfered with the right of the employer to enjoy freedom to contract, as he saw fit, with his workers. In short, the federal courts established an *unequal*, double standard: the property rights and liberties of workers would receive no protection, while the property rights and liberties of business owners were given substantial protection.

In the years after the Civil War, as more and more corporations were created, and as the largest corporations grew to the point that they engaged in operations in many different states across the nation, many citizens became alarmed at the immense economic and political power of big business and big businessmen. These people, mostly small businessmen (including *farmers, who were entrepreneurs*) and blue-collar laborers, thought that big business had eliminated opportunity for the small entrepreneur to operate successfully. It was also feared that the wealth of big business enabled it to buy political influence. In 1873, Frederick A. Ryan, Chief Justice of the Wisconsin Supreme Court, and hardly a radical, eloquently expressed these concerns about growing corporate power. In the future, he asked,

> Which shall rule—wealth or man; which shall lead—money or intellect; who shall fill public stations—educated and patriotic free men, or the feudal serfs of corporate capital?

Americans concerned about the threats big business posed to equality of economic opportunity and to republican political equality had different ideas about how to remedy the situation. To equalize opportunity, some, usually from agricultural regions, proposed breaking up large businesses into smaller, *competing* enterprises. Other critics wanted a graduated income tax, with high, *confiscatory* rates on wealthy individuals and large corporations. This would redistribute wealth, since the average person would see their property taxes reduced if government collected more money from the wealthy. A graduated income tax would also *break the economic and political power of large corporations and big businessmen.* The result: republican equality, both economic and political, would be preserved.

But few big corporations were ever broken up into units small enough to create meaningful price competition, and a steeply graduated income tax that drastically redistributed income was never enacted. (The 1943 income tax had very high rates on income for the affluent, but had loopholes that allowed corporate executives to be paid with tax-free stocks.) However, in 1914, Congress established the Federal Trade Commission, which was charged with halting *unfair competitive practices* by one business against another. The aim was to create equality of opportunity by making all businesses equally subject to the same rules of fair competition. Since 1914 the FTC has often acted to stop illegal competition, although different businesses have often disagreed sharply about the definition of fair competition.

During the Great Depression of the 1930s, Congress passed one law that was specifically intended to redistribute income, the National Labor Relations Act. While the passage of this law was something of an accident,* the effect was clearly *redistributive.* Why? By helping industrial workers form unions, the law enabled workers to bargain more effectively for higher wages. This involved some redistribution of income, which Senator Robert Wagner, who drafted the law, hoped would promote economic growth by putting more purchasing power in the hands of workers.

In the 1930s, President Franklin D. Roosevelt and many liberals who supported his policies insisted that the national

---

*Many congresspeople who voted for the National Labor Relations Act in 1935 expected the Supreme Court to declare the law unconstitutional. But late in 1936 the balance of power within the Supreme Court shifted, most likely in response to the huge majority President Roosevelt secured in his bid for reelection. In March 1937 the Supreme Court upheld the constitutionality of the NLRA. (See the discussion of the Supreme Court in Chapter 5.)

government establish a welfare state (see also Chapter 11). The principle behind the welfare state is that there should be a *minimum* level of income and social services for all citizens. No one should be allowed to fall below this level. To prevent such a decline, *income maintenance* and *free social service* programs were instituted. There is no question that such programs often involved redistributing income to the most unfortunate (and poorest) segments of our society. In the years since the 1930s, the amount of money transferred has increased, especially as food stamps were added to income maintenance payments and social service programs for those below the poverty line have been expanded to include medical care and legal aid. In one sense, the welfare state theoretically moves society toward a type of *equality of condition*, since welfare state programs ideally guarantee that *no matter how unequal citizens are in their total levels of income, they are all equal in that in theory the government will not allow any citizens to fall below a subsistence level* of income and basic social services.

The New Deal also strove to promote equality of economic opportunity by using the *credit* of the national government to help businesses. Historically, bank credit had always been more expensive in the less prosperous rural regions of the nation. And in many cases banks simply would not make any loans to small farmers. To give rural entrepreneurs the same access to credit as urban businessmen, the 1935 Rural Electrification Act provided for loans to electric companies, including nonprofit cooperatives, to enable them to put up the poles and wires necessary to transmit electricity to farmers. With electric power now available, farmers could buy electrical machinery that made their operations more efficient and more profitable. The Tennessee Valley Authority (TVA) built many new dams to generate hydroelectric power in the Southeast. This activity created more economic opportunity by supplying electricity at low rates to farmers and manufacturers in the poorest region of the country. The TVA also provided loans to rural consumers to enable them to buy electric appliances. Finally, throughout the New Deal years, the Reconstruction Finance Corporation, headed by Jesse

Jones of Texas, favored businesses in the South and Southwest when it made loans to help them avoid bankruptcy. This policy was a form of *equalization of access to credit,* since commercial banks in these two regions did not have as much money to loan as did the more established banks of the Northeast, the Midwest, and the West.

Since the 1930s, Congress has enacted additional programs designed to help small businessmen obtain loans and to provide small businesses with free expert advice that they cannot afford. In 1994, proponents of using government power to produce an equality of condition demanded that no citizen should be denied access to health insurance because she or he lacked the money to purchase an insurance policy. Legislation aimed at preventing insurance companies from refusing to sell benefits to people who had a preexisting illness was also debated in Congress. The aim of this legislation was to create equal access to health insurance for consumers who could afford to purchase insurance.

III

As noted in Chapter 1, the first clause of the Fourteenth Amendment to the U.S. Constitution was designed to prevent any state from denying basic rights and liberties to any citizen. The clause also held that no state could "deny to any person within its jurisdiction the equal protection of the laws." This clause, known as the equal protection clause, had great potential to prevent economic and political discrimination based on race, sex, national origin, and place of residence.

But women were initially not able to use this clause to obtain the right to vote. When women did secure the vote through the Nineteenth Amendment, they still were not able to get the federal courts to use the Fourteenth Amendment to eliminate wage discrimination and to prevent employers from refusing to hire women for many (usually high-paying) jobs. Despite the Fifteenth Amendment, by 1900 few African Americans were allowed to vote in southern states. Other people of color, whether Hispanic or Asian, encountered similar problems.

Early in 1776, an anonymous pamphlet writer who believed in a republican form of government speculated on the meaning of social equality. He wrote:

> Whenever any rank in society is invested with more than an equal share of the privileges and powers of that society, it must be at the expense of the other ranks.

Racial discrimination (and discrimination based on sex or age or sexual preference) created such inequalities because discrimination against one group also involved discrimination *in favor* of another group, white males. Put another way, racial and sex-based discrimination created *racial preferences* for white males.

Only in the 1930s did the Supreme Court, for the first time, apply the principle of equality before the law to people of color. In *Missouri Ex Rel. Gaines* v. *Canada* (1938), it ruled that if states chose to segregate college students racially, the states had to provide *equal* funds to black and white state colleges. Before the decision, most public black colleges in the South were grossly underfunded compared to their all-white counterparts, even though black citizens were taxed at higher *rates* than whites.

After World War II, the civil rights movement slowly gathered strength. Boycotts and demonstrations aimed at securing for nonwhites, especially African Americans and Hispanics, equal rights to buy seats in buses, baseball parks, theaters, and rooms in hospitals. The *Brown* v. *Board of Education* Supreme Court decision in 1954 held that racially segregated schools could never offer equal educational opportunity to nonwhites and whites. In the words of the Court,

> Separate educational facilities are inherently unequal. Therefore we hold that the plaintiffs . . . are, by reason of the segregation complained of, deprived of the equal protection of the laws guaranteed by the 14th Amendment.

Since education has a powerful impact on the kind of job and monetary earnings that a person will have when they enter the labor force, equal educational opportunity is related to equality of economic opportunity. As the schools were desegregated (and many were not), more nonwhite citizens had greater opportunities for economic advancement.

It is important to understand that discrimination against people who are members of a particular nationality, or of a racial, gender, religious, age, or disabled group not only denies them equality before the law but also denies them equal opportunity in the competition for economic rewards and social status. Job discrimination that favors a particular sex, race, or nationality *is a type of affirmative action policy* that helps the favored group. In the United States, white males, especially white males of English and Western European origin, have been the main beneficiaries of laws and customs that gave them superior economic and social opportunities.

In 1964, Congress began a major shift in government policy toward the existing patterns of economic inequality in the United States. Having previously addressed only class-based economic inequalities, the Congress elected in 1962 passed the Civil Rights Act of 1964, which specifically banned employment *discrimination* based on race and sex. (In 1964 Congress rejected proposals to also ban age-based employment discrimination.) As amended in 1972, the national civil rights law requires that *government* agencies, who are major employers, establish *training* programs to equalize opportunities for their employees to learn new skills and compete for promotions. Government agencies and businesses that sell to them are also required to draw up plans that (a) indicate how they plan to make efforts to advertise fairly job opportunities to all qualified persons and (b) establish targets for hiring more people from groups that were available and qualified, but were not being hired in numbers proportionate to their availability.

Antidiscrimination lawsuits filed by the Justice Department and (after 1972) the Equal Employment Opportunities Commission, led federal courts, *when they found evidence of racial and gender employment discrimination*, to award financial damages to the victims of race-based and sex-based employment discrimination. Such actions (and the threat of such actions) definitely pressured many private employers and government agencies to hire many non-whites and women for jobs that had previously been closed to them. In a small number of cases, where the federal courts were convinced that employers were actively discriminating, the courts imposed hiring quotas for *limited* periods of time.

Since 1964, our congresses and presidents have had different degrees of enthusiasm for enforcing this civil rights law. There have been many controversies over whether quotas should be used in situations where a business or government agency has discriminated based on race or sex. The Supreme Court has changed its mind about the kind of discrimination (deliberate action by an employer or the operation of general social processes) necessary to justify damages and to imposing hiring quotas. Nevertheless, thousands of people of color and women have benefited from antidiscrimination lawsuits, which were filed on their behalf by the agencies of the national government. The court verdicts and settlements of these lawsuits enabled many people of color and women to secure financial damages for past discrimination and to obtain new, more equal employment opportunities.

Public opinion polls show that Americans overwhelmingly believe in equal opportunity in theory. But when people realize that truly following the standard of equal opportunity means that groups formerly denied such opportunity will share the opportunities available, they often react fearfully, and use negative racial *and gender* stereotypes to suggest that these "new" beneficiaries of equal opportunity do not deserve their access to education or jobs. This is especially true when a slowly expanding economy creates a *zero-sum game*, in which one person's gain, in the short run, comes at the expense of a potential gain by another person. Racism is likely to intensify in such an environment.

In 1964, in _Baker v. Carr_, the Supreme Court ruled on the question of the fairness of legislative districts that overrepresented and underrepresented voters. Many southern states had not changed their legislative district lines since 1900; the old lines overrepresented rural areas. Since 1940, many African Americans living in the southern states had moved from rural to urban areas. This migration was a response to the decline in farm jobs (due to mechanization) and the growth of urban-industrial areas throughout the South. Civil rights groups were concerned that as African Americans gained the right to vote in the urban parts of the South, their voting power would be diminished by the old district lines. The Supreme Court applied the Fourteenth Amendment's equal protection clause, ruling that

> A citizen, a qualified voter, is no more nor no less so because he lives in the city or on the farm. We hold that, as a basic constitutional standard, the Equal Protection Clause requires that the seats in both houses of a bicameral state legislature must be apportioned on a population basis.

Note that the same _argument_ could be applied to the way the U.S. Senate is chosen. But since the equal protection clause applies only to _states_, there is no contradiction between this clause and the way the Constitution specifies that Senate seats shall be apportioned. Unless the Constitution is amended to alter the way voters elect the Senate, which is not likely, two standards of political equality will continue to exist in the nation.

Chapter 5 will explore the history of the idea that the powers of governments in the United States should be divided unequally, with state governments exercising most of the government power in the nation. During the first two-thirds of the twentieth century, an increasing number of people believed that in an urban-industrial society, only the national government had the resources to aid and protect citizens when their rights and livelihoods were threatened.

CHAPTER 5

Federalism

I

Three years after the Declaration of Independence was signed, the state legislatures (1779) ratified the Articles of Confederation. This constitution created a *federal* system of government. The new United States of America was a league of states that agreed to join together to create a central government, while each member state *retained much of its power to govern.* The central government of this federation was very weak, so weak that it was largely a servant of the state governments. Look at the chart that compares the powers of the states and the federal government under the Articles of Confederation.

NATIONAL GOVERNMENT	STATE GOVERNMENTS
Make treaties with foreign governments.	Full authority to determine how delegates to Congress are selected.
Can determine total amount of revenue to be raised for the national government.*	Each state legislature would determine the type of tax used to raise its share of the revenue due to the national government.
Exclusive control of military ships and armed land forces.	Each state retains all powers and rights not expressly delegated to the United States.
Right to coin money and regulate coinage of money by the states.	

---

*The actual ability of the national government (the Congress) to raise revenue was severely limited by the requirement that taxes had to be approved by a majority vote of *each* separate state delegation in Congress.

In 1787 a group of affluent, educated men who believed the central government of the Articles of Confederation was too weak gathered at an unauthorized constitutional convention in Philadelphia. To design a national government that would be able to protect the property, commerce, and physical security of the new nation against domestic and foreign challenges, the men at the convention wrote a new constitution that *increased the relative power of the national government*. Many complex compromises were necessary before the delegates agreed to a structure that they thought would strengthen the national government without going so far that voters worried about excessive national government power would refuse to ratify the Constitution. Since the delegates all *believed that special ratifying conventions of all voters should be called* to approve the Constitution, they understood that they had to draft a constitution that took the views of these voters into account.

Most of the delegates at the Constitutional Convention were alarmed by the recent passage of state laws that prevented creditors from collecting the money owed to them. The delegates, all substantial property owners, thought that the state legislatures were becoming too democratic, with too many ordinary men either voting for the candidates or getting elected to the legislatures. To block the feared radical action of popular majorities in the state legislature, many of the delegates, including James Madison, favored giving the president or the Congress of the new national government *a veto over laws passed by the state legislatures*. But as the delegates discussed this idea, even its backers became convinced that it would never be approved by the state ratifying conventions.

As they thought about the national republic they were creating in the draft of the Constitution, the delegates realized that the new national government would be the largest republic in history. Thinkers like James Madison concluded that in a geographically extensive republic, with a very diverse population, *national majorities would not be easily formed*. Thus the national government was not likely to be influenced by majorities of hard pressed debtor farmers, as were many state governments. Since the national government had sole authority to coin money, the kinds of inflationary, paper-money printing schemes that debtors favored would no longer be possible in the states and would be unlikely to be adopted by the national government.

The following chart compares the powers of the national government and the state governments enumerated in the Constitution of 1787.

NATIONAL GOVERNMENT	STATE GOVERNMENTS
Right to raise revenue by taxes.	States could charge fees to pay for cost of inspecting imports.
Exclusive right to regulate commerce between the states.	States could appoint the officers in the militia.
Exclusive right to charge tariffs on imports.	
Exclusive right to coin money.	
Right of the Supreme Court to decide the meaning of the Constitution and whether or not state and national laws were in violation of the Constitution.	
Establish post offices and post roads.	
Issue patents for inventions.	
Run the militia.	

Under the 1787 Constitution, the national government had many more *exclusive* rights than it had under the Articles of Confederation. It controlled tariffs, determined the amount of national taxes (besides tariffs) to be raised, and the type of tax to be used to obtain funds. (The Constitution imposed one requirement on the taxes voted by Congress: the amount of taxes due from the people of each state was to be proportional not to their wealth but to the population* of the state.) The national

---

*Slavery issue influenced the apportionment of taxes. The Constitution required that slaves count as three-fifths of a full person for purposes of

government was the only government allowed to coin money. It would also control almost every aspect of the militias. Of course, each state's constitution gave each state government authority to levy state taxes, to pass and enforce criminal and civil laws, to charter non-governmental organizations, and to determine the structure of county and city governments.

II

In making the national government stronger the delegates to the Constitutional Convention miscalculated. Too many voters were alarmed by the lack of specific restraints on the power of the national government. As one critic of the Constitution put it,

> the unlimited powers of the new Congress over the lives and property of their fellow citizens . . . [would] certainly be abused.

To win approval of the Constitution, its backers had to promise to support a series of constitutional amendments as soon as the new federal system took effect. James Madison took the lead in introducing the amendments in Congress. The first ten amendments became known as the Bill of Rights. These amendments protected two kinds of rights. First, most protected the basic natural rights of the individual against violations by the national government. Second, the Tenth Amendment dealt with a major objection of critics of the Constitution, that it had omitted an essential part of the Articles of Confederation: that each state *retained all powers and rights not expressly delegated to the central (national) government of the United States.*

The lack of this *constitutional* limit on national government power made many people who were willing to give the national government new powers very nervous. They feared that without

---

determining the tax liability of the people of each state. This formula gave taxpayers in the slave states a break, since their taxes would have been higher if each slave was counted as a full person.

a *specific reserved powers clause*, it would be possible for the national government to assert that it had additional governing powers, powers that were being exercised by the state governments. Supporters of the Constitution realized that they had to accept a reserved powers clause. This was the Tenth Amendment. It held that

> The powers not delegated to the United States by the Constitution nor prohibited by it to the States, are reserved to the States respectively, or to the people.

This clause went even further than the reserved powers clause of the Articles of Confederation, because the Tenth Amendment stated that powers not given to the national government by Constitution were retained not just by the states but *by the sovereign people*.

The relationship between the national government and the states proposed by the delegates at the Constitutional Convention was unprecedented. Never before had a true republic, without any aristocratic parts of government, been created in which there were two levels of government, *each deriving authority from the voters*. The *federal* structure of government in the new nation, in which the states and the national government divided up governing functions, had developed because of the lack of centralized control of the English colonies. The voters in each colony had become accustomed to exercising a significant amount of influence over their colonial governments. Colonial or state government helped preserve the distinctive interests of the people of each colony or state. The voters of each state did not want to abandon this power. But a majority concluded that their separate state governments had to have some kind of national organization to conduct diplomacy, provide for defense, settle commercial disputes between the states, ensure an effective monetary system, and serve as a protector of property rights. Hence, once the Bill of Rights was promised, they backed the Constitution and the federal system it established, giving the national government specific powers in the areas just mentioned, and reserving all other powers to the states and the people. *Federalism* is the term used to describe this system of two levels of government, with different powers assigned to each level.

James Madison, and most members of his generation who believed in a stronger national government, did not think the range of powers of the national government should be all-encompassing. In the United States, during the first century following the creation of the federal system of government by the Constitution of 1787, the state governments exercised many more powers than did the national government. This *inequality* was especially evident with respect to the exercise of the positive powers of government—to build new roads, finance education, and care for the poor. Here Madison believed that state governments would be the main players. Madison clearly wanted the level of national government activity to be far lower than the greatly intensified level that evolved in the 1930s and the years after World War II. Of course, Madison lived at a time when the economy was far simpler than it would later be.

III

Since the passage of the Bill of Rights, no constitutional amendment has limited the powers of the national government. The Fourteenth Amendment set a new precedent by applying some of the Fifth Amendment's restraints on federal government power to the states. Thus the 1868 amendment limited the power of state governments to make or enforce any law that deprived "any person of life, liberty or property without due process of law." The Fourteenth Amendment then added to the Constitution a new concept, applying only to the states. It said that the states could not deny to any person "the equal protection of the laws." This clause was intended to protect the civil rights of African Americans in the South.

The Sixteenth Amendment held that the national government's power to tax could be exercised by means of a particular kind of tax, an income tax "without apportionment among the several States, and without regard to any census or enumeration." It might be argued that in the long run, this amendment allowed the national government to raise a great deal of additional revenue, which increased its power compared to each individual state. But in theory the state governments that modified their constitutions to allow *state* income taxes had the same rights as the national government.

The Seventeenth Amendment (1913) took the power to *elect* U.S. senators away from the state legislatures. Direct election of senators by the voters of each state was now the law of the land. This did not change the governing powers assigned to the national government and the state governments. Rather, it *redistributed power* between two important groups *within each state*: the elected state officials and the voters. The powers of senators in the Senate remained the same; only the source of their authority changed. And the basic elements of republicanism had not been altered. Instead of being indirectly elected by a body that had been chosen by the sovereign voters in each state, senators now were to be chosen directly by the voters. Many voters believed that as a practical matter, the Seventeenth Amendment made the election of senators more democratic, since the amendment prevented powerful political bosses and corporate executives from manipulating state legislatures, thereby choosing U.S. senators. Direct voting for senators would, it was hoped, allow the views of the sovereign people to be honored.

The Eighteenth Amendment allowed *both* "the Congress and the several states" to ban the production and transportation (including importing and exporting) of "intoxicating liquors." Thus it did not change the balance of powers between the federal and state governments.

As the United States industrialized, many business groups and labor groups called on the national government to legislate to regulate the rates charged by railroads (including electric street railroads in cities), to bar children from working, to regulate the safety of the workplace, to bar employers from violating the civil rights of workers by forcing them to sign contracts promising not to strike or to join unions, and to limit the hours of labor for wage earners. But after 1890, a majority of the Supreme Court judges, fearful that increases in government power, and especially the power of the national government, would undermine the security of private property and pave the way for socialism, began to limit severely the authority of Congress and the state legislatures to regulate commerce, working conditions, and relationships between workers and employers.

By 1900 debate about the meaning of the Article I, Section 8, of the Constitution, which allowed Congress to regulate interstate commerce, had become fierce. Militant liberal reformers maintained that it authorized more regulatory action by the national government than just the regulation of rates charged by interstate railroads. But most lawyers and elected officials felt that this would upset the historically established balance of power between the national government and the state governments. In the 1920s the Supreme Court voided congressional legislation banning child labor, and gutted the 1914 Federal Trade Commission law that had created a regulatory agency protecting businesses and consumers against unfair business practices that discriminated against business competitors and raised prices to consumers.

The Depression in the 1930s led a majority of voters in the United States to look to the national government to solve the problems created by the collapse of the economy, which was the worst in the history of the nation. Huge numbers of middle-class people found themselves facing *prolonged* poverty for the first time in their lives. Overall, a majority consensus had emerged that with the state government treasuries empty, *the national government should expand its level of activity,* providing relief and regulating many types of economic activity. Different categories of voters looked to the national government for specific aid programs, although large numbers agreed on the need for the national government to create jobs for the unemployed and on the desirability of starting the Social Security system.

Congress responded to specific interest groups of voters with legislation to help them increase their earnings. For example, Congress levied a tax on the processing of farm goods to raise money for a system of payments to farmers to plant fewer crops and raise fewer animals. The end result was lower agricultural output, but higher prices for farmers' products. Congress created national government agencies to ensure the mortgages of business owners and private home owners, thereby preventing them from losing their properties. Congress passed the Social Security law, which financed old age pensions, unemployment insurance, and other income maintenance benefits by different combinations of taxes on workers and employers. It also passed legislation allowing the national government to regulate labor relations between workers and employers. The supporters of these programs argued that the Constitution's interstate commerce clause gave Congress the power to institute such regulation.

Overall, between 1933 and the present, the power of the national government to regulate individual behavior, to regulate the economy, and to use the power to tax to fund the distribution of welfare state benefits to citizens expanded greatly. As this trend developed, the spending of the national government *relative* to the state governments also increased. These changes created a much more powerful national government than had been desired by the citizens who ratified the Constitution of 1787.

But many Democratic senators and congressmen from southern states were very nervous about the increase in the spending activity and regulatory power of the national government during the 1930s. They worried that eventually the national government might use its power to end racial segregation in the South. The influence of many southern

Democrats on important committees, especially in the Senate, President Roosevelt's desire to avoid antagonizing southern Democrats, and Roosevelt's own enthusiasm for joint national-state government programs, led to the incorporation of the principle of federalism (i.e., power sharing between the national and state governments), in many reform laws passed in the 1930s. For example, one important part of the Social Security system—unemployment insurance—was controlled solely by the states. (Funding came from payroll taxes paid by employers.) Decisions about eligibility and benefit levels for income maintenance payments to mothers with dependent children were to be made exclusively by the states. The national government would simply pay for about half the cost of these benefits. Cash relief benefits for poor able-bodied adults without children were to be fixed by and paid for by the states. This allowed southern states to keep business costs low and to discriminate against African Americans who applied for relief.

Despite many important congressional compromises that took into account concerns about the general trend toward a more powerful national government, a constitutional crisis emerged in 1935 and 1936 over certain aspects of the increase in regulatory activity of the national government. By narrow 5–4 margins, in 1935 and 1936 the Supreme Court ruled that many of the regulatory laws passed by Congress exceeded the powers granted to it by the interstate commerce clause of the Constitution. This type of judicial interpretation of the Constitution is known as *strict construction*. Those who favored an expansion of the power of the national government believed in a loose construction of the interstate commerce clause, an interpretation that allowed the national government to pass laws regulating business activities that involved manufacturing and processing, but did not directly involve commerce between the states. The argument of the *loose constructionists* was that the supplies used by a business to make a product that it sold only within the borders of a single state came from a *stream* of *interstate* commerce. They argued that this brought such processing under the interstate commerce clause, and that Congress could regulate the activity. Advocates of strict construction argued that when a business processed materials received from the flow of interstate commerce, but sold such products only within the state in which the business was located, the "flow in interstate commerce had ceased." Hence regulation of the hours and wages of the processing business was unconstitutional.

IV

As indicated earlier, the views of the strict constructionists, who were a majority of the nation's lawyers and judges but a minority of the population, were closer to the views of the people who had ratified the Constitution in 1787. But a century and a half had passed since 1787. As all industrial societies—in Europe, Asia, and the Western Hemisphere—had expanded, different segments of the population—businessmen in specific manufacturing and service industries, consumers, and wage earners—had lobbied to get their state governments and national government to regulate economic activity, provide guarantees to help businesses avoid failing, and aid the poor. In the depths of the Depression, a majority of voters in the United States clearly approved of expanded government, including national government, activity. But a slim (5–4) majority of the Supreme Court thought the overall effect of the specific new national government programs desired by the majority would have taken the nation too far in the direction of socialism and would have upset the previous ratio of national government to state government power.

More than any other factor, it is likely that the results of the 1936 election convinced one member of the Supreme Court, Justice Owen Roberts, to abandon his opposition to the expansion of national government power. The election represented a voter mandate (a commitment or endorsement) in favor of the new national government programs put forward by

President Roosevelt and by a coalition of Democratic senators and congressmen and a handful of liberal midwestern Republicans. Roosevelt was reelected with 60.8 percent of the popular vote, the highest total in the history of the nation until Lyndon B. Johnson received 61.1 percent in 1964. And the Democrats increased their already dominant representation in Congress.

It appears that the size of the Democratic victory convinced Justice Roberts that the Court would risk serious attacks on its constitutional role if it completely resisted government programs desired by a strong majority. In December, less than a month after the November election results were in, Justice Roberts, whose views on national government regulation had not changed, began voting to uphold the constitutionality of regulatory laws that had been passed by Congress in 1934 and 1935. This switch marked an important turning point. *Never again would the Supreme Court oppose Congress when it increased the regulatory powers of the national government.*

But the legacy of the shared power between the national and state governments can still be seen in the structure of many government programs. Workers' compensation, the income-maintenance program that provides funds for workers injured on the job, began as a state program. During the 1930s, the team President Roosevelt appointed to draft the Social Security Act did not even consider trying to combine the relief of injured workers into the system to provide for those who were physically and mentally disabled. They were afraid of being accused of trying to take over state government programs, thereby reducing the absolute power of state government. When Congress passed the Occupational Safety and Health Act in 1970, it created a new force of national government workplace health and safety inspectors. But, mindful of the tradition of federalism, Congress allowed states that had a program of safety inspection that met national standards to use state inspectors instead of national government inspectors.

President Bill Clinton recognized the political necessity of accommodating this tradition when he put forward his health insurance reform plan in 1993. His plan would have allowed each *state* government to determine the membership of the *state*-level health care alliances that were proposed to make many decisions about the kind of health insurance plans that would be available. On the other hand, the power to require employers to offer workers insurance coverage would be the result of national legislation, and the national government would set maximum rates on all health insurance policies authorized by the state health care alliances. Overall, the Clinton health insurance proposal assigned some important functions to each state government, but delegated most of the power to shape the health care system to the national government. This kind of power sharing is the logical outcome of the federalism that is written into the Constitution.

As this essay is being written (1995), it appears that the Congress and the president will back a significant, but as yet undetermined amount of transfer of power, from the national government to the state governments. This will be done by giving states bloc grants of money for income-maintenance programs and by eliminating requirements in national law that the states offer specific educational services to their residents. These shifts in power show that the Constitution's federal structure allows for changes in the location of government authority.

The following chapter is the first in a series of three chapters that discuss the prejudices that led to the denial of legal and economic equality to specific social groups. We begin with an analysis of racism because it has proven to be the strongest, most enduring prejudice held by human beings.

CHAPTER 6

Racism

I

Nigeria. 1756. Olaudah Equiano, the 11-year-old son of a village chief, had been kidnapped by Africans. Carried to the Atlantic Ocean, he was put on board a European slave ship. Seeing white people for the first time in his life, Equiano was fearful that he would

> be eaten by those white men with horrible looks, red faces, and long hair.

Reassured by other Africans that he would kept alive so that his labor could be used by the owner to whom he would be sold, Equiano was still worried about being executed, because

> the white people looked . . . so savage.

To an African accustomed to seeing only people who were black-skinned and short-haired, the European white men looked so different that he reacted negatively to their appearance, concluding that the Europeans were uncivilized savages. Equiano's reactions are a good illustration of the great sixteenth-century French essayist Montaigne's observation that because humans were usually self-centered and therefore easily prejudiced, "each man calls barbarism whatever is not his own practice."

The word "prejudice" comes from the Latin words that mean to judge someone or something before the facts are known. Prejudice also refers to opinions held because someone has not accepted known facts that contradict the judgments that cause a person to form the opinion. A prejudice can lead to a positive or negative judgment. *Racism** is a form of prejudice based on the assumption that humans of some groups are members of *superior* "races" and others are members of *inferior* "races."

In the past, humans categorized each other by noting differences in external appearance. People focused *especially on differences in skin color*, as well as variations in body height and body proportions, and the shape of facial bones, lips, nose flesh, and eye flesh. A group of humans whose appearance seemed similar would consider itself to be of the same race and would regard a second group, whose members looked different from the first group, as a another race. In the mid-1700s, *white*-skinned scientists developed supposedly scientific classification schemes for different human races. For the next 150 years, most scientists believed that there were three basic races: white-skinned Caucasians; brown- and black-skinned members of the Negroid race; and yellowish-skinned people in the Mongoloid race. The scientists of Europe and the United States, virtually all Caucasians, thought their race was superior to all other races.

Today most scientists are not comfortable when asked to define the concept of race. They are not sure that race is a valid *scientific* category for distinguishing between human beings. Why? If race is to have any meaning, it must refer to a group that is genetically uniform, with no crossbreeding that would allow genes from other groups to enter into the genetic makeup of the race. But there has been so much crossbreeding among humans that it is doubtful any pure race exists.

---

*This essay uses the terms racial prejudice and racism interchangeably, and calls racism based on alleged scientific facts *scientific racism*. Some writers define racism differently, equating racism only with prejudice based on alleged scientific facts. Such writers use racial prejudice to describe nonscientific racism.

Advances in electronics and chemistry have enabled scientists to describe the *structure of human genes*, the chemicals that determine our biological makeup, including the capabilities of our brains. But it is clear that *many* different genes, most of which have not yet been identified, are responsible for intelligence. This makes it impossible to determine precisely whether or not there is any genetic difference between human groups that might be correlated with differences in the average basic brain reasoning capacity of each group. But since 1972 geneticists have repeatedly discovered evidence that suggests that it is highly unlikely that such differences do exist. Overall, geneticists have found that there is more variation when they compare the genetic makeup of the members of a single alleged racial group than there is variation between the overall genetic makeup of different races. *Genetically* speaking, different alleged racial groups are more or less similar to each other, while *within* each alleged racial group there are significant genetic differences. *The History and Geography of Human Genes*, a 1994 study by three geneticists (L. Luca Cavalli-Storza, Paolo Menozzi, and Alberto Piazza), concludes that "once genes for . . . traits such as coloration and stature are discounted, the human races are remarkably alike. . . . The diversity among individuals is so enormous. . . . [that race is] meaningless at the genetic level."

Scientists have reached these conclusions by experiments that involve the following kind of comparisons: They choose peoples of two very different skin colors. Let us call these groups skin color A and skin color B. Then, at random, the geneticists select two people from skin color A and one person from skin color B. Examining the genetic makeup* of all three persons, the geneticists have found that the genetic makeup of the two persons of skin color A is likely to be very different. But the genetic makeup of the person of skin color B will be more *similar* to the genetic makeup of any person of skin color A than the genetic makeup of that person of skin color A will be similar

---

*To compare the genetic makeup of different groups of people, scientists examine specific genes and segments of DNA that are not found in genes.

to the genetic makeup of the other person of skin color A. Overall, the members of the same color/nationality group will vary *from each other*, but as a group, they will be genetically similar to other such defined groups.

Geneticists have discovered that single genes can explain the likelihood of a person developing some diseases. But overall brain functioning (intelligence) *cannot be explained by any single gene*. Complex mixtures of genes—mixtures that are not yet understood by scientists—determine the growth of the brain and the way it functions. Why have past and present scientists paid so much attention to the trait of mental ability or intelligence?* Because the most important bias of people prejudiced against other alleged races is usually the belief that members of other "races" are not as intelligent, and therefore their "race" is inferior to the "race" that contains the supposedly more intelligent peoples.

II

Historians cannot be sure when racism first emerged. Certainly, the records of the Greek city-states and of ancient Rome are

---

*Note that I have not used the term IQ. This term stands for an intelligence quotient, and is measured by a written test. There is no evidence that such tests measure the basic, genetic capabilities for the types of reasoning they ask each test taker to attempt. Between the time a person is born and the time they start taking such tests, they are exposed to different kinds of social environments, some of which are focused on teaching the kind of reasoning measured by IQ tests, others of which are not. Thus cultural factors can produce variations in IQ scores that do not reflect the basic, or intrinsic, mental ability of a person.

IQ tests measure *only certain kind* of human mental abilities. These tests measure the ability to compare words and different shapes, reading comprehension, and arithmetical skills. These kinds of mental activities may not be superior to other mental activities, like those involved in carrying out complex verbal negotiations or those used to judge quickly the types of physical reactions necessary to overcome physical obstacles as a person maneuvers towards a basketball hoop.

filled with examples of racism. Both the Greeks and the Romans looked down on darker-skinned peoples, whom they viewed as inferior, but still as *human beings who had the capacity for justice, religious faith, and wisdom.* The physical differences between lighter-and darker-skinned peoples were believed to be the result of *environmental* factors—the different climate, land, and topography in the regions inhabited by darker-skinned peoples. It was assumed that if peoples of "inferior" races and cultures lived in the presence of people with superior cultures, the former could improve their behaviors by adopting the cultural practices of the "superior" group.

The religions of the Greeks and the Romans were highly syncretic, combining the belief in many different Gods and rituals. Thus they were relatively tolerant of foreign peoples whose religions were different. Consequently, the Greeks and the Romans rarely applied to foreigners a *double* bias, based on differences in race *and* religion.

Medieval Christians were not as tolerant. They considered non-Christians to be infidels and heathens, uncivilized and evil because they were not Christian. It is likely that the Crusades to capture the Holy Land for Christendom intensified the racism of Europeans, as did the conquest of Spain and other parts of Islamic Southern Europe by the dark-skinned Moors of Northern Africa. Fighting with darker-skinned peoples who were identified as enemies of the Christian religion deepened the hostility of Christian, white-skinned Europeans toward such peoples. And the Christians of medieval Europe also developed a cultural outlook that *defined dark skin color very negatively*, much more so than had the Greeks and the Romans. This view was part of a general European cultural orientation that portrayed white colors as symbols of goodness and Godliness and black colors as symbols of evil and the Devil. By the time the white peoples of Western Europe sought to exploit the resources of the rest of the world, many popular playwrights had created dark-skinned characters who were associated with evil actions, including sexual lust.

When the sailing ships of Western Europe brought Europeans into contact with peoples on the coast of Western Africa and India, the Europeans often remarked on the very dark skin color (and relative nakedness) of the indigenous peoples. European travelers were strongly influenced by what they thought were visual similarities between the apes they saw in Africa and the humans they encountered there. The Europeans' judgment was influenced by the negative ideas they already had about black colors and dark-skinned humans. And so the Europeans developed a series of largely negative beliefs about black Africans, who were portrayed as heathen (not Christian), technologically backward, superstitious, and ferocious (including cannibalistic). (A minority of Europeans saw Africans as noble, polite, and uncorrupted because they lived a life that was close to nature.) Overall, the Europeans were convinced that the Africans were *less* civilized and more barbaric than white Caucasian peoples.

To explain the skin color and the alleged inferior cultures of Africans, Europeans and their New World descendants relied on a form of environmental racism: climatological determinism. They claimed that the heat of the sun darkened the skin of the Africans and made them lazy. Other Europeans were cultural determinists, believing that the inferiority of Africans could be explained by the supposedly unsophisticated, "primitive" political and social organization of their society. This view left open the possibility that Africans could be "civilized" by contact with the "superior" organization (and technology) of European societies.

When the Europeans came into contact with the natives of the Western Hemisphere, it was *not skin color* but the relative lack of body hair of the American Indians that impressed the explorers and colonizers. At first, the English thought of the Indians as gentle pagans, not savages, who lived in a civil society. They thought of the Indians as members of the same racial stock as the English. Until the 1640s, the English assumed that it would be possible to convert the Indians to Christianity and in general to teach them how to *raise their "inferior" social and political practices to the level of English society.*

But as time passed, circumstances and the Europeans' views changed. Initially outnumbered, the settlers slowly became more numerous and self-confident. Native peoples and the Europeans argued over damages to each other's property. (The courts created by New England's English settlers established a discriminatory standard for damages caused by pigs and cows that ran loose and ate the crops of others, refusing to allow damages unless the owner of the crop had fenced in her/his field. But because Native American agriculture did not use fenced fields, this standard favored the English settlers.) As European intentions to expand their landholdings and their political rule became clear, the native peoples began to use force to resist what they saw as illegal European land grabbing. And as time passed it became clear to the English colonists that most native peoples would refuse to convert to Christianity. This resistance to European religious "truth" convinced the settlers that Native Americans were hopelessly degenerate.

In 1637, Roger Williams, who would be banished from Massachusetts for his belief in freedom of religious worship *for Christians*, attacked the Narragansetts of Rhode Island as "another miserable drove of Adam's degenerate seed" and as "beasts wallowing in idleness, stealing, lying, whoring, treacherous witchcrafts, blasphemies, and idolatries." *By 1650 and thereafter, racist portrayals of American Indians began to predominate in the writings of English settlers.* The image of the gentle pagan was replaced by venomous descriptions of the Indians:

> consider what these creatures are (I cannot call them men) . . . no character of God in them . . . rooted in evil, the very dregs, garbage and spawne of Earth . . . fathered by Satan and the sonnes of hell.

And the skin color of the Native Americans was increasingly noted by the colonists. By 1700, Indians were described as "red" men. By the time of the American Revolution, white racial prejudice against American Indians was fully developed, with Indians being depicted as a race of inferior, devilish, red men.

White Americans also condemned the Indians because, as Benjamin Franklin charged, they were lazy and could rarely be raised to the level of whites:

> The proneness of human Nature to a life of ease, or freedom from care and labour, appears strongly in the little success that has hitherto attended every attempt to civilize our American Indians.

The Eurocentric notion that a people was inferior because its culture did not stress the ownership of private property and incessant labor *to accumulate more wealth* was very common among the European settlers in the Western Hemisphere and was embraced by their descendants. This notion enabled them to *justify robbing the lands of the different indigenous peoples of the New World.* Because American Indians did not want to spend as much time as Europeans did in improving their land's wealth-generating capability, the whites concluded that the Indians were lazy. This notion persisted into the nineteenth and twentieth centuries. Thus President Theodore Roosevelt would exclaim: "This great continent could not have been kept as nothing but a game preserve for squalid savages."

Supposedly lazy people had to be concentrated on reservations so that their lands could be developed by allegedly more energetic white people. And the preference of most of the surviving North American Indians for their own culture, and especially for their own religions, continued to infuriate white Christians, who believed that all other religions were inferior and encouraged immoral behavior. Thus, in 1869, Amanda Miller wrote in *Overland Monthly,* about viewing an

> assemblage of hideously painted savages, whose countenances were rendered still the more revolting by their efforts to intensify their passions of hatred and revenge in their incantations of demonaltry.

The best indication of the effect of color prejudice on the behavior of European settlers in the Western Hemisphere is the fact that they *never thought of enslaving white-skinned*

Europeans. Africans were enslaved. Some Indians (mostly women and children) were enslaved. But white men and women were not. Of course, white men and women who emigrated as temporarily unfree labor—indentured servants—were sometimes exploited by their masters, who hit and molested them, while conniving to extend the length of their period of servitude. However, even indentured servants had the liberties of the English. Thus *white* servants could bring lawsuits against abusive masters. Such lawsuits were an important deterrent to truly barbaric treatment.

Slaves had no legal rights. It was that simple. They could not own real estate. *The mainland English colonies never allowed people of color to bring suit in a court of law*, let alone testify in a lawsuit brought by a white person. Denied any recourse to the courts, by 1660 slaves in most of the English colonies, who were all people of color, were declared, by law, to be the property, for life, of their owners. And the children of slaves were also the legal property of their owners. This total lack of legally protected liberties and freedoms made it possible for slave owners to deny slaves their freedom and to abuse them physically and psychologically. But since African and Indian slaves (and free people of color, who did own property) were clearly human, whites developed justifications—based on prior prejudices—for the way people of color were denied their liberty and due process under law. Racist stereotypes were used in spoken and written justifications for enslavement of Africans, robbing the land of the American Indians (see pages 177-178), physical brutality, and legal controls ranging from lifetime enslavement to forced residence on reservations to the prohibition of the teaching of reading (to slaves).

The legal distinctions between the perceived races of people in the Western Hemisphere were summarized by an English official in a 1675 report on the social structure of the Caribbean island of Barbados. Freeholders, who owned land, were Englishmen who had been given their land by an agent of the King. Then came freemen (and women), especially of English and Scottish background, who had "served out the time they contracted for" as indentured servants. Those still serving as indentured servants had the status of "Christian Servants." At the bottom of the social ladder were men and women who were neither free nor Christian, "the negroes . . . who live as absolute slaves to their masters."

III

This section will describe the emergence of "scientific" racism in the second half of the eighteenth century. But the use of modern science to justify racism did not necessarily lead to harsher treatment of people of color or of allegedly inferior nationality groups. While environmental/cultural racism (prescientific racism) left open the possibility of improvement in the behavior and status of despised racial groups, *it had emphasized the initial inferiority of the nonwhite peoples of Africa and the Western Hemisphere, justifying the brutal treatment the Europeans meted out to these peoples.*

As the biological sciences developed at a rapid pace during the eighteenth century, naturalists began to develop schemes for classifying living forms. In 1735, Carolus Linnaeus, a Swedish botanist, developed the first modern system for classifying living organisms. The classification systems used by Linnaeus and other scientists arranged organisms by degree of complexity. At the top of the ladder of complexity stood human beings. Instead of classifying different groups of human beings into *nations* or *peoples,* the eighteenth-century scientists began to use the category of *race.* Linnaeus believed that Europeans, Africans, and American Indians belonged to *separate* races. He was a pre-Darwinian scientific racist.

Eighteenth-century scientists believed that God created all organisms at the same time. This view is called monogenesis (one origin). Scientists who were monogenesists did not argue that higher-level organisms were more evolved than lower-level organisms. But eighteenth-century scientists definitely believed that organisms could be classified as being inferior and superior. And they believed that the white races of Western Europe were superior to all other races on Earth. However, like the Greeks and Romans, *Linnaeus and other eighteenth-century biologists believed that different races of humans could be changed by changing the climate or social environment in which they lived.*

Not all laymen agreed. In 1767, Pierre Marie François de Pages, a French naval officer, decided to explore the area that is now Texas. He portrayed the Indians in the area as living in a state of "rustic simplicity," embracing "a native love of justice and fair dealing." The Frenchman attributed these virtues to the physical environment. But he clearly indicated that he did not believe that "reason" could "*ever* enter into the character or conduct of the savage [s]." [emphasis added]

By the era of the American Revolution, racism based on cultural stereotypes and disdain for the nonwhite color of the skins of Africans, African Americans, and Native Americans was deeply ingrained in white society. Thus Arthur Lee, a Virginia slaveholder, claimed that African slaves were "utterly devoid of virtue," had a view of life that was "generally shallow," had cruel hearts, and were "vindictive, stubborn, base and wicked." Southerners like Lee believed that African Americans were naturally lazy, and did not want to work hard. Whites concluded that African Americans could only be controlled by enslavement, would not work without the supervision of whites, and could not be allowed to participate as voters in a republican society that depended on virtuous voters.

In the early nineteenth century, some biologists developed the specialty of *craniology*, which categorized different human races by the volume their brains occupied in the skull. Craniologists immediately concluded that the white Caucasian races of Western Europe and North America were the most advanced race because their skulls had the highest cranial capacity. Craniology was the first allegedly *biological* proof of the superiority of white races.

Did African Americans living in the pre-Civil War years conclude that the biological condition of whites explained their hostile, often barbaric treatment of people of color? No. It is more likely that religious black people agreed with the views of David Walker, an ex-slave who migrated to Boston and began publishing an abolitionist newspaper. Like many African Americans who had been mistreated by whites, Walker developed a strong set of negative feelings about whites as a group. Walker's *Appeal to the Coloured Citizens of the World* (1829) referred to whites as

> an unjust, jealous, unmerciful, avaricious and blood-thirsty set of beings, always seeking after power and authority . . . we see them acting more like *devils* than accountable men. [emphasis added]

(Walker's outspoken public criticism of whites probably led to his murder in 1830.) Frederick Douglass was an escaped slave who became a famous writer and abolitionist. In a poem written in 1854, Douglass used animal images to describe the whites who persecuted two African-American slaves:

> They crack old Tony on the skull,
> And preach and roar like Bashan bull,
> Or braying ass, of mischief full,
> Then seize old Jacob by the wool [hair].

But Douglass did not suggest that whites were actually a different species from blacks.

In 1828, the members of the Connecticut Colonization Society stated that the degradation of free and enslaved African Americans was

> inevitable and incurable. The African in this country belongs by birth to the lowest station in society; and from that station he can *never* rise, be his talent, his enterprise, his virtues what they may. [emphasis added]

The abolitionists agreed that free African Americans lived in a degraded status, but attributed this to racial discrimination. However, like Linnaeus, who argued that new environments would improve the capacities of different human groups, the abolitionists believed that African Americans could be *raised to a higher level of civilization* if the social and legal environment in which they lived was altered. Applying a view of *equality* that was based on the religiously inspired idea that blacks and whites were "of the same species" and were "God's rational creatures," abolitionist William Lloyd Garrison believed that whites and blacks could live "in harmony together."

As the abolitionist movement spread throughout the north and the midwest after 1830, attacking slavery as un-Christian and economically backward, southerners fearful of the end of slavery—and the bloody race war that they assumed would begin with abolition—began an ideological counterattack. Increasing numbers of southerners began to argue that the inferior condition of blacks was *permanent* because the behavior of blacks was determined by racial traits that were *biologically*, not culturally, determined.

In the mid-1830s, many southern writers began to argue that the African Americans were *by nature* savages, with "brutish propensities" that could only be contained if the African Americans were enslaved and controlled by white slaveowners. To justify the physical assaults whites often made on slaves, it was argued that the African American's skull was so thick that it was physically impossible for a master to knock a slave senseless. Other writers claimed that it was impossible to overwork blacks because the black race had a "peculiar [biological] instinct" that protected African Americans "against the abuses of arbitrary power." Supposedly, African Americans were only capable of the emotions of "lust and beastly cruelty." Hence, the breakup of slave families was justified on the grounds that the "black's natural affections are not strong, and consequently he is cruel to his offspring, and suffers little by separation from them."

By the 1850s, Josiah C. Nott, an American anthropologist, summarized the views of the pre-Darwinian scientific racists. Maintaining that "lofty civilization has been achieved solely by the 'Caucasian' group," Nott described a hierarchy of nonwhite races. Mongolian races were still "semi-civilized," although Nott conceded that the Chinese had achieved civilization. He argued that American Indians were "savage," "barbarous," and "untameable" peoples. Only if the Indians intermarried with whites could their offspring, "mixed breeds," amount to anything. Nott ranked African Americans somewhat lower than American Indians, because the "Black races" were so "low in intellect."

But in California and New Mexico, white (i.e., Anglo-American) settlers who had migrated from other regions of the country did not believe that people of mixed Spanish and Indian ancestry were "white" people. In 1846, the territorial governor of New Mexico referred to "sullen reaction of the mongrels"* [elite Hispanics] to Anglo-American rule." In 1849, a Sacramento, California businessman considered Hispanics of Mexican and Spanish ancestry to be

> devoid of intelligence, sufficient to appreciate the true principles of free government; vicious and dishonest, to an extent rendering them obnoxious to our citizens; [with] . . . an intellect but one degree above the beast in the field, and not susceptible of elevation.

Such attitudes helped Americans justify vicious violent assaults on the Hispanic residents of the Southwest, and the manipulation of the land laws and tax systems either to steal the land owned by Hispanics or to force Hispanics to sell their land to Anglo-Americans at low prices. The racism that pervaded California after Anglo-Americans took over its government was also reflected in legislation (1850) that prohibited Chinese immigrants and Native Americans from testifying against whites. Thus, many affluent Hispanic persons who were of mixed Indian and Spanish blood were prevented from testifying on their own behalf in lawsuits involving attempts by Anglo-Americans to challenge the Hispanics' title to their land. Handicapped in this way, many Hispanics lost their land to the Anglo-Americans.

Visiting the United States in the 1830s, Alexis de Tocqueville, who believed all humans were members of the same race, was overwhelmed by the racism that pervaded U.S. society. He was especially impressed by the importance of prejudice

---

*Mongrel comes from a Greek word that means mixed. Mongrel was usually a term of contempt used to describe dogs that were mixed breeds.

based on skin color. De Tocqueville summarized the racial prejudices of most white Americans, who believed that the appearance of the typical African American was

> to our eyes hideous . . . his understanding weak, his tastes low; and we are almost inclined to look upon him as a being intermediate between man and the brutes.

De Tocqueville also noted that white racism created a vicious, self-fulfilling cycle: prophecy of the inferiority of African Americans; treatment of African Americans as inferiors, with limited economic and social rights; and the consequent inferior economic and social conditions of African Americans.

Justification of the *enslavement* of people of color was an important effect of racism in the United States. Slavery was an immensely profitable form of economic exploitation. A slave lacked the bargaining power of a free laborer, and consequently had to accept a lower standard of living. In a 1854 editorial, the Richmond, Virginia *Examiner* suggested how white slaveholders had come to view their slaves as forms of property, rather than equal human beings:

> Let us . . . glory in and profit to the utmost by what [God] . . . has done for them in transplanting them here, and setting them to work on our plantations . . . *the Negro is here, and here forever; is our property, and ours forever.*

The notion that people of color were *helped* by being enslaved was based on the assumption that they were of inferior races and lacked the ability to take care of themselves.

IV

Scientific racism, both pre- and post-Darwinian, developed during a century (1750–1850) *when theories of equal rights and democracy were emerging throughout the Western World and especially in the United States.* Yet the earnings of many farmers and other businessmen in the United States depended on the social, political, and economic subjugation (including enslavement) of Indians, Hispanics, and African Americans. And the social status of white Americans throughout the nation was boosted by their feelings of superiority to peoples of color. How could white Americans who embraced theories of human rights and democracy justify denying such rights to an important part of the nation's population? *By denying that certain peoples were truly human.* By convincing themselves—with the aid of racist stereotypes and theories—that peoples of color were savage and bestial, *sub*human creatures who had to be controlled, white Americans could rationalize denying basic human rights to people of color.

Scientific racism convinced white Americans that they were justified in treating people of color unequally, a treatment that brought economic and social gains to white people. Succeeding scientific research provided supposedly more convincing evidence, and more sophisticated theories, that allegedly *inferior groups were so biologically different that they could never be raised to the level of the civilized races.*

Charles Darwin's theory about the role of natural selection in producing the evolution of the species was first published in 1859. Many other scientists and social commentators applied Darwin's theories of natural selection and evolution to explain the origins of, and *differences within,* the human species. Darwinian scientific racists, concentrated in the nations of Western Europe and among the white-skinned people of the United States, would claim that certain "races"—the nonwhite races—within the species *Homo sapiens*, were significantly *less evolved* than others. These races were depicted as closer on the evolutionary scale to our ape ancestors. Darwinian scientific racists assumed that the process of natural selection ensured that the allegedly more evolved races were more adaptable than the other races, and that superior intelligence was the main contributor to that adaptability.

Two major conclusions emerged from this analysis:

1. The less evolved human races were incapable of acting in the rational, sensible manner that made an adult entitled to full legal and political rights.

2. Since evolutionary processes had been shown by Darwin to take such a long time, in the short run nothing could be done to help the members of an inferior race to evolve into a superior race. They would remain inferior and had to be treated as such.

As we have seen, most of the white people living in the United States in the nineteenth century believed that African Americans were inferior to whites. Among the abolitionists before the Civil War began, only Wendell Phillips advocated going beyond freeing black slaves to pressing for allowing blacks to vote. Even Abraham Lincoln thought that blacks were mentally inferior to whites, and that blacks were socially undesirable in a white society.

John William De Forest was a Connecticut businessman who went to South Carolina after the Civil War to work for the Freedman's Bureau, a relief agency set up by the national government to help the newly emancipated slaves. He thought that African Americans were inferior to whites, but were humans who deserved decent treatment. Like many well-educated, mid-nineteenth-century Americans, De Forest had been influenced by evolutionary theory. He did not think African Americans were members of a different biological species than white Caucasians. But De Forest thought that the process of *evolution was also taking place within the human societies* that were created by different races of *Homo sapiens*. Human experiences with advances in government and technology allowed the allegedly more evolved races of humans to reach higher levels of "civilization." De Forest believed that newly freed black slaves were now engaged in a "struggle to be at once like a race [Caucasians] which has passed through a two thousand years' growth in civilization." De Forest felt free blacks were not as evolved as Caucasians because they had not been Christians for a

John William De Forest

long time, and because they did not know how to live as self-governing free men since they had, he believed, not been given chances to govern themselves. Thus De Forest believed it was futile for free black men and women to aspire to match the achievements of free whites:

> It is doubtless well for his chances of existence that his color keeps him a plebeian [a common person], so that, like the European peasant held down by caste, he is less tempted to destroy himself in the struggle to become a patrician.

Until 1935, almost all of the historians who wrote about the Civil War and Reconstruction believed in the racial inferiority of African Americans. This bias blinded the historians to the scope of efforts made by the newly freed African Americans in the South to gain rights and liberties equal to those enjoyed by whites. These efforts were described in 1935 by the African American historian W. E. B. Du Bois, in a book titled *Black Reconstruction*. Du Bois acknowledged in his preface that his account would be dismissed by readers who embraced scientific racism and therefore viewed "the Negro as a distinctly inferior creation, who can never successfully take part in modern civilization and whose emancipation and enfranchisement were gestures against nature."

While federal troops were present in the South during Reconstruction, African Americans could vote. Using the franchise, they elected black and white judges, mayors, state legislators, and congressmen. These government officials appropriated money for schools for African Americans and gave black people equal justice when they appeared in court to press economic claims against white employers (non payment of wages) or white businessmen who had violated contracts they had signed with African Americans. But once it was clear that slavery would not be reestablished, most Republican congressmen quickly lost interest in protecting the civil liberties of African Americans in the South. The "Redeemer" governments that came to power in the South allowed white vigilantes to use violence against blacks to prevent them from voting. In many rural communities, whites used arson and gunfire to destroy black schools.

The racial creed of most white southerners was not changed by the Civil War and congressional reconstruction. They believed social and political equality for African Americans was a mistake and that even the poorest white should have a status higher than that of the highest black. How was this accomplished, since there were many black ministers, doctors, and landowning farmers who were *economically* superior to poor, landless white people? By custom and then by law, white southerners required racial segregation in all public places: schools, hospitals, baseball parks, movie theaters, hotels, trains, and buses.

The enactment of segregation laws also was designed to prevent black and white industrial workers from cooperating, despite their mutual racial antagonisms, in union efforts to advance the wages and protect the working conditions of workers. The cooperation of black and white farmers in the Populist movement in the 1890s (See Chapter 11) worried southern economic elites, who backed "grandfather clause" laws that made voting legal only if a man's grandfather had been a voter, making voting an impossibility for African American men whose grandfathers had been slaves. These same elites secured poll tax laws that charged all voters a fee. In many instances these voting fees were used to discourage poor white men, as well as blacks, from voting.

Many white southerners used Darwinian evolution to justify the racial distinctions they drew between "superior" whites and "inferior" blacks. In 1908, a group of Mississippi farmers who had formed an organization to market their cotton crops decided to exclude black farmers. Placing African Americans on the evolutionary level of the apes, one farmer asserted that

> the monkey and the negro, are in their tendencies imitative. . . . So all we need to do . . . is to set a good example . . . As soon as the negro[es] see that we are moving upon a higher plane of prosperity, they will not be slow in organizing their forces, imitating the precepts we must first establish.

Three years later, Louis Gray, an agricultural historian born in Missouri, justified the repression of blacks by the social and governmental institutions dominated by white southerners because blacks were "thriftless," ignorant, and required supervision. At the same time, most northern trade union leaders favored excluding blacks from their unions. In 1898, the president of the American Federation of Labor endorsed the following comments made about blacks by a union organizer in Georgia. Blacks, whom he wanted to sent to Liberia or Cuba, did not possess

> those peculiarities of temperament such as patriotism, sympathy, etc., which are peculiar to most of the Caucasian race, and which alone make an organization of the character and complexity of the modern trade union possible.

In 1909, a group of black and white Americans who believed in racial equality founded the National Association for the Advancement of Colored People. The NAACP published a magazine that challenged racial segregation. The NAACP also filed lawsuits to challenge the constitutionality of racial inequality, whether it took the form of racially restrictive zoning laws, the unequal [lower] payment of African-American school teachers, or social segregation. In its early years, the NAACP met with little success because the racial attitudes of white judges were still strongly influenced by scientific racism.

Japanese immigration to California was concentrated between 1890 and 1910. White Californians, already predisposed to consider Native Americans, Chinese, Hispanic Americans, and African Americans inferior peoples, exhibited a racist reaction to the Japanese. In 1900, the California legislature passed a resolution that condemned "Japanese laborers, by reason of race habits," as "immoral, intemperate [and] quarrelsome." Reflecting the scientific racism of the day, the Asiatic Exclusion League argued that the whites "cannot assimilate them [the Japanese] without injury to ourselves." The reason: the Japanese were too different, possessing "distinct racial, social and religious prejudices." This analysis reflected the "scientific" notion that biological intermingling between superior [white] and inferior [nonwhite] races would lower the genetic quality of the superior race. It also reflected a belief that major differences in appearance and religion would never be eliminated and would continuously create social conflict between Christian whites and nonwhite Asians.

European and Asian immigrants to the United States often quickly absorbed the racism that was so widespread in their new homeland. A Filipino Methodist minister remembered how the desire to be accepted in a strange, new land in which whites were often hostile to people of color influenced his views about African Americans:

> Somehow, . . . by osmosis, you begin to say Negroes must be terrible to [have been] . . . enslaved and to be treated like that, so I'm not going to associate with such people who are relegated to being almost animals. And if I'm going to be acceptable to the American white[s], I better share their prejudice. Otherwise, if I associate with the blacks against whom they [whites] are prejudiced, I'll be included in that. I have enough prejudice [against me] as an Oriental. Why should I add some more by associating with the blacks.

V

Franz Boas, a German-born anthropologist who had emigrated to the United States in 1886, became the first prestigious twentieth-century scientist to challenge the theories of scientific racism. By the 1920s, Boas' work was influencing many anthropologists in the United States. Boas argued that environmental forces exerted such strong influence on the condition and behavior of individual humans that it was unscientific to argue that hereditary (genetic) forces could determine the condition and behavior of *large population groups, (i.e., races)*. Indeed, Boas pointed out, there was so much *interbreeding* between humans of different skin colors (supposed races) that there were no pure populations equivalent to the pure breeds of other species:

> All the evidence available argues against the theory that a people must conduct itself in a certain way merely because of its physique . . . To prove their point [biologists] cite different breeds of dogs, brought up under similar conditions and environment, yet adhering to their own pronounced types. Because the bulldog invariably maintains his racial traits distinct from those of a French poodle, it does not follow that human groups do the same. Obviously the dog in this instance corresponds not to a nondescript population but to an inbred family line. What we have here is merely the result of long inbreeding. . . . Our populations are *so mixed and consist of so many family lines* that their common likes and dislikes, their common interests and hopes are not to be accounted for by any simple biological formula. [emphasis added]

By the 1930s, many scientists, social scientists, and journalists began using the term "racism" to describe a set of false beliefs based on prejudices. By the start of World War II, most anthropologists and geneticists in Western Europe (except Germany) and the United States rejected the validity of scientific racism. The rejection of scientific racism by Western scientists was hastened by the fact the Germany, the leading proponent of such theories, was a brutal dictatorship. Many of the Christian English and American scientists who were influenced in this way had at first been reluctant to accept the work of many of the scientists who challenged scientific racism because those scientists were Jewish and the Christian scientists were anti-Semitic.

During World War II, the training manuals given to all the men and women in the armed forces of the United States included specific criticisms of the Nazi doctrine of racial (Aryan) supremacy, which was termed inconsistent with the principles of a democracy based on the concept of equal rights for all. An increasing number of college and high school teachers explicitly rejected the validity of scientific racism. One important effect of these developments on U.S. history was the impact they had on the thinking of Supreme Court judges. Racism was rejected by every Supreme Court judge appointed between 1938 and 1965, whether a Democrat or Republican, whether they believed in a strong national government or in keeping power in the hands of the states. From 1938 through the 1970s, the Supreme Court struck down discriminatory laws and practices with increasing frequency.

Of course, as we noted earlier, racism had flourished well before full-blown scientific racism had emerged. *Even after scientific racism was rejected by most intellectuals, many white-skinned members of the general public continued to believe that nonwhite peoples had inferior intelligence*. Polls show that about one-fifth of whites believe that Hispanics and African Americans do not have the same basic intelligence as whites. It is likely that even more people agree with this view, but are embarrassed to admit it. The existence of such prejudice suggests that the legacy of scientific racism is a living legacy, not a relic of the past.

Intellectual challenges to theories of racism reduced but did not eliminate racial prejudice. The public challenge by civil rights demonstrators in the 1960s to the racial *discrimination* that was the product of a long historical legacy of racism led virtually all public officials and many other business and organizational leaders to *avoid public statements that expressed notions of racial inferiority*. But the civil rights movement and the governmental response that enforced laws that required equal opportunities for employment, housing, and education generated a backlash that intensified racism throughout the nation. Speaking in 1987, Kwame Turé, who had been a leader of the Student Nonviolent Coordinating Committee in the 1960s (under the name of Stokley Carmichael), observed that civil rights activists had not anticipated these developments: "Having succeeded in driving racism underground, we became comfortable and complacent, falsely believing this hidden creature was dead or dying." But Turé believed that politicians and intellectuals who were racists or who wanted to capitalize on many voters' racial prejudices were using

> a new and far more sophisticated form of racism . . . Where the old racism was overt [open], frankly announcing its hatred and opposition to all peoples of color, the new racism smiles and insists it is our friend. . . . [and] parades itself about, cloaked in the garb of anti-racism.

While Turé makes a good point, it is also clear that overt assertions of scientific racism were part of the backlash against the civil rights movement in the 1960s. Recently, newspapers and magazines have publicized assertions (made by academics who are not genetic scientists) that genetic differences, rather than social environment, account for the lower *average* IQ test scores of most groups of nonwhite people when compared to whites. These unsubstantiated claims reflect the way in which racism, and nativism, tend to intensify during periods of social stress.

Chapter 7 analyzes nativism, which often reflected racial prejudice, but also drew on religious prejudice and concerns that persons immigrating from nations with political and social cultures very different from and supposedly inferior to those of the United States would not easily be converted to the customs of the American nation.

CHAPTER 7

Nativism

I

> Whereas, The record of immigration to the United States shows that more than 800,000 foreign born persons landed upon American soil during the past year—not the sturdy people who came before the sixties to find a place where they might "worship God according to the dictates of their own conscience," to build up homes for themselves and their families, and if necessary, to die in defense of the stars and stripes, OLD GLORY, our flag—but from the pauper districts of Southern Europe and Oriental Countries, the incubators of nihilism, anarchy, disease and crime . . . THEREFORE BE IT RESOLVED, that we demand the enactment of such laws as will shield us from the depressing effects of unrestricted immigration, to the end that the American laborer may not only be protected against the product of the foreign pauper labor, but that we may be protected against direct competition in our own country by the incoming of the COMPETITIVE ALIEN—the foreign pauper laborers themselves.

This statement, taken from a petition printed in 1905 by the Scranton, Pennsylvania chapter of the Junior Order United American Mechanics, is a good example of nativist sentiments. Attacking immigrants for their national background, race, beliefs, and habits, which are *alleged to be inferior* to the culture of the population groups already occupying a territory, is the main characteristic of nativism.* Nativism invariably involves xenophobia—the fear of foreigners. Nativism is often accompanied both by demands to exclude undesired immigrants and by an insistence that suspect immigrants be forced to adopt the culture of the groups that dominate the territory to which the migrants are moving.

We can find cultural and racial bias in the attitudes of the European settlers in the Western Hemisphere toward the Indians, but it would be incorrect to call this viewpoint nativistic since the Europeans were actually the foreigners and the Indians were the true native Americans. The indigenous peoples of the Western Hemisphere were overcome by the newcomers, and by the 1760s the white descendants of the original European settlers and subsequent European immigrants had begun to identify themselves as "Americans." Since most immigrants to the colonies in the eighteenth century were English Protestants, who shared the same culture and nationality as the majority of the colonists, there was little nativism directed at the immigrants. In fact, one of the complaints the colonists had about British policies, expressed in the eleventh paragraph of the Declaration of Independence, was that they

> had endeavored to prevent the population of these states; for that purpose obstructing the laws for naturalization of foreigners; refusing to pass others [laws] to encourage their migration hither.

II

English Protestants were deeply suspicious of Catholics (see pages 6-7), believing them all agents of the Pope and inclined to support England's major European rivals—Spain and France, both *Catholic* nations that claimed lands in the Western

---

*Nativism comes from *nasci,* the same Latin root as the word native, which means "be born." Thus the nativist is someone who is concerned about the presence of those who were not born in the same nation.

Hemisphere, including land that Great Britain wanted. Throughout the history of the United States, militant nativists emphasized that the Protestant religion and democratic republicanism (See Chapter 3) were the main native values that were threatened by immigrants. This kind of *cultural* nativism was often combined with *economic* nativism, the fear that immigrants would lower the wages and threaten the jobs of native-born workers and diminish the sales and profits of native businessmen. The Boston Massacre (1774) was an example of primarily economic nativism. It was caused by the friction that developed in the 1770s between English soldiers stationed in Boston, who during their time off worked at common manual labor jobs in the port, and native-born dock workers, who resented losing some of their jobs to the British.

Fear of the negative effects of immigration on the culture of the United States became an issue during the 1790s, as elitist Federalists attacked immigrants, especially English artisans and French immigrants, who were militant republicans and supported the French Revolution. The Federalists worried that these immigrants would demand radical changes in the United States, demands similar to those of the more radical groups in the French Revolution who advocated confiscation of the land of the nobility, refusal to pay taxes levied by a government that did not let all men vote, and equal political rights for all people irrespective of their wealth. The Alien Act (1798) empowered the president to deport aliens who were suspected of "treasonable or secret" views and of planning to help French revolutionaries. The Sedition Act was also used by the elitist Federalists to intimidate immigrant journalists, most of them English, who were tied to Democratic-Republican societies and were very critical of President John Adams and his cabinet officers.

By 1820, democratic republicanism was the consensus ideology of most Americans and most elected officials. Proud of their form of government, Americans contrasted it with the corrupt, decadent monarchies of Europe. (The first republic in modern Europe was created in France in 1848. It lasted until 1853, when Napoleon III created a dictatorship. In 1871 he was overthrown and a republic was reestablished. Germany and the nations of central and Eastern Europe did not establish republics until the end of World War I. Italy did not become a republic until after World War II.)

In the years before the Civil War, Americans linked the development of their democratic political system with the ethnicity—Anglo-Saxon*—and the religion—Protestant—of the overwhelming majority of the nation's white settlers and early nineteenth-century population. Thus, Protestant cultural nativists charged that large scale European immigration, including immigration from Germany, was forcing American "Republicanism . . . to swallow the whole serpent brood of [European] monarchies." Many American Protestants viewed the Catholicism of Irish, German, Italian, East European, and French Canadian immigrants as a threat to these traditions. Militant Protestants especially feared that Catholic immigrants would be agents of the Pope, instead of being loyal to the United States. In 1829, a Boston mob spent three days stoning and burning the homes of Irish Catholics, and anti-Catholic nativism began intensifying in the United States. Protestant novelists and newspaper editors began warning Americans of the dangers of alleged "Popish" plots and of Catholic priests, who supposedly invited Protestant women and children to Catholic religious schools and convents, where they were seduced and murdered. Members of the American Bible Society worried about alleged Catholic plans to dominate the territories of the Mississippi River Valley. Criticism of republicanism by Catholic Austrian government officials, who opposed democracy and favored monarchy, deepened the anti-Catholicism of many Americans.

Protestant nativism mounted in the 1830s and 1840s, when increasing numbers of Irish and German immigrants began arriving in the United States. The Irish immigrants were largely Catholic, as were about 40 percent of the Germans. In the 1840s

---

*This term was used but was not accurate. The settlers from England and Scotland were the descendants of a variety of nationalities: Angles, Scots, Saxons, Normans, Danes, Norsemen, Britons, and Picts.

nativist organizations often petitioned Congress to repeal the existing five-year naturalization period in favor of a longer time span. While Congress did not approve such measures, many state legislatures passed laws requiring all aliens to wait 20 or 21 years after emigrating to the United States before they could be naturalized and gain the right to vote.

Political competition—for electoral offices and patronage appointments—quickly developed, especially between Irish Catholics, who were concentrated in urban areas and were overwhelmingly affiliated with the Democratic party's urban political organizations, and Protestants, most of whom were affiliated with the Whig party (and later on with the Republican party). However, the Democratic party had a large rural Protestant constituency; and significant numbers of affluent urban Democrats were Protestants who viewed Catholics as rivals for political power within their own party.

During the 1840s, bitter conflicts arose in many large American cities, particularly New York and Philadelphia, over Catholic demands that the Catholic Bible, rather than the Protestant King James Bible, be used for religious services for Catholic children who attended public schools. Many Protestant ministers and laypeople furiously opposed these demands for individual choice in worshipping. The conflict was complicated by the fact that some state governments gave financial aid to urban public schools, including those which had Catholic children in attendance. The use of public money to provide non-Protestant religious education angered Protestants. Some Catholics who resented the religious intolerance of the Protestants publicly burned the King James Bible. In Philadelphia in 1844, Protestant crowds fought pitched street battles with Catholics and burned a Catholic church.

In the early 1850s, as Irish and German immigration swelled to unprecedented levels, antiforeign sentiment, and especially anti-Catholic sentiment, reached a new level of intensity. By this time, substantial numbers of foreign-born people had emigrated to the United States, increasing economic competition between native-born Americans and immigrants. Significant price inflation also increased social tensions in urban areas. Some of the German immigrants were socialists who began to agitate for a worldwide, revolutionary movement that would found a universal, anti-Christian democratic state. Other, nonradical Germans aroused hostility because they had a tradition of military clubs that paraded in public. Crowds of native-born people often attacked parading Germans in city streets. Meanwhile, the American Catholic hierarchy became more militant in its public statements because heavy Irish and German Catholic immigration after 1843 convinced them that Catholics would soon have the numbers to overwhelm native-born Protestants in the contest for political and religious supremacy.

Since it appeared to be impossible to expel most undesired Catholic immigrants from the country, nativists insisted that American schools and businesses had to "Americanize" the immigrants and their children. (It was assumed that the immigrants could not teach "American" values to their offspring.) Immigrants had to be taught English, respect for democracy, the futility of economic radicalism that demanded the redistribution of wealth or the abolition of private property, and obedience to authority. In 1852, the *New York Times* demanded that immigrants help with the process:

> [They have] the duty of thoroughly *Americanizing* themselves . . .
> they should imbue themselves with American feelings. They should
> not herd themselves together for the preservation of the customs,
> habits, and languages of the countries from which they came.

The rapid rise of the Know-Nothing* party (1853–1856), (also called the American Party) reflected these growing social and economic tensions. The Know-Nothing party advocated immigration restriction, longer naturalization periods or permanent alien status for those not born in the United States, and laws banning foreign-born citizens and non-Protestants from holding public office. The Know-Nothing candidate for president

---

*This term developed because the party originally was a secret society. When asked about the party's activities, members replied, "I know nothing."

in 1856, Millard Fillmore, secured 21.6 percent of the popular vote, the second highest third-party candidate total in the history of the United States. (In 1912 Theodore Roosevelt, running as the Progressive party candidate, obtained 27.4 percent of the total vote.) In Connecticut, the Know-Nothings disbanded state militia units dominated by Irish immigrants and passed legislation making it difficult for Catholic bishops to own real estate. Some Know-Nothings advocated giving women the vote, in part so that native, Protestant women, who were more likely to vote than naturalized immigrant women, could counterbalance the voting of immigrant men.

The Know-Nothing movement collapsed after 1856, as the slavery issue became the main concern of more and more voters. The newly founded Republican party absorbed many voters who had been strongly influenced by nativism. In the 1880s, when questions of post-Civil War reconstruction of the defeated South began to fade from prominence in national political debates, nativists within the Republican party, especially those who were influenced by evangelical Protestantism, lobbied successfully in Iowa and Wisconsin for laws stipulating that only English could be used to teach subjects in public schools like history and government.

But in the late 1880s, a new group of Republicans, led by William McKinley, the governor of Ohio, opposed nativism. They argued that the Republican party could not win elections in a nation of immigrants if it did not make the nation a house for all peoples. Urban Republicans especially targeted French-Canadian Catholic and Italian Catholic voters, hoping to take advantage of the alienation these ethnics felt from the U.S. Catholic Church, which was dominated by Irish and German Catholics. The McKinley Republicans triumphed; until the post-World War I "red scare," the dominant groups in the Republican party were against immigration restriction and opposed legislation that tried to force immigrants to give up their distinctive cultures.

III

In the years after the Civil War, a new variant of nativism emerged, based on Darwinian theories of evolution. Foreigners were now stigmatized by the *assertion* that *scientific research had proven that they belonged to inferior races*, races that were not as highly evolved as the superior Anglo-Saxon and Nordic races (see Chapter 6). Samuel Gompers, president of the American Federation of Labor, absorbed this kind of thinking. Remarking on the immigrants from Southern and Eastern Europe, referred to by historians as the "new immigration," Gompers called them "beaten men of beaten races." Elite Protestants, who dominated the major Eastern universities and literary circles, complained in the years between 1890 and 1920 that the nation would experience "race suicide" if the "inferior" new immigrants married and had children with "Americans" of Anglo-Saxon and Teutonic background. The Protestants believed scientists had demonstrated that the genes of the inferior immigrants would overwhelm the superior genes of natives of Anglo-Saxon and Teutonic racial stock.

Economic nativism continued to be strong in the last quarter of the nineteenth century. A Wisconsin blacksmith lamented in 1887 that " . . . immigrants work for almost nothing and seem to be able to live on wind—something which I cannot do." Workers who worried that immigration would lower their wages were right about the short-run effect of adding more women and men to the labor force. But in the long run, *as long as the U.S. economy was expanding rapidly*, immigration provided increased labor power and more consumers to purchase goods, which actually promoted faster economic growth.

The immigration of Asians to the West Coast, from 1849–1906, helped the regional and national economy. Chinese immigrants—many of them contract laborers who were forced to emigrate and were severely exploited by their follow countrymen —helped build the transcontinental railroads. Japanese immigrants were all voluntary immigrants. They applied the backbreaking, labor-intensive farming techniques used in Japan to the fruit and vegetable farms they created in California. The reaction of the white population of the West Coast to the Chinese and Japanese was clearly influenced by the racism that was so strong throughout the United States. Congress banned Chinese immigration in 1882.

Japanese immigration was halted in 1906. Yet the racially based hatred and envy of the Japanese immigrants, many of whom had established successful fruit and vegetable farms, led the California legislature, in 1913, to pass a law that barred Japanese immigrants from buying additional agricultural land. Japanese immigrant farmers evaded this law's limitations by creating trusts to buy land, and then having the land given to their children when they became adults.

Nativistic rhetoric and organization increased whenever economic or social crises developed in the United States. Periods of massive immigration, economic depression, and labor unrest stimulated nativistic attacks on immigrants, who were blamed for threats to the national culture, unemployment, and labor radicalism. Treating foreign-born residents as *scapegoats*, and blaming them for the nation's economic problems and social tensions was a way to ignore social inequities and basic economic forces that had nothing to do with foreigners.

No single social class or group in the United States had a monopoly on nativism. Elites, middle-class people, and wage earners often felt threatened by immigration and the presence of diverse ethnic groups in the nation. Elite, middle-class, and working-class nativists all advocated the use of literacy tests and nationality quotas to exclude undesired immigrants, especially those who held socialist or anarchist political views, or who came from Southern and Eastern Europe. A native-born hat maker in Danbury, Connecticut complained in 1917 that the owners of the city's hat shops were hiring nonunion, immigrant workers—the "scum of Europe" who were "a low class of people." Of course, the hatters' union, dominated by native-born workers, excluded many of the immigrants from membership. Mainstream labor leaders, generally of Yankee, English, German, and Irish ethnicity, believed that the immigrants from

Southern and Eastern Europe who dominated the immigration stream after 1900—Italians, Poles, Russians, and Jews—were too prone to political radicalism and too inclined to militancy and violence during strikes to be worth incorporating into existing labor unions. Samuel Gompers wrote in 1910 that immigrants had been responsible for the "undermining of American labor in certain industries . . . and much of the increase in whatever is permanent in the American Socialist vote."

American socialists talked about the unity of the working class, yet many socialists were nativists. In 1914, the Socialist mayor of Martin's Ferry, Ohio complained about the problem of keeping law and order in a city that

> now has a population of about 2,000 foreigners, most of whom have a wrong impression of the laws governing this country, and are of the opinion that they can do most anything they please in this land of Liberty and Freedom . . . Ninety percent of arrests are made among this class of people who, no doubt, will ultimately make good citizens but they *must* be taught that the customs and laws of this country must be respected.

At its 1910 convention, the Socialist Party of America split on the question of allowing unrestricted immigration to the United States. Nativistic socialists argued for the exclusion of Asian and "new immigrant" workers on the grounds that they were not easily convinced to vote Socialist, while nonnativistic socialists asserted that "new immigrant" workers were very militant and would constructively participate in the activities of the Socialist party if they were actively encouraged to join.

Not all opponents of immigration were nativists. In some cases members of a particular nationality group opposed further immigration of their fellow countrymen. For example, in the 1870s, Scottish immigrant coal miners in Illinois, worried about limited work opportunities during slumps in the coal business, opposed the immigration of more *Scottish* miners, and worked out a scheme to send cash payments to Scotland to prevent the emigration of their fellow countrymen.

While many industrial employers believed that immigrant workers were animalistic brutes who had to be controlled by Americanization schemes, *these businessmen adamantly opposed any immigration restriction*, since *labor shortages would raise wages and make it easier for workers to strike* for union recognition and improved working conditions. "Americanization" of foreigners was promoted by employers who pressured their workers to take English-language classes at night, and by labor unions that refused to conduct meetings in any language except English. In 1918, the AFL union of hotel and restaurant workers told foreign-born workers that they had to "Americanize" if they wanted to join the union:

> If you are an American at heart, speak our language. If you don't know it, learn it. If you don't like it, MOVE.

Many activists in the Prohibition movement, which achieved success in many states before the passage of the Eighteenth Amendment in 1919, thought of Prohibition as a technique for controlling the alleged violent propensities of foreigners. In the 1920s, American eugenicists, who wanted to improve the quality of the gene pool of the population, demanded sterilization of people from "inferior" ethnic groups. Many proponents of the dissemination of birth control technology stressed the value of limiting the number of children produced by immigrants with "inferior" genes. Margaret Sanger, who did more than any other person in the United States to secure for women the right to use birth control technologies, used such arguments in the 1920s when she tried to get affluent middle-class people to contribute money to the American Birth Control League.

In 1919, horrible race riots broke out in Charleston, South Carolina, Washington, D.C., and Chicago. Race hatred between whites and blacks was the primary cause of the riots. Yet U.S. Army Intelligence agents blamed the Chicago race riot on the influence of immigrants who were allegedly agents of the new socialist government in Russia. The 1919 strike wave, the largest in the nation's history, was attributed by many newspaper editors, businessmen, and government officials to the alleged agitation of politically radical foreign-born workers, especially those of Russian and Polish nationality. This kind of nativistic bias ignored the legitimate complaints striking foreign-born workers, most of whom were not revolutionaries, had about ethnic discrimination and economic exploitation. Nevertheless, during the "red scare" that lasted from November 1919 to January 1920, government agents throughout the United States arrested thousands of alleged radical immigrants. Hardly any of the arrested were ever convicted of a crime in a court of law, although about 500 were deported after administrative hearings in which they were not allowed any of the rights that would have been accorded to a person tried in a regular court.

Throughout the 1920s, the Ku Klux Klan organized native-born workers in the Midwest—especially Indiana, Ohio, Illinois, and Minnesota—to intimidate Catholic immigrant workers. Business owners financed the Klan's nativistic rallies and terrorism because these activities were often directed against attempts to unionize semi-skilled and low-skilled Catholic workers. The Klan's demand for immigrant exclusion appealed to many Protestant workers, since in many firms there was strong competition between Protestant and Catholic workers for promotion to better-paying, skilled-labor jobs.

In 1924, Congress enacted a comprehensive immigration law. Hitherto, only Chinese (1882) and Japanese (1906) immigrants had been banned from coming to the United States Now total immigration was limited to 150,000 a year. (In the period between 1840 and 1920, immigration had averaged 500,000 a year.) The ethnic bias of the 1924 law was deliberate: quotas were set up for each nation, with the overwhelming majority of the places assigned to people from Western European countries, who were of largely Anglo-Saxon, Teutonic, and Scandinavian background. Congress wanted to exclude immigrants from Eastern and Southern Europe because such peoples were believed to be likely to advocate economic and political radicalism.

As the nation's economy expanded during the 1920s, severe labor shortages would have developed if the 1924 law had been enforced strictly. But *immigration officials allowed one significant violation of the law*: Mexican men and women were allowed to cross the border in large numbers. When the U.S. economy collapsed in 1929, large numbers of Mexican immigrants were deported because city and state governments did not want to pay for relief for unemployed people *who were not citizens*. Moreover, unemployed "white" workers did not want to have to compete with Mexicans for scarce jobs. Racial prejudice led the authorities to deport many Mexican-American *citizens* of the United States, since the authorities did not try to distinguish between citizens and noncitizens when they staged mass roundups of people who *looked like Mexicans*.

As the Depression of the 1930s worsened, increasing amounts of anti-Semitic propaganda was disseminated throughout the country, blaming the nation's economic crisis on international Jewish bankers and "gold-bugs," and especially the French banking company of F. Rothschild and Sons. Father Coughlin, a Detroit priest who had a nationally syndicated radio show, broadcast attacks on Jewish bankers all over the world, accusing them of financial manipulations that hurt the American economy. People who joined the Liberty League, which opposed U.S. preparation to fight against Germany and Japan, thought that Hitler's persecution of Jews and communists (many falsely assumed that all Jews in the United States and Europe were radicals) was a good thing.

The Japanese attack on Pearl Harbor on December 7, 1941 began a panic, as many racial nativists believed that even American-born citizens of immigrant Japanese parents would be loyal to Japan, not the United States. (There was no evidence to support this claim.) The federal government caved in to pressure from military leaders and West Coast nativists, some of whom were very envious of the successful agricultural businesses that had been developed by second-generation Japanese-American vegetable and fruit farmers. Virtually all West Coast people of Japanese extraction were forcibly removed to internment camps for the duration of World War II. The property of the interred Japanese was confiscated, and hardly any of this property was returned after the war ended. Meanwhile, neither German-Americans nor Italian-Americans were jailed, even though the United States was also at war with Germany and Italy.

During World War II, many racist advertisements were printed in national magazines like *Life*, including one that praised the virtues of Du Pont gunpowder in the bombs that would destroy the "slant-eyes" who were our adversaries. Social tensions increased in many communities during World War II. Internal migration brought large numbers of newcomers to the cities and towns where new factories were being built to manufacture military products. Established residents of these communities often resented the newcomers. Furthermore, the rapid growth of war industries created many local housing shortages. Overcrowded housing created tension and aggressive behavior. People of different ethnic and racial groups often competed for scarce apartments.

Wartime tensions led groups of whites on the West Coast to attack people of color. For example, on June 3, 1943, U.S. Marines in Oakland, California went into the Mexican/Mexican-American section of the city and assaulted young gang members who were wearing a faddish type of clothing, the "zootsuit." Four days later, thousands of sailors and civilians in Los Angeles descended on East Los Angeles, where they indiscriminately assaulted people of color—Mexican Americans, African Americans, and Filipinos. The Los Angeles police did nothing to stop the attacks, which were ended by the dispatch of military police to East Los Angeles.

In the decade following World War II, there were additional surges of anti-Mexican nativism in the Southwest and on the West Coast. As the Cold War intensified, many militant Mexican and Mexican American labor leaders were accused of being Soviet agents. Between 1945 and the early 1950s, many antiunion businessmen and politicians charged that foreign-born radical labor leaders were corrupting American workers with "un-American" ideas like trade unionism, national health insurance, and government-financed public housing. Attempts were made to deport militant foreign-born labor leaders such as the Australian citizen Harry Bridges, who headed the West Coast Longshoremen's Union. During the McCarthy years, teachers, intellectuals, and union leaders who advocated pacifism, peaceful coexistence with the Soviet Union, or anticolonial foreign policies were often attacked for spreading "foreign" ideas. When such views were publicly expressed by men and women who had been born abroad, many of whom had been victims of Fascist and Communist persecution, their "Americanism" was impugned, and demands were made for their incarceration or deportation.

IV

Since the early 1970s, real incomes have been stagnant or declining for most American adults. Improvements in the productivity of the technologies used to manufacture goods and provide services have been so great that in the U.S., Western European, and Japanese economies, more and more jobs are being eliminated. This is the result of the fact that an increased number of nations are rapidly adopting the latest, most efficient production technologies. Consequently, by 1993, the number of jobs created for each billion dollars of growth in our gross domestic product had fallen by 45% compared to 1988.

The next 20 years are likely to be a period of slow economic growth in Western Europe, Eastern Europe, Japan, and the United States. With new job creation limited and real wages static or declining, *competition for jobs, especially for the less numerous high-paying jobs, is likely to be fierce.* The tensions created by this competition have already led to increases in ethnic, racial, and religious prejudices in the United States, Western Europe, and Japan.

Nativistic reactions to foreign businesses' investments in American factories and real estate have become prominent in the press and on television talk shows. Hostility has especially focused on Asian—particularly Japanese—companies, even though most investments in American real estate and businesses have been made by Europeans. Vocal critics of the Asians have called for higher tariffs on foreign imports and reverse quotas (in California universities) to reduce the number of Asian-stock students (most of these students are American-born citizens). On college campuses and elsewhere, the number of verbal attacks and physical assaults on people of Asian background has increased markedly.

In the United States, the tendency to blame minority social groups for the nation's economic problems is increasing. Consider the lyrics of *One in A Million,* a song by the internationally-known rock group, Guns 'N Roses:

> Immigrants and faggots
> They make no sense to me
> They come to our country
> And think they'll do as they please.

Immigration from Latin America—both legal and illegal— has picked up considerably since 1983. Evidence of nativistic reactions to Spanish-speaking immigrants and their offspring is evident in the demands of some educators and politicians for abandoning bilingual educational programs. Some nativists have argued against printing signs in any language other than English. As this essay is being written (summer 1995), an intense public debate is going on in California and other southwestern states about the desirability of restricting immigration—especially the immigration of Hispanic peoples from Central and South America—and the constitutionality of Proposition 187, a California law that denies schooling and Medicaid coverage to illegal immigrants and their children born in this country (who are legal citizens).

In June 1995, Congress was debating a bill that would deny income maintenance benefits (Aid to Families with Dependent Children, food stamps, Supplemental Security Income, and Medicaid) to most *legal* immigrants who are not U.S. citizens and to many immigrants who have *become citizens*. In the fall of

1995, Congress will vote on a significant immigration restriction bill that has obtained bipartisan backing.

The advocates of immigration restriction and of limiting the rights of immigrants have not accused illegal aliens of representing a devious foreign power, as nativists did in the nineteenth century. Rather, immigration restrictionists— including some Hispanic and Asian immigrants who have been longtime residents of the United States—have focused on the economic impact of immigration at a time when the California economy is shrinking, with hundreds of thousands of workers finding themselves unemployed. Many people are unhappy that their taxes are being increased to provide social services to illegal immigrants. Other advocates of immigration restriction and the withholding of social services from illegal immigrants are racial nativists, who are most likely prejudiced against darker-skinned immigrants. Some racial nativists are now claiming that the majority status of white people in the United States is threatened by high levels of legal and illegal immigration from Latin American and Asian nations. The high birthrates of many immigrants from these parts of the globe can be expected to add to the proportion of nonwhite peoples in the United States. Nativists believe that nonwhite peoples are culturally and genetically inferior to whites, and warn that whites will not feel comfortable in a nation with a nonwhite majority.

Although some immigrants work in agricultural and manufacturing businesses that have to face low wages and foreign competition, most immigrants work in jobs that provide services to homeowners or businesses *in this country*. Workers outside the United States *cannot provide such services*. Businesses employing low-wage workers want high levels of immigration, since immigration creates a larger surplus of unemployed low-wage workers in the nation, which *helps prevent the wages of low-income wage earners from rising*. One study estimates that present levels of immigration have lowered overall U.S. wage rates by about $120,000,000,000 yearly, or two percent of the Gross Domestic Product.

It is possible that in the future, anti-immigrant groups may, as they did in the nineteenth century, form a new, anti-immigration political party that will be active in states that are the destinations of large numbers of immigrants. Nativism is likely to intensify in the United States if our economy does not grow vigorously, and if the flow of legal and illegal immigrants continues at present levels.

Prejudice based on sex often existed alongside racial and nationality-based prejudice. But in the Christian world, male prejudice against women of the same race and nationality had a long history that reached back to the period when the Old Testament was written. As the next chapter explains, in the late eighteenth century, and especially after 1830, an increasing number of women in the United State began to challenge the prejudices that were used to justify male domination.

CHAPTER 8

Women's Rights

I

In 1775, Thomas Paine wrote a poem, *Liberty Tree*, to remind the English North American colonists about the rights and liberties British actions threatened to limit. In his poem, liberty was brought to humankind by a woman, the Goddess of Liberty:

> In a chariot of light from the regions of day,
>   The Goddess of Liberty came;
> Ten thousand celestials directed the way,
>   And hither conducted the dame . . .
> She brought in her hand as a pledge of her love,
>   And the plant she named *Liberty Tree*.

But Paine seemed unaware that his poem depicted only men as the beneficiaries of this gift from a woman god.

> The fame of its fruit drew the nations around,
>   To seek out this peaceable shore.
> Unmindful of names or distinction they came,
>   For free*men* like *brothers* agree . . .
> Beneath this fair tree, like the *patriarchs* of old,
>   Their bread in contentment they ate.

The English colonies were patriarchal societies. English men and most women believed that women were intellectually inferior to men, incapable of rational, unemotional judgment, and therefore best off as wards of their husbands, grandfathers, uncles, and brothers. Consequently, women were placed in a second-class legal position. Single women who had reached the age of 18 could own property, as could widows. But married women were dominated economically by their husbands. With few exceptions, the laws of the patriarchal colonial governments gave married men total control over all earnings and property brought into a marriage or earned and accumulated by their wives. (However, property that a women owned before marriage, including her dowry, could not be sold by her husband without her permission.) Married women were not allowed to sign contracts. Their husbands had to sign for them. (Husbands could choose to give their wives a legal power of attorney, granting them the power to conduct business in the husband's absence.) Lack of legal rights prevented married women from acting autonomously to start a business or to make a will specifying, if they were to die before their husbands, the distribution of the property they had brought into the marriage.

Women unhappy with their marriages found divorce almost impossible to obtain from the male-monopolized courts. Verbal abuse and physical cruelty were not generally recognized as adequate grounds for divorce by the courts. (English common law allowed husbands to give wives "moderate [physical] correction" for misbehavior.) However, when women could prove their husbands had committed adultery or abandoned them, the courts usually granted divorces, although in abandonment cases the delay could be considerable. Such delay made the abandoned woman vulnerable to adultery prosecutions for having sexual relationships with men and often left her impoverished, especially since remarriage to a man who could support her was illegal without a divorce.

Some widows who inherited enough property to support themselves decided to avoid remarrying (and having to share control over their property with a new husband). But the colonial courts sometimes voided wills, preventing single women from receiving inheritances that would make them independent of men. In a patriarchal culture, men (and women dependent on men) were suspicious of and envious of women who gained financial independence because they had been lucky enough (because of the lack of male heirs) to escape from the standard inheritance practice of giving the bulk of the wealth of the deceased to men. In the seventeenth century, many such women would be accused of witchcraft.

The colonists were reared in a Christian tradition that blamed women for humankind's fall from grace and expulsion from the Garden of Eden. In the Bible story, the serpent had tricked Eve into eating the fruit God had forbidden Adam and Eve to eat. The serpent had tempted Eve with the promise of power: eating the fruit would allow her and Adam to become Gods. Eve ate the fruit and gave it to Adam, who also partook. When God discovered that they had eaten the forbidden fruit, he chastised Adam, who replied, blaming Eve: "The woman whom thou gavest to be with me, she gave me of the tree, and I did eat." Written by men who lived in a highly patriarchal society, the Old Testament version of creation served as a powerful religious justification for male supremacy: women were responsible for the origin of sin. Elizabeth Cady Stanton, one of the foremost proponents of equal rights for women in the history of the United States, believed that these beliefs were so harmful to the effort to advance women's rights that she wrote an entire book (*The Women's Bible*) attacking the Bible's patriarchal biases.

Double standards also persisted in the social relationships between men and women. During courtship, women were expected to be passive, while men were encouraged to be aggressively open about their feelings. In 1736 a Virginia woman, who was afraid to admit her identity, complained about this disparity:

> They plainly can their Thoughts disclose,
> While ours must burn within:
> We have got Tongues, and Eyes, in Vain,
> And Truth from us is Sin.

In the first written demand for male/female equality to survive in the colonies, the woman insisted upon a leveling of the status of both sexes:

> Then Equal Laws let Custom find,
> And neither Sex oppress;
> More Freedom give to Womankind,
> Or give to Mankind less.

But men born and raised in patriarchal cultures were hardly interested in sharing the exclusive powers that gave them social and economic supremacy.

In contrast, among Native American peoples, there was wide variation in the roles and rights of women. The eastern and southwestern tribes that engaged in significant amounts of agriculture gave women important official powers, including the authority to veto decisions to go to war. The more mobile tribes of the West and Southwest appear to have given women fewer powers. In the religions of many Native American peoples, accounts of the creation of the world were less hostile to women and assigned to women a greater role in the creation process than Christianity did. Prolonged contact with the patriarchal Europeans influenced some tribes, like the Cherokees, to end the voting powers women had exercised at tribal councils.

II

The American Revolution was led by a coalition of economic elites and "middling" artisans and farmers. The intellectual arguments used by the educated elites to justify independence from England to preserve the liberties of the colonists—the Lockean language of all men being created equal—were later taken up by non-elites, who argued that equality meant equality for their group, not just for the substantial propertied person. Men who were small farmers and artisans insisted that in the new republic, political equality for all *free men* was essential (see Chapter 2 on Democracy). In the eighteenth century, a small number of American women dared to make the same argument, challenging patriarchal beliefs.

In 1790, Judith Sargent Murray, the first American woman to develop a consistent critique of women's subordination, wrote an article in *Massachusetts Magazine* that asserted in Lockean rhetoric that

> our souls are by nature *equal* to yours; the same breath of God animates, enlivens, and invigorates us.

Addressing the patriarchal notion that men's superior physical strength was accompanied by superior mental ability, Murray pointed out that there were many mammals who were stronger than *homo sapiens*, yet clearly had inferior mental. powers. Murray pointed out that lack of educational opportunities made it appear that many women were not as intellectually gifted as men. Speaking largely to literate, educated men and women, Murray argued that marriages would be improved if women received education equal to that of men and did not feel "a mortifying consciousness of inferiority" that made it hard to enjoy sharing experiences with their husbands. To those who believed that educated women would not have time to learn domestic skills, Murray bluntly asserted that "every requisite in female economy is easily attained; and . . . once attained, they require no further *mental attention.*"

Murray had begun a challenge to patriarchal ideas that is still being debated. Most women and men in the new nation accepted the patriarchal framework. They believed women's abilities were best suited for the domestic sphere, the sphere of the household, where they would provide the basic services necessary to run the household and raise the children who were present. Women were also responsible for economic production in their homes and in the barnyards of their farms. On most farms, at critical times in the year, women, at the direction of men, planted and harvested.

The *republican* ideology of the new American nation had a profound influence on one aspect of women's lives. Whereas in the colonial period it was generally believed that too much education would confuse the allegedly "weaker" minds of women, it was now believed that women needed to have a basic education to enable them to *raise the wise and virtuous men who would be the future voters of the republic*. These sentiments led to the founding of more private women's high schools and colleges in the United States in the nineteenth century than in any other country in the world. An increasing number of the daughters of *middle-class* parents attended these schools.

Although the right of free white men to vote and run for office was slowly extended, and was largely achieved by 1840, nowhere in the republic could women vote or run for public office. (For a brief period after the Revolutionary War women were allowed to vote in New Jersey.) During the state constitutional conventions of the 1820s, which decided to abolish property qualifications for voting, the delegates never considered giving the vote to women. The image of women that was upheld in these conventions was that they were *dependent* children who needed the protection of men. In Massachusetts in 1821, Josiah Quincy spoke against universal manhood suffrage by claiming that it was not a mistake to exclude men who owned no property, since "extreme poverty . . . is inconsistent with independence." Only self-sufficient voters would be free from the manipulation of the rich. Likening women and children to the dependent pauper, Quincy argued that women and children had been denied "the right of suffrage, without any injustice."

How did women come to challenge patriarchal notions? Women's participation in a major religious revival movement, the Second Great Awakening (1820–1850), would play a crucial role in encouraging significant numbers of women to challenge men's monopoly to be present at, and to *speak to audiences* in the public sphere of the meeting hall, the street rally, the church, and the university. During the Second Great Awakening, ministers began to preach that men and women could will themselves out of sin and could directly experience the saving grace of God. Each person who had this kind of spiritual rebirth did so by means of a *one-to-one* relationship with God, without any authority intervening. Those who believed themselves saved viewed themselves as *equals* in the eyes of God to any other person who was saved. Charles G. Finney, the most influential evangelical minister in the 1830s, went out of his way to encourage women to be active in the public sphere by describing their conversion experiences at church meetings.

Women who experienced religious conversion by taking God's spirit into themselves were often enthusiastic about spreading God's word and doing God's work in their local communities and on a national level. Many of these women joined antislavery organizations. Attending meetings at which slavery was criticized as creating an inequality that God had not intended for humans, some women were emboldened to *speak to public audiences on the slavery question*. But it was not easy for these pioneers.

When eight women students at Oberlin College formed a debating group in the 1830s, they were so afraid of being criticized or punished that they decided to meet secretly in the woods and in a house on the outskirts of town. In 1838, when Angelina Grimké, a Quaker* abolitionist, addressed an abolitionist meeting in Boston, she felt the strain of going against established custom. Describing her feelings before her first public address, she wrote "I never was so near fainting under the tremendous pressure of feeling. My heart almost died within me. The novelty of the scene, the weight of responsibility . . . all together sunk me to the earth."

Grimké's speeches aroused criticism from many men. A newspaper editor complained

> She exhibited considerable talent for a female, as an orator; appeared not at all abashed in exhibiting herself in a position so unsuitable to her sex, totally disregarding the doctrine of St. Paul, who says, "Is it not a shame for a woman to speak in public?"

---

*Quaker congregations had no ministers and allowed women an equal right to speak during services. It is not accidental that many of the women who would play leading roles in the nineteenth century antislavery and women's suffrage movements were Quakers, since their religious experiences had taught them that they were equal to men in one sphere of life—that of religion—and they resented the unequal treatment of others and themselves in other ways.

And the congregational ministers of Massachusetts issued a pastoral letter condemning Grimké for her temerity.

Many of the women active in the abolitionist movement gained confidence in their ability to participate in social policy debates that took place in the public sphere. Influenced by the rhetoric of the abolitionist movement, which called for justice for slaves, some of the women abolitionists became aware of the depth of the legal injustices visited upon women, especially the way married women lost rights to their own property and were denied the right to vote. Women active in the abolitionist movement also absorbed an important lesson from the way William Lloyd Garrison attacked clergymen who were not abolitionists. Garrison's example in *challenging religious officials* helped women who wanted to publicly demand equal rights for women to face the hostility of large numbers of ministers (including many abolitionist ministers) to women's equality. Angelina Grimké asserted that

> it is woman's right to have a voice in all the laws and regulations by which she is to be governed, whether in Church or State. . . . and that the present arrangements of society . . . are a *violation of human rights, a rank usurpation of power*, a violent seizure of what is sacredly and inalienably hers.

But not all women agreed. Writing in 1836, Catherine Beecher, one of the most capable intellectuals of the nineteenth century, argued that God had ordained

> different stations of superiority and subordination [for women and men], and it is impossible to annihilate this beneficent and immutable law.

Beecher did not believe that women were intellectually or morally inferior to men. She maintained that if women did not enter the public sphere of partisan politics and business, but remained within the domestic sphere, they could maintain their *superior* moral abilities. Then the activities of women could morally redeem a nation divided by debates over slavery and by the harangues of self-seeking politicians. Staying in the domestic sphere would enable woman's morality to "be infused into the mass of the nation, and then truth may be sought, defended, and propagated, and errors detected, and its evils exposed." Beecher had developed an argument that would be enthusiastically accepted by many American women for the next 100 years.

Women concerned that their basic rights were not equal to those of men decided in 1848 to call a Women's Rights Convention. Meeting at Seneca Falls, New York, the convention adopted a Declaration of Sentiments modeled on the Declaration of Independence. Claiming that "the laws of nature and of nature's God entitle" women to equality, the women argued that laws denying married women equal property rights to their husbands should be repealed, that women should have equal access to education, and that in divorce cases men should not automatically be awarded custody of their children. The Declaration also asserted the "inalienable right" of women to vote and proclaimed as unjust that fact that women were "compelled . . . to submit to laws, in the formation of which [women] . . . had no voice [in the passage of those laws]." The second statement was clearly based on the principle of "no taxation without representation" that had led the colonists to declare their independence from England. But the demand for the vote was the only plank of the Declaration that was not unanimously approved by the convention.

The Declaration of Sentiments also criticized patriarchy for excluding women from professional vocations. It charged that men had "monopolized nearly all the profitable employments. . . As a teacher of theology, medicine, or law, . . . [woman] is not known." Addressing the notion that women did not belong in active roles in the public sphere, the Declaration lamented that men claimed

> the right to assign for her a sphere of action, when that belongs to her conscience and to her God.

The Seneca Falls convention also marked the public debut of Elizabeth Cady Stanton, who was the most eloquent orator of the women's movement in the nineteenth century. In her first public speech, Stanton maintained that women should have equal rights to men in all matters. She attacked the belief systems that convinced men that women deserved their subordinate legal and social position:

> Man's intellectual superiority cannot be a question until woman has had a fair trial. When we shall have had our freedom to find out our own sphere, when we shall have had our colleges, our professions, our trades for a century, a comparison then may be justly instituted.

By 1869, Stanton had developed strong, vehement critique of patriarchal rule. She contended that throughout history, men's behavior—in warfare and at election time—demonstrated that men *were morally inferior to women*. Governments of men had brought human society nothing but misery:

> The male element is destructive force, stern, selfish, aggrandizing, loving war, violence, conquest . . . acquisition . . . overpowering the feminine element everywhere, crushing out all the diviner qualities in human nature.

Stanton believed that enfranchising morally superior women would improve the operation of government:

> We ask woman's enfranchisement, as the first step towards the recognition of that essential element in government that can only secure the health, strength, and prosperity of the nation . . . that great conservator of woman's love, if permitted to assert itself, as it naturally would in freedom against oppression, violence, and war, would hold all these destructive forces in check.

In 1872 Susan B. Anthony, Stanton's friend and partner in reform efforts, pointed to the dangerous, anti-democratic precedent set by denying the vote to women, most of whom were *citizens*, a precedent that encouraged

> the petty tricks and cunning devices which will be attempted to exclude one and another class of citizens from the right of suffrage. It will not always be the men combining to disfranchise all women. . . . There is and can be but one safe principle of government—equal rights to all.

But the women's suffrage movement did not secure the vote for women in all states until 1920. Many women continued to embrace patriarchal ideas. Numerous women married to affluent middle- and upper-income husbands were fearful of leaving the security of their comfortable homes and competing in the world of business. In 1896 Amelia Barr, an educated woman who embraced the notion of the domestic sphere, insisted that housekeeping "is a woman's first natural duty and answers to the needs of her best nature. . . . that there is a most intimate connection between food and virtue, and food and health, and food and thought." Other women who hesitated to demand the vote were impressed by arguments that if they entered the world of politics men would no longer "retain their chivalrous deference to them [women] and refrain from using their brute force in an emergency."

In the years between 1848 and 1880, many states responded to the lobbying of proponents of equal rights for women by passing laws giving married women the same property rights as their husbands, as well as the right to sign business contracts without their husbands' permission. By 1880, seven prestigious men's colleges (starting with Oberlin in 1833) admitted women students and four women's undergraduate colleges (Mount Holyoke, Vassar, Wellesley, and Smith) had been established. By 1900, 85,000 women were enrolled in colleges. Significant numbers of women were obtaining law degrees and several women's medical schools had been founded. Professional women trained at these colleges and an increasing number of graduate schools began to accept women. However, many professional schools (like Stanford's law school, MIT's engineering program, and Harvard's business school) discriminated against women by establishing quotas that limited the number of women who would be admitted, by deciding not to build additional on-campus housing for women students, which effectively excluded them, and by forcing women students to leave the library at an earlier hour than male students.

Sex-based hiring discrimination forced most women with professional degrees to practice as self-employed specialists.

Hospitals refused to allow women doctors to admit patients, let alone get staff appointments. Law firms would not hire women lawyers. In 1916, the American Society of Civil Engineers voted to expel women members and ban future admissions of women. Most high school administrative jobs were closed to women teachers. Only those institutions in which women played a major administrative role—women's colleges and settlement houses—were willing to employ large numbers of professional women.

In the last quarter of the nineteenth century, the strongest social movement organized in the United States by white women was the temperance movement. Women enrolled in the Women's Christian Temperance Union pointed to the way male breadwinners often drank away a large part of the wages they earned, depleting the already meager financial resources of families of poor or modest means. Alcoholism also increased male violence, including sexual violence, against women and children. Many women (and their children) subsisted on whatever earnings they could get from alcoholic male breadwinners.

Women's economic dependency was worsened by discrimination against women in the labor market. If a woman wanted to divorce an alcoholic husband, she would have great difficulty getting a job that would allow her to match her husband's income. Most employers and male wage earners distinguished between "men's jobs" and "women's jobs." The former were higher-paying jobs that often required on-the-job training. In the late nineteenth century, the jobs made available to women paid, on average, about 40 percent less than the jobs available to men. An 1895 study of 150,000 manufacturing jobs revealed that women and men were employed in the same job classification in only 800 cases. In 600 of the 800 cases, the men in the same classification were paid an average of 30 percent more than the women. While some women desirous of earning "men's wages" fooled their employers by dressing like men, most women did not employ this strategy. (Some women were jailed for violating laws that banned "cross dressing.")

Male wage earners generally did not want to compete with women for better-paying jobs. Men argued that their masculinity would be undermined if they could not earn a family wage, a wage enabling them to be the main source of support for their families. Allowing women to compete for jobs that paid a family wage would deny some men access to these jobs and would lower wage rates, since more workers would be seeking the same jobs. To justify the exclusion of women from the better-paying jobs, male wage earners and/or employers claimed that women lacked the intelligence or physical strength and stamina to perform high-skilled jobs that were mentally and physically demanding. Employers claimed that most women workers did not *need* wages equal to men, since they assumed that the women were single women who were not supporting households. While many women who worked in wage labor jobs outside their homes were young women who were supported by their families (and in turn gave their families some of their earnings), at least one of every six women who worked as a wage laborer *headed a household*. Such women were widows supporting their children and/or women relatives, or married women supporting disabled husbands.

By 1900, an increasing number of women labored outside the home (or, to be more accurate, the rented single-family house or apartment). The best paid women were stenographers, university-trained professionals, and women who were the supervisors of secretaries and clerks in businesses with large office staffs, especially insurance companies and department stores. However, women who worked in white-collar jobs were almost always fired if they married, since even most women supervisors believed that marriage would increase absenteeism, among women workers. The lowest paid working women labored in homes (as domestic workers), on farms, in factories (including small garment shops), and in retail stores. Many of these women believed that they would receive higher pay and labor under better conditions if they were voters and could pressure legislators for minimum wage laws, sanitary and safety codes, and fire codes. The male relatives and husbands of the growing number of working women often sympathized with the arguments the women made for the suffrage, since it was clear that the families of women workers would benefit from the economic gains women expected from gaining the vote.

In their public statements, most twentieth-century women's suffrage reformers did not strongly attack men and patriarchal culture. The suffragists knew that they needed the votes of many men who would oppose goals like *full social equality* for women (including unimpeded rights to personal self-development) and would have been offended by the kinds of attacks that Elizabeth Cady Stanton made on patriarchal religious culture. A study of the arguments used by California suffrage groups in 1916 revealed that when their *public* propaganda mentioned sex-based discrimination, it did not suggest the remedies that could eliminate the discrimination. This tactic avoided antagonizing men.

The most common arguments used to advocate women's suffrage were based on the traditional notion that women had special maternal instincts that would lead them to improve the moral quality of the electorate. Women would extend their "housekeeping" talents and the "instinct of motherhood" from the domestic sphere into the public political sphere. This line of argument also mobilized many women to join in suffrage agitation.

More and more women were concluding that voting was not inconsistent with the performance of their domestic duties. In urban areas, households run by women were increasingly dependent on the services provided by government institutions: fire prevention services, garbage collection, and street cleaning services were necessary to protect life and property and to ensure hygiene and prevent contagious diseases. Supporters of women's political involvement argued that if women voted, they would seek to improve the quality of home life by backing efforts to improve public health, reduce government corruption, and combat prostitution, drug use, and the sale of impure food.

After 1905, the revived American women's suffrage movement gained increased effectiveness from the new *tactics* it adopted. Nineteenth-century suffragists had petitioned legislatures, testified at hearings, lobbied influential legislators and members of the social elite, and held unadvertised, private, indoor meetings before invited audiences. Rarely did early suffragists threaten to oppose elected officials who were against women's suffrage.

In 1903, one group of women suffragettes in England, led by Emmeline G. Pankhurst and her daughters Crystabel and Sylvia, began to use especially militant tactics to demand the vote for women. During their *public* demonstrations, these English suffragettes sometimes burned down homes, slashed campaign posters, and threw stones through store windows to protest the refusal of the police to issue parade permits. The English suffragettes also interrupted all-male political meetings, shouting challenges at candidates who were opposed to women's suffrage. The militant English suffragettes were physically assaulted by male bystanders and were often treated roughly by the police.

Many of the American women who would play leading roles in the militant wing of the suffrage movement in the United States either personally witnessed the demonstrations of the English suffragettes in London or, like Katherine Houghton Hepburn (mother of the famous actress), heard the Pankhursts during their speaking tours of the United States. The American suffragists were not inclined to be as physically aggressive as their English counterparts, but they embraced the militant use of the *public* sphere pioneered by their English counterparts. By 1909, Massachusetts suffragists were holding innumerable street corner rallies, in small towns and large cities, at which speakers talked to people passing by and distributed prosuffrage leaflets. By 1912, the National American Women's Suffrage Association (NAWSA) had decided to abandon its neutral political stance and allow local chapters to support the election of pro-suffrage candidates for public office. In Massachusetts in 1912 and 1913, suffragists defeated a considerable number of antisuffrage Republicans, a performance that converted the leaders of the state's Democratic party to a guarded prosuffrage position. In 1913, NAWSA organized 8,000 women to march in Washington,

D.C., at Woodrow Wilson's inaugural parade. The women carried banners calling on the president to support giving all women the vote. In May 1913, in New York City, 30,000 woman's suffrage advocates, female and male, marched up Fifth Avenue.

But one group of suffragists, led by Alice Paul and women who were younger than the other active women suffragists, wanted to adopt some of the ultra-militant tactics of the English suffragettes. Splitting off from NAWSA (1916), they formed the National Women's Party (NWP). The primary tactic used by the members of the National Women's Party was the nonviolent, illegal informational picket against opponents of women's suffrage. They used this kind of civil disobedience to great effect against President Woodrow Wilson. Marching outside the White House on January 10, 1917 and throughout the year, the members of the NWP chided Wilson for his antisuffrage stance. After the United States entered World War I in April, the NWP pickets challenged Wilson's hypocrisy, reminding him that while he had described the war effort as a "fight for democracy" and a crusade to give all the peoples of Europe "a voice in their own governments," he favored denying American women such a voice. Arrests of NWP pickets backfired, as the newspaper stories about their maltreatment in prison developed public sympathy for the suffrage cause. By November 1917, Wilson, who was also being pressured by his daughters, both of whom were suffrage supporters, came out for the women's suffrage constitutional amendment.

In 1910, the National American Women's Suffrage Association appointed a talented executive director, Carrie Chapman Catt, who organized nationwide lobbying and election efforts to support prosuffrage politicians and punish antisuffrage ones. Many wealthy women, who felt insulted by the fact that poor, uneducated men could vote while no women could, helped finance the NAWSA. The entry of the United States into World War I also affected the campaign for women's suffrage. Many men became more sympathetic to the notion of giving women the vote because women were making a major contribution to the war effort, by working in jobs vacated by men who were in the armed forces and by participating in War Bond and Red Cross fund-raising drives that helped the nation's fighting men. Carrie Chapman Catt and NAWSA vigorously supported American entry into World War I, a position that appealed to many men who had been lukewarm about women's suffrage. Responding to the pressure from the National Women's Party and the National American Women's Suffrage Association, Congress passed the Nineteenth Amendment by June 1919. The state legislatures approved the amendment quickly, allowing all white women citizens to vote in the 1920 presidential election.

III

By 1920 women had attained legal equality to men with respect to their ability to vote and run for public office. Yet patriarchal social biases remained strong, and women who tried to become active in political parties still were not *treated equally to men*. For example, in 1924, at the Democratic party's presidential nominating convention, Eleanor Roosevelt, who headed the Democratic party's Women's Platform Committee, was not even allowed to present the demands of her committee in person. Belle Moskowitz, who was the top political advisor to Governor Alfred Smith of New York, felt that she had to keep herself in the background to avoid antagonizing the male voting public. Until the 1980s, the number of women running for public office was relatively small.

In 1920, congressmen concerned about the emergence of a women's voting bloc were afraid to oppose the Sheppard-Towner Act, which began a program of national government-funding (to states that chose to participate and make matching grants) of medical care for pregnant low-income women and their newborn children. But only 17 states chose to participate. A strong women's lobby on behalf of the program did not emerge and Congress allowed the program to lapse in 1929.

Even after the suffrage victory, economic discrimination against women remained strong. Most employers continued to refuse to hire women for high-skill blue-collar and professional jobs. In social life too, women encountered significant social and legal obstacles when they sought access to new birth control technologies that promised women the ability to control an important aspect of their lives.

Under legislation that had been passed by Congress in 1873 (the Comstock Law), the advertising and sale of any birth control technology or printed material that described birth control technologies were crimes. Yet women especially wanted to know how they could exercise control over their reproductive functions. Women, not men, took the considerable physical risk of carrying and giving birth to babies; and women, not men, were the primary caregivers who raised children. Highly effective, *woman-controlled* birth technology was not available anywhere in the world until the early twentieth century, when European physicians developed the rubber pessary, or cervical diaphragm. *However, only a medical examination* could determine which size diaphragm would effectively inhibit conception. While a small number of European physicians were willing to prescribe diaphragms, at first no male physicians (and most physicians were men) in the United States were willing to follow suit. The doctors in the United States did not want to run the risk of losing their licenses if they violated the Comstock Law. In Europe, as well as in the United States, male physicians also opposed woman-controlled birth control technology because they believed it would allow women more sexual freedom.

Emma Goldman, an anarchist who stressed the need for individuals to have total freedom to control their lives, and members of the Industrial Workers of the World, a radical labor organization that advocated worker control of business, were the first to publicize the existence of diaphragms. Shortly thereafter, Margaret Sanger, who had been trained as a nurse, decided to commit herself to promoting woman-controlled birth control. Her advocacy was based on the *rights* she believed women should have. Above all, Sanger argued, women had a basic *right* to control their bodies. Exercising that right would allow women to protect their health by avoiding unwanted pregnancies. Moreover, Sanger argued that sex should be a source of personal pleasure, not just a means of reproduction. And because the fear of undesired conception placed stress on women when they had sexual relations, Sanger maintained that woman-controlled birth control technology would enhance the ability of women to enjoy sexual relations.

In 1914, Margaret Sanger started a magazine, *The Woman Rebel*, to promote her ideas about women's reproductive rights. She fled the country after the publication of the first issue led to her arrest for violating the Comstock Law. But she arranged for the distribution of several hundred thousand copies of a pamphlet, *Family Limitation*, which presented her ideas. When the charges were dropped, Sanger returned to the United States and on October 16, 1916, opened the first birth control clinic in the nation. But the police quickly raided the clinic and closed it down.

Throughout the 1920s, Sanger continued to work to legalize woman-controlled contraception. She founded the American Birth Control League, which was funded by affluent men and women who believed that population limitation and sexual freedom were desirable goals. With the support of a small number of male physicians, and significant funding from the Rockefeller Foundation, Sanger opened a birth control clinic in 1925 (in New York City). The clinic was staffed by women physicians and nurses. By 1930 it was treating 20,000 women yearly. The clinic's staff developed excellent data about the effectiveness of the cervical diaphragm as a birth control technology. But the *Journal of the American Medical Association* refused to publish the information. The editors of this medical publication refused to print any article on birth control until 1934.

By the mid-1930s, it was clear that American men and women were developing new views about the freedom to choose to have sexual relations, irrespective of parental and social prohibitions. Increased support for birth control was one consequence of these changing views. By 1936, 60 percent of Americans of both sexes favored legalizing birth control. A 1937 poll showed that 79 percent of women in the United States were pro-birth control, a figure that rose to 85 percent in 1943.

In 1936, the New York Federal Court of Appeals heard a landmark birth control case. It ruled that the Comstock Law did not apply to physicians, who were free to prescribe any medically acceptable birth control technology to their patients. This decision led an increased number of physicians to prescribe cervical diaphragms. But the New York decision did not apply to other parts of the nation. In many states, the courts upheld state laws modeled on the Comstock Law. Proponents of the legalization of birth control technology in these states tried in vain to secure the enactment of new state laws that would give women reproductive freedom.

After World War II, the American Birth Control League changed its name to Planned Parenthood of America. While continuing, in vain, to try to get states to pass legislation legalizing the prescription of birth control technology, Planned Parenthood also challenged existing laws by opening up clinics to dispense birth control technology. But many state courts upheld police actions that closed these clinics. At the beginning of the 1960s the members of the Connecticut Planned Parenthood League became convinced that the Supreme Court might be likely, given its strong support of civil liberties since 1940, to legalize women's freedom of access to woman-controlled birth control technologies. The Connecticut League opened a clinic in New Haven. The state attorney general directed the local police to close the clinic. The resulting court case, *Griswold* v. *Connecticut*, was decided by the Supreme Court in 1965. The Court held that even though privacy was not mentioned in the Bill of Rights, the overall effect of these amendments was to create a right of privacy. Thus the Court held that the decisions men and women made to use birth control technologies were protected by the Constitution. This decision, coming when a highly effective estrogen birth-control pill had been developed, made it much easier for all women to gain access to woman-controlled birth control. And this new right to one aspect of reproductive freedom came at a time when more and more women wanted to be free to control their childbearing so that they could more easily work outside the home. However, many women found that widespread access to effective birth control also created a new problem: since there was less danger of conception, many men now expected women to agree more readily to having sexual relations. Feminists pointed out that many men did not understand that women had a *right* to say "no" to attempts to "use" their bodies.

There was another dimension of women's reproductive rights that was influenced by the Supreme Court's willingness in the 1960s and 1970s to expand the rights of Americans: abortion. Historically, many women who had become pregnant had sought abortions. The list of folk remedies that were used for such abortions fills several books. Many women secretly went to physicians, midwives, or untrained abortionists for mechanical abortions or chemical potions. Many of these abortions ended with serious damage, including loss of life, to the aborting mother.

In the English North American colonies, it appears that mostly single women sought abortions. (We cannot be sure, since few women told anyone about their efforts to abort a fetus.) Women's rights advocates in the nineteenth century opposed abortion, as they opposed contraception, because they feared that these two methods of preventing women from having babies encouraged men to be sexually aggressive toward women, and in the process violated the right of women to control their bodies. By the late nineteenth century most states had passed laws that made hitherto legal abortions illegal, unless the life of the mother was threatened. Yet millions of women were so afraid of the economic, physical, or psychological cost of carrying an unwanted child that they were willing to risk breaking the law.

In the 1965 Griswold decision, the Supreme Court held that the Constitution created for citizens a right to privacy that governments could not be allowed to violate, unless there was a compelling societal need to do so. In 1973, in *Roe* v. *Wade*, the

U.S. Supreme Court ruled that states could not ban abortions in the first three months of pregnancy, and could regulate abortions only during the last three months of pregnancy (see page 29). The freedom given to women to have abortions during the first three months of pregnancy, and with the consent of their doctor during the next three months of pregnancy, was expanded by many state legislatures when they appropriated funds for abortion clinics to serve poor women.

Critics of this policy, and of the preference the Supreme Court gave to the rights of mothers during the first six months of their pregnancies, began mobilizing. In the 1990s, opponents of abortion targeted abortion clinics for repeated picketing. In cases where antiabortion picketers have used threatening verbal taunts directed at women entering abortion clinics, the Supreme Court has ruled that the free speech rights of picketers were not violated when city and state governments ordered an increase in the distance between the picketers and abortion clinics. Abortion critics also pressured many state legislatures into banning the use of public money for abortion. President Ronald Reagan ruled that the health insurance plans of employees of the national government would not pay for abortions. President Bill Clinton restored abortion coverage. Legislation introduced in the House of Representatives in 1995 would partially restore the Reagan policy.

IV

Several years after World War II ended, the percentage of women working outside the home began to increase. Many women who worked at high-paying industrial jobs during World War II experienced a sense of psychological empowerment because they were earning more money and could control the way they spent the money. In the years after the war, these women had a strong desire to continue to work outside the home. This slowly became possible, and necessary, for a variety of reasons: Increased opportunities for professional women as hiring discrimination subsided; expansion of service sector jobs that had usually been considered "women's" jobs (and were generally low-paying jobs); higher rates of divorce that made it necessary for single women to work to support themselves (and any dependents); and the development of new production technologies (especially after 1975) that eliminated many high-paying blue-collar and middle-range white-collar jobs, forcing wives to seek work to augment their husbands' lower incomes.

During World War II, many women did the same kind of work as men, but were paid lower wages. By the end of the war, some agencies of the U.S. government were pressuring employers of women to pay women equal wages for equal work (done by men). Professional women working in Washington, D.C. for the federal government took the initiative in lobbying Congress to correct this inequality. A generation later Congress passed the Equal Pay Act (1963), which applied to women working for government.

This law helped a limited number of women gain pay equity. But the main cause of the gap between women's and men's earnings has always been the *exclusion* of women from the higher-paying blue-collar and white-collar jobs, which have been monopolized by men. (Women in offices were sometimes made office managers, and women stenographers were paid more than secretaries. These jobs paid well for "women's jobs." But women in these jobs generally hit the "glass ceiling" and could not compete for the higher-level supervisory and technical jobs in their companies.)

The 1964 Civil Rights Law banned sex-based employment discrimination. Ironically, the law included this ban because congressmen opposed to ending racial discrimination had amended the original bill to include sex-based discrimination in the hope that more congressmen would vote against the entire civil rights bill. But the tactic failed. Despite the absence of any large national women's rights organization, women had made a major legal gain. The Civil Rights Act of 1964 set up equal hiring and promotion rights for women (and people of color) as a legal standard. Enforcement of the antisex and antirace employment discrimination parts of the Civil Rights Law began slowly. It was strengthened by the 1972 amendments to the 1964 Civil Rights Act, which gave the federal Equal Employment Opportunities Commission power to sue persons or firms that practiced employment discrimination.

Between 1950 and 1970, women made their greatest gains in securing professional jobs. In 1950, 12.2 percent of employed women were professionals; 20 years later the figure was 15.5 percent, a proportion that was relatively constant for the next seventeen years. (In 1987 it was 15.6 percent.) Significant gains for women in the access to managerial jobs came between 1970 and 1987, rising from 3.6 percent of employed women to 12.2 percent. But within these two high-income job categories, women did not make significant gains in their pay, relative to men, which suggests that they encountered barriers to promotion and pay inequities. Thus in 1960 the ratio of the median earnings of year-round, full-time women professionals to male professionals' earnings was .64, while 27 years later it was .68. For women in managerial positions, the 1960 ratio was .58 and the 1987 figure was .59.

In 1939, those women lucky enough to be employed year round, earned, on average, 59 percent of the total amount earned by men. In 1950, women's earnings were 45 percent of men's, but rose to 64.5 percent in 1955. However, this ratio fell to 58 percent in 1965, rose to 59 percent in 1971, and then fell to 57 percent in 1973. After 1973 the ratio began to climb, reaching 1955 levels by 1986. In 1990, the earnings of women employed year round, full time were 71.5 percent of men's.* Looking at the *top earnings* categories, in 1979 .22 percent of women and 2.59 percent of men *employed* full time, year round earned $50,000 or

---

*The decline in this percentage reflected the entry of more women into the labor force during this period. Most of the "new" women workers could only find low-paying jobs. Hence their earnings lowered the ratio of women's to men's wages. It is likely that the increase in the ratio after 1973 reflected antidiscrimination legislation and the declining number of high-paying men's jobs.

more. In 1987, .17 percent of women and 1.67 percent of men employed year round earned $99,999 or more. (These figures do not include self-employed business owners and professionals.) While women gained slightly relative to men in these top income categories, *fewer* women and *fewer* men were employed in the top income categories because the entire economy was in the midst of a restructuring that produced a decline in the total number of high-paid salaried and wage employees. 1995 figures for men and women ages 20–24, who tend disproportionately to be hired for the *lowest-paying* jobs, show that the sex-based wage gap is small, with women averaging 94 percent of men's wages.

Qualifying for a job requires a person to have the skills necessary to do the job well. If a society's educational institutions discriminate against any part of the population, it is likely that such persons will not have an *equal chance to learn* the skills needed for employment. In jobs where the only way to learn job skills was by getting "educated" on the job, employers and wage earners often were agreed that women or racial minorities would not be hired and trained. As our society has increasingly relied on elementary, secondary, and higher education institutions to give people the job skills they need to enter the labor market and to advance to better-paying jobs, the existence of equity in education has become more important.

Attaining equal educational rights is not a simple matter. Students react to the attitudes of their teachers. If teachers discourage young women from entering "male" occupations, like engineering and science, women do not have equal educational opportunity. If teachers are more likely to call on male students during class discussions, which is frequently the case, then female students do not develop confidence in their intellectual abilities. Female students also react to the attitudes of their male peers. Some studies have suggested that during adolescence, when young women are in the same school classroom as young men, the women are reluctant to express their views about social issues and are fearful of being embarrassed if they give wrong answers in math and science classes. These findings have led some educators to conclude that young women would benefit from sex-segregated classes in junior high school and high school.

In 1966, a group of women activists, many of whom had been members of the Students for a Democratic Society, formed the National Organization for Women (NOW). Many other women's liberation organizations were founded in the 1960s. The women's rights movement was not typified by any single organization. The newly formed women's groups sought to take advantage of the new egalitarian legal climate created by the civil rights movement, a climate in which lawyers, judges (especially on the Supreme Court), and intellectuals were increasingly concerned with promoting equal rights and liberties for all Americans. Many of the women in these groups had participated in reform organizations in which men had resisted allowing women to speak at public meetings and in which male leaders expected women to assume responsibility for cooking and cleaning chores.

Women's groups supported many reforms that would give women rights equal to those of men. Most women's groups defended the rights of lesbians to equal employment opportunities and to adopt children. They stressed the rights of women to have access to abortions, with government funding for poor women who wanted abortions. Equal opportunities for women to borrow money were written into national law by Congress in 1974. Feminists also argued that women students should have equal access to sports programs. In 1972, Congress specified that college athletic departments had to spend *equal* amounts on women's and men's sports.

Some state governments responded positively to women's groups that called for comparable worth pay schemes, which would end the undervaluation of women's job skills and provide equal pay for different jobs that had the same *level* of skills. Thus a skilled woman administrative assistant would not be paid less than a skilled male auto mechanic. These states passed such legislation, but only for their own employees. Private sector workers were not covered.

During its first decade, the post-World War II women's movement had a very significant effect on the way women thought about themselves. For example, in 1971 the majority of American women did not believe women should publicly protest (through marching or speechmaking) to increase the rights enjoyed by women. By 1975, 65 percent of American women backed such direct actions. In 1962 the number of married women who worked steadily outside the home was 37 percent. By 1978 it was 58 percent.

To promote the overall goal of equality of rights for women, the leaders of NOW decided to make a major effort to secure the enactment of the Equal Rights Amendment (ERA) to the Constitution. First proposed by the National Women's Party in 1923, the ERA applied *only to government actions, whether national or state*. It would have banned any government administrative policies or laws that put women on an unequal legal plane with men. NOW's campaign for the ERA bore fruit when Congress passed the amendment in 1972. While a majority of Americans supported the ERA, and a majority of the state legislatures passed the ERA, it fell three states short of the *three-fourths* vote needed for ratification. An active minority of men and women who opposed the ERA was successful in blocking its passage. Some opponents of the ERA were men uncomfortable with the notion of legal and social equality for women. Some women who opposed the ERA were fearful of getting drafted or were concerned that the ERA would promote abortion. Other women, generally of low and lower-middle income families, feared that of the ERA would convince men who had loose emotional ties to their families that they could provide less support to their wives, ex-wives, and children since women would supposedly be able to earn more money. (A 1977 poll indicated that 42 percent of American women believed that the women's movement was a cause of the breakdown in the stability of the family.)

By 1983, when the effort to pass the ERA was abandoned, congressional legislation and Supreme Court decisions had produced most of the legal changes that the proponents of ERA desired. A large body of law and legal opinion endorsed the notion of equal rights for women. Women began entering the armed forces in larger numbers. Limited numbers were placed in combat units (in the Navy).

But many iniquitous practices remain. For example, women who can prove to a court that they have suffered from employment discrimination cannot collect triple damages, whereas nonwhites who have been similarly treated can collect these punitive damages. The threat of such damages is a major deterrent to discrimination. Many women believe that police forces and courts do not offer equal protection to women who are the victims of certain kinds of crime, especially rape and physical assault. Women who want to work do not have a legal right (an entitlement) to obtain child care for their children, which often makes it impossible for them to compete with men on an even playing field. Only a minority of men equally share housework and child care responsibilities with their female partners. Only a very few of the vastly increased number of women with degrees in law, medicine, and business are ever promoted to top management positions within their professions.

The essays in this book demonstrate that customs and laws change *slowly*. Groups that benefit from existing, discriminatory social structures and common beliefs do not see the need for changes that will promote full equality of rights, especially if such changes threaten the power and status of those who benefit from existing practices. Those women and men who want to attain equal legal and social rights for women will have to make significant efforts to alter social beliefs and eliminate the legal barriers that are responsible for the unequal treatment of women in our society.

The next chapter examines the historic faith of the majority of our nation's people in the availability of a unique abundance of natural resources. The chapter also analyzes the way people deny the existence of the negative effects of our historical abundance of resources.

CHAPTER 9

Abundance

I

From the first late fifteenth-century European contacts to the present, the abundant natural resources in the land that would become the United States have impressed its native peoples, new immigrants and foreign visitors. Emigrating to the British North American colonies in 1775, the English writer Thomas Paine soon expressed his wonderment at these resources:

> Lands are the real riches of the habitable world, and the natural funds of America. The funds of other countries are, in general artificially constructed; the creatures of necessity and contrivance dependent on credit, and always exposed to hazard and uncertainty. But lands can neither be annihilated nor lose their value; on the contrary, they [land values] universally rise with [increased] population, and rapidly so when under the security of effectual government.

The North American continent was endowed with vast tracts of fertile soil, immense forests, huge numbers of game animals and fish, numerous rivers and plentiful, strategically located mineral resources.

Ample *human* resources (slaves and voluntary immigrants) were soon transferred to the continent from the rest of the globe. Huge amounts of foreign capital (money) would be invested in the businesses European immigrants and their descendants established on the continent. For three and a half centuries most of the free peoples living in the North American European colonies and the United States believed that their nation was blessed with such abundance that they would never lack the resources necessary for economic expansion and an ever-increasing standard of living.

This expectation encouraged risk taking, rapid technological innovation, and unusually wasteful practices in exploiting natural and human resources. These practices were so common that Americans would find it hard to change their wasteful actions. When a national movement to end environmental pollution became very active in the late 1960s, many Americans found it hard to accept scientific research that demonstrated that the wasteful use of resources was a threat to their health and quality of life.

II

The peoples of the native nations of North America, numbering about 1,000,000 in 1600, knew full well that they lived in a region of plenty. Their agricultural practices emphasized clearing land through forest fires and using only light fertilizers that could not sustain crop cultivation for more than seven years. Exhausted soil was allowed to lie fallow and rejuvenate. Native Americans did not try to conserve the soil, since they had abundant lands that could be cultivated while natural processes restored the fertility of soils that had been depleted of nutrients. (In areas with scarce rainfall, the Pueblo peoples developed labor-intensive techniques to allow soils to retain moisture.) Before contact with Europeans, the animal hunting practices of the native peoples were never so intensive that the continent's animal food supply was endangered.

The Europeans and their offspring developed a prosperous trade in animal furs. Many Native Americans were drawn into the fur trade. Tragically, the intensive trapping of animals led to a sharp reduction of their numbers by the mid-eighteenth century. This loss of abundance deprived many groups of Indians of their supply of food. Thereafter they were dependent on trading with the English for food. When some Indian nations could not provide any more furs in exchange for food they sometimes had to hire out as military mercenaries. All these changes drastically reduced the social stability of the Native American tribes. But there was an even greater threat to the abundance of land and food resources enjoyed by the native peoples of the Western Hemisphere.

The Europeans who migrated to the Western Hemisphere came to conquer. As in Europe itself, the government of each European nation sought *abundance through plunder*. Military force and trade were both used to acquire land that was endowed with important resources. In North America, the European settlers expected that Native Americans would be willing to sell land to the newcomers. When the Indians resisted, or agreed only to lease land, the Europeans became enraged, and often used military force and terrorist tactics to seize land.

When the Indians lost their lands, or had their hunting activities restricted on the lands they were allowed to occupy, their lack of access to abundant natural resources severely restricted their ability to support themselves economically. Being separated from the land (including the burial grounds that contained their ancestors) made many Native Americans depressed and psychologically disoriented. These traumas made Indians vulnerable to alcoholism and disease.

The European settlers sought financial profits from the development of the colonies' agricultural resources. Free people who wanted to farm generally were able to acquire land, since there was so much land available that the price of buying or renting land was much lower than the price of land in Europe. During the first century of the settlement of New England many immigrants received free grants of land from the colonial governments. During the second century of settlement, colonial governments in the middle and southern colonies gave men land as a reward for migrating to the colonies. Since the value of land could be increased only if people cleared it and farmed it, many private landowners rented their land at very low rates.

Cultivators of the rich, heavy soils of the middle colonies developed many prosperous farms, and especially many medium- and small-sized farms that were profitable for three centuries to come. The fertile, but shallow topsoil of the southern colonies was more easily cleared, but was exhausted more quickly, especially by the cultivation (with minimal use of fertilizer) of tobacco crops. But in the New England colonies, where the soil was generally not as fertile as in the southern and middle colonies, within 200 years soil exhaustion became a serious problem, leading farmers to migrate westward, looking for new land to farm. Farmland was not the only natural resource exploited by the colonists. The abundant forests of the eastern seaboard colonies were an important source of wood products that were exported or used to build merchant ships that made large profits for their owners.

To extract this wealth, human labor was necessary. Initially, there were enough European migrants to satisfy the demand for labor of the people who owned large farms. But in the 1680s, in Virginia and Maryland, the tobacco farmers' harsh treatment of their English indentured servants scared off new English immigrants, creating a labor shortage. At just this time, English, Dutch, French, and Portuguese merchants came into contact with a plentiful supply of slaves in the countries of Western Africa. African slave laborers were forced to migrate to the Western Hemisphere. The African "settlers" and their children provided the abundant labor power necessary to the development of plantation agriculture (growing tobacco, sugar cane, rice, and cotton) in the South and in the Caribbean.

By the middle of the eighteenth century many colonists were worried because the supply of good agricultural land was no longer abundant in the colonies. The English government's mercantilist policy of developing a colonial market for English exports had led to a ban on any migration west of the line established by Parliament's Proclamation of 1763. This barred colonists from economically exploiting the large tracts of land in the "West" that lay ripe for the picking—assuming, of course, that the land could be taken from the native nations which controlled the territory in the interior part of the continent. Friction over the British policy was an important factor in the rising tension between Americans and England after 1763.

The 1783 Treaty of Paris that ended the War for Independence allowed Americans to settle west of the Proclamation line of 1763. During the next 100 years the United States acquired substantial amounts of additional land. The major additions came in 1803 (the Louisiana Purchase), in 1848 (the Mexican-American War), in 1854 (acquiring Oregon by means of a treaty with England), and in 1861 (the purchase of Alaska from Russia). But the process of transferring legal ownership of the newly acquired resources to white Americans required military action, vigilante terrorism, and legal fraud. Native Americans were forced to sign treaties that removed Indians from lands on which whites wanted to settle. Pushed westward, the displaced Native Americans were assigned to new territories by the Department of the Interior of the national government. In these territories they sometimes came into conflict with the Native Americans who were already living on these lands. Friction often developed, since hitherto abundant resources now became overtaxed. When valuable metals or oil and gas resources were discovered on the lands that had been assigned to Indians, they were generally removed from these lands, in clear violation of the treaties that the U. S. government had signed.

In the Southwest, the U.S. Army and the armed forces recruited by the Republic of Texas drove Mexicans of Spanish descent, mixed Spanish-Indian blood, and native peoples off the lands they occupied. In New Mexico and California, Anglo-Americans controlled the legal system, and deliberately rigged the laws governing land ownership and land taxation to allow Anglo-Americans to defraud most Hispanic landowners, including many affluent, large landowners, of the title to their lands. In California in the 1850s, at least 10,000 Indians were illegally forced to serve as indentured servants for gold miners and ranchers. Indians who complained could obtain no justice in California's courts, which were run by whites and did not allow Indians to testify. In the 1880s, 300 hundred years of separating

Native Americans from their natural resources ended with the slaughter of the buffalo herds and the destruction of the lifestyle of the plains Indians. In 1900, the 300,000 Native Americans in the United States who had survived disease and genocidal* slaughter were concentrated on a limited number of reservations run by the Department of the Interior.

America's abundant natural resources were acquired, in large part, by the use of brute force. Thomas Paine, the apostle of freedom, was ironically right when he had stated that land values would rapidly rise "under the security of effectual government." The majority of Americans backed their government's effective use of military power to seize the abundant resources once owned by the Indians and by Mexicans. Government power was also essential to maintaining the property rights of the owners of the large numbers of slave workers who were compelled to migrate from Africa to the Western Hemisphere.

III

In 1793 Eli Whitney invented an effective cotton gin machine. This innovation increased the value of land in the South, bringing great wealth to the region. Much of the South did not have the kind of soil necessary to grow long-fiber cotton plants, from which it was relatively easy to remove the seeds by hand. The cotton gin made it possible to quickly deseed short staple cotton, which could be grown almost anywhere in the South, but could not easily be deseeded. This development also stimulated

---

*Genocide is a term that was developed in 1944. It refers to the deliberate destruction of a whole people or nation. Murder and deprivation of access to natural resources were the two techniques used by Anglo-Americans to destroy the Native American nations. Huge numbers of Native Americans also died from exposure to the bacterial and viral diseases the Europeans brought with them. As they came to understand the Indians' lack of resistance to European diseases, some English settlers in North America consciously presented the Indians with blankets rubbed against the smallpox sores on cattle.

the westward movement of southerners, who sought to grow cotton on the fertile virgin lands of the Southwest (Alabama, Mississippi, Arkansas, Louisiana, and Texas).

Cotton exports swelled, and by the late 1850s accounted for more than half of the value of the exports of the entire United States. Without these exports, which were based on the abundance of land and slave labor in the United States, the nation would have had a severe balance of payments problem, and European investors would have been much less willing to buy the stocks and bonds of U.S. railroad, mining, and manufacturing companies. European investments, especially in railroads, lowered the price of transporting crops to market, which made it profitable for farmers in nonslave states in the Midwest and central western states to clear and plant large amounts of fertile land. Increased farmer profits in these states created more demand for the products of the factories of the Northeast, stimulating industrial growth. Thus the abundance of land and exploited, unfree slave labor helped stimulate the economic development of the whole nation.

The high wages paid to free workers in the English colonies encouraged the emigration of many skilled craftsmen from Europe. In the nineteenth century, skilled and low-skilled industrial workers, many of them young people who were ideally suited for hard physical labor, were attracted to the United States by its high real wages and by the abundance of civil freedoms: the freedom to worship as one chose, the absence of a regular army draft, the freedom to move from one part of the country to another, and the absence of the requirement common in so many central and eastern European nations that citizens had to carry internal passports and register with the police every time they changed residences. High levels of immigration, beginning with the surge of the 1840s and continuing until 1930, gave the United States an ample supply of skilled workers and young, highly productive workers who took jobs that required a great deal of physical stamina.

The East Coast of the British colonies that would become the United States was blessed with a large number of natural ports, resources that facilitated the export of raw materials and the importing of human labor. The large number of swiftly flowing rivers and streams in the New England and mid-Atlantic colonies encouraged the construction of many flour mills, and made it easier to ship lumber to coastal towns and cities, where shipbuilding flourished. The trade in whole grains and flour, as well as the expanding production of wooden sailing ships, attracted immigrant artisans and encouraged all artisans to take on and train many apprentices. Thus when entrepreneurs began to build textile, paper, gun, and shoe factories—especially after 1815—there was an ample supply of skilled workers available to build and operate the industrial machinery that made these factories so profitable. The metal-working skills that were developed by machinists, blacksmiths, and welders in these factories were essential to the building and repair of steam engines. Steam engines—which were, in essence, complex machines with metal parts—powered the next generation of industrial factories, the steamboats and ocean liners that facilitated domestic and international commerce, and the railroads.

The combination of abundant natural resources and skilled human workers helped stimulate the *mechanization* of production in the United States. American factory owners were confident about the future demand for their products, since the nation's consumer population received the highest real wages in the world and was growing rapidly. Indeed, the United States developed the largest domestic market of any industrial nation in the world. Consequently, American manufacturers were more willing than their European counterparts to replace existing machinery rapidly with newly invented, more productive mass-production technologies. A positive attitude toward technological innovation was one of the effects of American abundance; consequently, industries in the United States developed an unmatched abundance of the most efficient production technologies available in the world.

Railroads used steam engines and railroad cars made of metal and wood. Railroads promoted the development of more of the nation's agricultural land and transported the iron and coal needed for the growth of the nation's iron and steel industry. While canals, which actually provided cheaper—but slower—transportation, could only be built when land elevations allowed water to flow from one location to another, railroad lines could be built almost anywhere. Thus railroads could connect coal fields and iron mines to iron and steel factories that could be located to minimize the cost of transporting these raw materials: The United States was fortunate because the iron and coal fields tapped for mid- and-late nineteenth-century industrialization held vast amounts of iron and coal and were located in places where rail or water transportation could bring these raw materials to steel mills.

American railroads had to cover much larger distances than their European counterparts. European nations were smaller than the United States and their populations were more concentrated. American railroad builders had to lay down so many miles of track that they decided to save money by using cheaper rails than European railroads. These rails had to be replaced more frequently. But since large supplies of wood and iron and steel were available in the United States at reasonable prices (especially because American metal producers used the most efficient machinery available and generally had lower raw materials transportation costs than their European counterparts), this practice appeared to be sensible. Of course, it contributed to a habit of using natural resources without any worry about their availability in the future.

By the time the Industrial Revolution was in full swing in the nineteenth century, England and many western European nations had already used so much of their forests for heat and housing that they had a serious shortage of wood products, which meant that as their populations expanded, housing had to be built from stone products. This housing was expensive, but it lasted longer than wood frame houses and was less likely to be destroyed by fires. In the United States, where great supplies of wood were available, housing was much more likely to be built from wood. Especially in densely populated urban areas, wood frame dwellings contributed to the rapid spread of great fires, like the one that destroyed Chicago in 1871. Of course, when fire-ravaged cities had to be rebuilt, wood supplies were available at low cost. And workers in the building trades had steady employment in the aftermath of urban disasters, whether fires or earthquakes (which usually also started destructive fires).

Because the United States was richly endowed with natural resources and had an abundant labor supply, many European banks and individual investors were very willing to invest their money in American business enterprises. Europeans were especially interested in railroads, mines, and factories. Some Europeans invested heavily in land in the Plains states (especially Kansas and Oklahoma). The money Europeans invested in the stocks and bonds of American companies was supplemented by the businesses European firms started in the United States. All these activities increased the supply of investment capital in the United States, which helped growth in two ways: by providing the funds necessary for new production facilities and by keeping interest rates lower than they would otherwise have been. Lower interest rates reduced the *cost of borrowing money* to build a new factory or open up a new mine. Lower costs meant that expected profits would be higher. The expectation of high profits led investors to be willing to loan their money to business firms. Because investment capital in the United States was both abundant and relatively less expensive than it was in Europe, there was less demand in the United States for the formation of government-owned central banks of the kind created in France, Austria-Hungary, and Italy.

The millions of men and women who immigrated to this country and became farmers and wage earners were, like the farmers and wage-earners born in the United States, *consumers* of the goods and services produced in the nation. By the last quarter of the nineteenth century, the United States, of all the world's industrial nations, had the largest, most affluent group of consumers. Millions of landowning farmers bought agricultural machinery and, in the twentieth century, automobiles. City-dwelling wage earners bought many consumer products and, when possible, bought or built their own houses. The massed purchasing power of farmers and wage earners was an important factor in the growth of very large industrial companies in the United States, companies whose size allowed them to take advantage of what economists call *economies of scale* to produce more efficiently (i.e., at lower cost) than smaller firms. For example, a very large company can bargain with suppliers of raw materials for lower prices because it buys in such large volume. An oil company that knows it can sell all its output to a big consumer population will build refineries that are so large that they produce oil products at a cost that is significantly lower than that of smaller refineries. And a giant company with huge cash reserves has the funds to build the machinery necessary to mass produce new inventions.

Nineteenth-century American craftsmen and factory workers labored for longer hours and worked more rapidly than their European counterparts. Consequently, American workers were injured more often than the workers of England, Germany, France, and Italy. Moreover, because immigration made the supply of labor so plentiful in the United States, employers were less willing to spend money to make mines, railroads, and factories safer places to work, since they knew that they could *easily replace one injured worker with another energetic, undamaged worker.* A tragic variant of this phenomenon was evident in the policy of steel manufacturers who recruited black steelworkers from the large numbers of desperately poor black farm workers who lived in the South. These black steelworkers were assigned to the most unhealthy, dangerous jobs in steel making: the operation and cleaning of blast furnaces that gave off highly toxic fumes and that had many explosions that killed hundreds of steelworkers.

IV

By the end of the nineteenth century, some Americans were beginning to worry about the rapid, *unplanned*, use of the nation's natural resources and about the pollution of the nation's air, soil, and water resources. Wasteful resource exploitation, concerned only with short-term profits, led to overlogging and mining practices that produced serious soil erosion. Conservationists like Theodore Roosevelt and Gifford Pinchot were less worried about preserving the beauty of nature than they were about making sure that in the future there would be enough forests, underground minerals, and topsoil to allow Americans to have the abundant supplies of natural resources to which they had become accustomed. These conservationists were not antibusiness; their goal was to promote business prosperity in the long run by having the national and state governments regulate resource use. Conservationists argued that by mandating that wood and coal producers follow scientific principles of resource exploitation, the nation would avoid overlogging and serious soil erosion. This process would *preserve jobs* and the supply of raw materials for succeeding generations of Americans.

As industrialization advanced, new products and production processes utilized more complex technologies that increasingly depended on the research of scientists and engineers' efforts to design products and new production processes. The United States developed a unique system of training technical specialists, the land grant colleges, after Congress passed the Morrill Act (1863). This law authorized each state to found a land grant college dedicated to training experts in agricultural and industrial technologies. The abundance of land still owned by the United States government allowed Congress to fund these new colleges without raising taxes. The proceeds from the sale of federal lands were to be made available to state governments for the specific purpose of funding the land grant colleges. Land grant colleges like the University of Iowa and the University of Wisconsin trained large numbers of agricultural scientists whose efforts were critical in making American agriculture the most technologically advanced and productive in the world. Engineers trained in the land grant colleges, many of which became universities, augmented the supply of engineers trained in private colleges and universities. With ample numbers of engineers,* the U.S. industrial sector was able to maintain its position of world leadership in product development and efficient production technology until the 1960s.

The abundant domestic supply of gasoline had a major effect on the kind of transportation system that emerged in the United States as its industrial society matured. In 1900 France had more cars per person than the United States. But the discovery of the Spindletop oil fields in Texas in 1903 initiated an era of cheap gasoline, which led to a thriving domestic automobile industry. Mass production techniques were applied to auto production in 1913 and thereafter, substantially lowering the cost of cars. By the 1920s, skilled blue-collar workers could afford to buy new cars, and less highly paid workers purchased used cars.

In Europe, mass production techniques were not widely applied to automobile production until after World War II. Gasoline was much more expensive in Europe and average European incomes were lower than incomes in the United States. Consequently, many fewer Europeans could afford to buy and pay the operational costs of automobiles. Recognizing this, European governments encouraged investment in railroad, urban subway, and trolley car transportation. In the United States, the gasoline-powered automobile and gas- and diesel-powered trucks

---

*In the late 1950s, the Russian challenge in the space race and the arms race led to new federal government programs that funded the training of more scientists and engineers. But large numbers of these engineers were hired by military producers. This development created, for the first time in American history, a scarcity of engineers in the nonmilitary sectors of the economy. Much of the decline of the competitiveness of American businesses in the nonmilitary sector can be attributed to this shortage of engineers. Another development that contributed to this shortage was the increasing amount of money being made by lawyers after World War II. Many bright, ambitious Americans decided to pursue careers in law, rather than in science and engineering.

became the dominant types of inland transportation. Widespread ownership of automobiles comparable to that in the United States did not emerge in Europe until after World War II.

In the first half of the twentieth century, the United States developed the most extensive automobile road system in the world. The wealth of the nation allowed city, state, and local governments to finance the construction of paved roads. In 1956, Congress initiated the construction of the interstate highway system, which was intended to move military vehicles in the event of nuclear war and to stimulate car and truck travel. The interstate highways were especially important to farmers who depended on roads to transport their crops to increasingly distant urban and suburban markets. Tourism was also stimulated by the interstate road system. As the number of roads for automobiles and trucks mushroomed, the nation's railroad transportation system declined. Railroad companies had to pay for the cost of maintaining their tracks, tunnels, and bridges. Trucking companies received a free subsidy, since taxes paid by auto owners financed the construction and repair of the highways that trucks used.

In European nations, lower incomes and high gasoline costs led developers to build housing within walking distance of train, trolley, and bus lines. The typical European housing pattern was *denser* than the American, because in the United States, the automobile allowed access to dispersed suburban housing. The automobile also provided privacy while traveling.

Americans owned and operated more cars and trucks per person than the citizens of any other nation. But the plentiful supply of transportation vehicles powered by the internal combustion engine led to very high levels of air pollution. Cheap gasoline and mass-produced cars, which were much lower in price than the typical European car, led to much more rapid suburbanization in the United States than anywhere else in the world. The abundance of land outside American cities, combined with a low-cost, individualized travel technology, made the cost of moving to the suburbs less expensive than in the industrial nations of Europe. In the 1970s, Americans realized for the first time that the low cost of suburban living might be in jeopardy. Oil embargoes and sharp increases in the price of oil raised (albeit for only about a decade) the cost of commuting to work. It has become increasingly clear that Americans' widely dispersed homes and workplaces, made possible by the abundance of land and gasoline, pose another threat. Car exhaust fumes contaminate the atmosphere, causing increases in cancer and lung disease. The governments of most of the major industrial nations in the world have concluded that auto exhaust contributes greatly to "global warming" (see page 189).

As the Industrial Revolution developed, American manufacturing firms produced increasing amounts of toxic chemicals that were emitted into the air and into streams, rivers, lakes, and oceans. By 1900, the use of coal to power manufacturing and to heat homes had brought serious pollution problems to American cities. There was so much coal soot in the air that white-collar workers had to change their collars several times a day to avoid having gray rings at the creases of their collar. Fortunately, by the 1920s the increasing use of oil to supply industrial power and home heat reduced particle pollution (and carbon monoxide hazards) in most cities. One abundant resource solved a problem that had been created by another abundant resource.

Many Americans have always assumed that a technological fix could always be found to solve a problem created by another technology. Put another way, many assumed that an abundance of scientific and engineering talent would always develop a solution to a technological problem. This same kind of reasoning was applied by those who were uncomfortable with proposals for the redistribution of income and the elimination of social and economic discrimination. Rather, the argument was made that *economic growth*, facilitated by our abundant natural and technological resources, would raise the real incomes (and standard of living) of all people. It was hoped that steadily rising real incomes would reduce the demand for more far-reaching, and disruptive, economic and social changes. Many of the liberal

New Deal programs described in Chapter 11 were based on such a strategy (see pages 235-236 especially).

World War II ushered in a true revolution in chemistry. Each year thousands of new chemicals were created, which were used in factories and in consumer products. Hardly any of these chemicals were tested to determine whether or not they might hurt people if released into the air or water. Tragically, we now know that one cost of this kind of abundance has been a significant increase in many cancer rates since 1945.

American consumers, with incomes higher than the consumers of most other large industrial nations, bought more products than other consumers. And they discarded record numbers of these products and the materials that had been used to package them. An abundance of resources and wealth had produced an abundance of pollutants. In a 1931 novel, *A Cool Million*, Nathanael West created a character, Chief Israel Satinpenny, who described this development:

> The paleface came in and in his wisdom filled the sky with smoke and the rivers with refuse. . . . All the powers of water, air and earth he made to turn his wheels within wheels within wheels within wheels. They turned, sure enough, and the land was flooded with toilet paper, painted boxes to keep pins in, key rings, watch fobs, leatherette satchels. . . . Now even the secret places of the earth are full. Now even the Grand Canyon will no longer hold razor blades. Now the dam, O warriors, has broken and he is up to his neck in the articles of his manufacture.

As modern technologies evolved and became more sophisticated, new metals and chemicals were needed to produce them. Increasingly these materials were found in foreign nations. The territory of the United States had contained abundant quantities of the raw materials needed for the early and middle phases of the Industrial Revolution. But American manufacturers had to go abroad to obtain many of the materials needed for the most advanced phases of industrial production. All the world's industrial nations faced a similar problem, since most of the new raw materials needed for their economies were to be found in the nations of the Third World. The need for oil was a special example of this general tendency. Europe's industrial nations had always had to rely on foreign (mostly Middle Eastern) oil. But after 1980 the United States, once virtually self-sufficient in oil, increasingly became dependent on imported oil. By 1992, about half the oil used in the United States was imported.

Today, scientists in the United States and the other nations of the world are doing research aimed at developing sources of energy based on raw materials that are inexpensive and are found in abundance in many places. Clearly solar power is one of these technologies. Energy based on thermonuclear fusion is another, since the basic raw material, water, is cheap and plentiful. Of course, if we solve the problem of supplying all the energy demanded by the world's peoples, we will create an increased demand for material products. This threatens, in turn, to deplete the world's supply of industrial raw materials and to increase the pollution caused by the industrial processes used to make consumer products.

The majority of the world's climate scientists believe that as more and more countries throughout the world have industrialized, and as the major industrial nations of the world have burned more coal and oil products, the phenomenon of "global warming," an increase in the temperature of the Earth's atmosphere, has become inevitable. Hotter temperatures will raise the level of the oceans, flooding millions of acres of land where people live and produce food. "Global warming" will also produce major variations in rainfall from year to year. These unpredictable extremes will undermine the effectiveness of efforts to shift food production from arid areas to areas with increased rainfall. Immediate efforts to reduce global fuel use may limit the damage done by global warming. But will the industrial nations of the world adopt such a policy?

Since the end of World War II, the citizens of Japan and of many Western European countries have attained average incomes comparable to those in the United States. Movies, television, and advertising have spread images of material abundance throughout the world. The peoples of the world's industrial nations have enjoyed rising levels of material abundance and increasingly, the peoples of the rest of the world have been exposed to the images of such abundance. It is difficult for people to give up the material abundance that is now available to them for the first time, especially in societies in which media advertising creates attractive images designed to make people buy the products made by modern industrial technologies. If the Earth is to avoid horrible economic dislocation, plagues, and political conflict, people must understand an important paradox: an abundance of material goods has produced an abundance of environmental pollutants. Some scientists and philosophers have suggested that the peoples of the world need to reverse their acceptance of the goal of material abundance and adopt a new frame of reference, summed up by slogans like "Small is beautiful" and "Less is more."

As a whole, Americans have historically enjoyed more material abundance than the peoples of any other nation. This abundance encouraged particularly wasteful practices in using raw materials. We chose technologies that used up these materials at a rapid rate. And the vast amount of land, water, wood, metal ores, coal, and oil available in most places encouraged a "pollute now, maybe we'll do something later attitude." Americans thought our air and rivers and lakes could painlessly absorb our industrial wastes. These historically conditioned attitudes make it especially difficult for Americans to come to grips with the harmful effects of abundance.

It could be argued that in the United States, the emergence of a capitalist economic system attracted labor and capital to the nation, and generally facilitated the economic development that created an abundance of goods and services. The next chapter shows that some groups whose labor contributed to this abundance did not believe they received fair rewards. By the 1930s, many economists believed that capitalism could not promote economic growth and abundance unless it was stimulated by government spending and was regulated by government when specific businesses produced an overabundance of services and materials.

CHAPTER 10

Capitalism and Socialism

I

Capitalism is a relatively new economic system. It began to emerge in the 1700s. Although capitalism has come to be associated with industrial production, it originated before there were mechanized factories. *Capital* is any kind of wealth, including money, that can be used to produce more wealth. In this essay, capital will generally be used to describe productive resources, especially machinery, or money that is used to construct or buy such productive property.

At the heart of the system of capitalism that matured during the last century is (1) the ability of owners of capital to buy and sell their productive property (i.e., *capital) freely*; (2) the right of the business owner to start up a business *freely*; and (3) the existence of large numbers of wage earners, who are *not bound legally* to their jobs or to any work site. The ability to borrow money to buy capital, or to do scientific research to improve the productivity of capital, is also important to the success of capitalist enterprise. In short, entrepreneurial *freedom* to hire and fire labor and *freedom* to move capital are essential to capitalism. They make capitalism a dynamic economic system that can react to the opportunities offered by new technologies and changes in consumer demand.

A procapitalist, liberal commentator recently observed that capitalism was and is

> the greatest engine of prosperity in history . . . [however] capitalism does other things badly or not at all, such as ensuring social equality, protecting the environment, correcting the imbalance of power between employer and employee, guaranteeing universal education. . . . and providing security for needy people.

These conflicting aspects of capitalism generated support for its maintenance and also led to demands for different types of government action to alter the way it influences the lives of businesspeople, workers, and consumers.

II

How did capitalism begin? In medieval Europe land was the most important productive resource. But land could not be sold easily. It was not a commodity—a thing that could be freely bought and sold. Feudal rules restricted the sale of land. These rules reflected the fact that most land was owned by a king or nobleman or noblewoman who had given another person the *right* to occupy and use the land. (This lifetime right to use land was to be inherited by the heirs of the person to whom the right was given.) In return, the nonowner pledged to provide services (military forces and/or labor) and to pay feudal taxes. The king or noble, the technical owner of the land, could *block* the sale or transfer of rights to the land. Even land that was not subject to feudal taxes could not be sold without the permission of the manor lord.

These rules created significant costs for anyone who wanted to purchase land, since several persons often had to agree to the transfer of use and ownership rights to the land. The actual landowner might demand extra fees for agreeing to the sale of the land and the use rights that were attached to it. Buyers might be stuck with feudal service obligations to the former landowner, obligations that could be increased at any time. All these circumstances interfered with the free sale of land.

Slowly, between 1300 and 1900, these restrictions were removed in most European nations. In England, a law passed in 1290 allowed owners of land that was not subject to feudal taxes to sell the land without the manor lord's permission. Beginning in 1400, English courts allowed owners of lifetime leases to farm land to *sell* the leases without securing the lord's permission. The new freedom to treat economic assets (leases) as commodities was an important step towards full-blown capitalism. Land ownership gradually became more concentrated and the profits made by landowners (and leaseholders) increased. After 1750, Parliament permitted large landowners in any area to concentrate their holdings by petitioning Parliament to pass a special enclosure bill that forced small landowners and holders of lifetime land leases to sell their land or farming rights (for cash or other parcels of land). This allowed large landowners to earn more money from the land they farmed, concentrating wealth in their hands.

Between 1680 and 1700, Parliament also passed laws that allowed landowners to take out *long*-term mortgages (loans) to buy land or to borrow money (with their land as security) for investment in industry, commerce, or more land. Mortgages were made renewable. And the former practice of confiscating land (and *still* requiring repayment of the loaned money) if mortgage payments were late was ended. These changes allowed landowners more economic flexibility (freedom), which in turn reduced the risk of investing capital in trading and manufacturing enterprises, whether on their own land or in more distant places. Trade of land as a commodity encouraged the growth of agricultural, mercantile, and industrial capitalism.

Medieval merchants were city dwellers. The merchants and their city governments, unless they were city-states like Venice, were not free agents. They had to follow the dictates of nobles or monarchs, who granted trading and producing charters to businessmen. In turn, the merchants of medieval cities monopolized trading and producing rights. Traders and artisans who were not members of the city merchant and artisan guilds (associations) were *barred from selling goods at the city market*. This kind of monopolistic privilege, granted by a monarch or a government, was common in Europe (and in some European settlements in the Western Hemisphere) until the end of the eighteenth century. Then, influenced by Adam Smith's *The Wealth of Nations*, which argued that business monopolies limited economic growth, many governments began to stop granting legal monopolies to specific businesses. Consequently, if individuals had enough capital, they could more easily start up a business. And capitalism flourished.

In feudal Europe, many producers were attached to specific geographic locales. Serfs were legally tied to the villages where their families had rights to farm specific plots of land. Leaving meant losing the most important assets a serf had—his land-use rights. (Serfs did not own land; they had rights to farm parcels of land and to use their village's common lands for grazing animals, for hunting and food gathering, and for obtaining wood.) Artisans were often reluctant to leave the towns in which they resided, since medieval towns were closed communities in which strangers from other towns were not allowed to settle or sell their wares. As feudalism slowly declined after 1300, many of these restrictions were eliminated.

By the time England began founding colonies in North America, capitalism and a genuine *free labor* system had begun to emerge in England. Many agricultural workers, artisans, and laborers were legally free to change jobs to travel in search of work. But the practice of servitude, by which workers, female and male, young and old, pledged themselves to labor for a master for a period of one year or longer, meant that many laborers were only free *at the time their contracts expired*.

Most of the English colonists migrated to North America as free men and women, but agreed to become temporary servants. Too poor to pay for the cost of crossing the Atlantic, they indentured themselves to more affluent masters, and pledged their labor services for four to seven years in return for payment of the cost of the ocean crossing. Many slaves were imported into the colonies, largely from Africa. Slaveowners claimed title to children of their slaves, since they regarded both slave parents and children as a form of property. Almost from the time slaves were first brought to the English North American (and Caribbean) colonies, they were freely bought and sold in the same way that any other type of property would be in a capitalist system.

Colonial businesses—whether agricultural, mercantile, industrial or service—were individual proprietorships or joint partnerships. In virtually every part of the colonies where good transportation allowed landowners to ship crops and timber to distant markets, capitalism flourished. However, colonial merchant capitalists were subject to England's mercantilist restrictions on where they could ship and sell goods, restrictions which eventually led merchants who wanted to trade directly with France and the French West Indies to favor independence from England. American merchants would enthusiastically support the 1787 Constitution because they believed that without a strong navy, U.S. merchant ships would be attacked by European naval vessels and the U.S. government would be too weak to prevent foreign nations from barring U.S. merchants from trading with merchants in Europe and in the colonies controlled by European nations.

As the nation's economy grew, the amount of commerce increased, the distances people and products needed to travel became greater, and the potential market for products became larger. The size of many capitalist businesses, including the transportation businesses necessary to link businessmen (especially farmers) to the markets for their goods and/or the raw materials they needed, increased. As expensive machinery was developed to manufacture products more efficiently, the cost of starting up or expanding a business rose. Many individual businessmen found *they could not finance expansion of their activities because investors were afraid to risk their money by buying into the businesses* (becoming a partner). The risk to the investor was that if a partnership failed and went bankrupt, its creditors had a legal right to recover the money they had lent the business by confiscating the assets of the business and as much of the wealth (cash, land, houses, and personal effects) of each partner as was necessary. Thus partners risked much *more than the actual cash they invested* in a business.

Shortly after the new nation was founded, state legislatures began to charter a new form of business, the corporation. The corporation was based on the principle of the *limited* liability of all its investors. Incorporation allowed *more money to be raised* for costly, *large*-scale projects because each investor risked only the actual cash he or she put up when they bought the stocks or bonds issued by the corporation. Initially, a separate law had to be passed by a state legislature to charter each corporation, a requirement that was correctly criticized as favoring those businessmen who had the funds to lobby a legislature to get a special interest bill passed. In the 1830s, most businessmen argued that it was democratic to make the privileges of the corporation easily available to all businessmen who wanted to incorporate. Starting with New York in 1838, the states began to pass "free" incorporation laws that required only the filing of an application (and payment of a small fee) with the state government. Incorporation, and then free incorporation, promoted a very dynamic development of capitalist enterprise in the United States. Incorporation was essential if capitalist enterprises were to raise *large* amounts of capital.

But large transportation (and communication) improvements, which we call *infrastructure* projects, often required so much capital that private companies could not find enough investors willing to risk their funds on building a canal or a railroad. In the nineteenth century, state, city, and county governments financed and sometimes even constructed and operated large-scale canal projects and railroads. In 1825, New York State completed and then operated the Erie Canal, the most costly single infrastructure project of the nineteenth century. The state's economy boomed when the Erie Canal was finished. Pennsylvania's state government joined with private capitalists to build and operate a canal. This was an example of *mixed* (government and private sector) enterprise. To finance other transportation projects, county, city, and state governments *invested* in capitalist transportation companies, but did not play any role in their operation. Government financing of infrastructure development was usually done by borrowing money from investors by selling them government bonds that later would be paid off by means of state and local taxes.

Government investments gave capitalist development a great boost by speeding the completion of transportation facilities that benefited private sector farmers, craftsmen, manufacturers, and retailers. As more and more parts of the nation were reached by canals and railroads, new areas were opened up that supplied the raw materials needed for further industrialization. These areas grew crops that could be exported, allowing the nation to pay for the imports of industrial technology and investment capital that were needed for still more economic development.

Some capitalist enterprises were aided by government *subsidies*—payments of cash or land. Four transcontinental railroads were given millions of acres of land owned by the national government. The assumption behind the land subsidies was that the railroad companies would not be willing to build expensive railroad lines if they did not receive resources that they could sell to make quick profits. The Homestead Act (1862) was a program of grants designed to aid small farmers, each of whom received 160 acres of land owned by the national government. In 1862, the federal government also gave the states huge grants of public lands to sell to raise money to finance state colleges that taught and researched agricultural science. Eventually 69 land-grant colleges were founded. Most also became important centers for applied engineering and basic scientific research, activities that benefited business enterprise. Many shipping companies that were owned by U.S. citizens were subsidized, since they were the only companies allowed to earn money by carrying the U.S. mail. In 1902, Congress passed the Reclamation Act, which earmarked the money from the sale of the remaining U.S. government lands in 16 western and southwestern states for the construction and maintenance, by the federal Reclamation Service, of irrigation facilities that would help farmers prosper and would facilitate the growth of cities. Farmers were supposed to pay back the national government for the money spent to irrigate their lands, but most did not, and the Reclamation Service rarely tried to collect the money due the government. Thus, many capitalist enterprises grew with the assistance of the services provided by government-operated infrastructure activities and by means of government subsidies.

III

Proponents of capitalism argued that *free labor* was essential to the success of capitalism. If a business was failing, if demand for its product was slow, or if the owner to close one enterprise and invest in another, the capitalist wanted to be able to dismiss his workers immediately. The capitalist had no legal responsibility for dismissed workers and generally had no economic reason to provide them with resources. An unemployed free laborer was free to starve. In this sense, a slave was better off, since a slaveowner had to protect his investment in the slaves he had purchased by providing them with food, clothing, and shelter, *even when he had no work for them.* An indentured servant was also entitled to basic economic support from her or his master.

Free labor offered some benefits to wage earners. Men and women were *legally* free to move from one firm to another, searching for higher pay, a less domineering supervisor, safer working conditions, or a more varied job that helped to reduce the monotony of their labor. Clearly serfs and slaves did not have this right. But under capitalism, *the individual laborer, while free, was not nearly as powerful,* either economically or, in most instances, politically, *as the capitalist.*

The capitalist owned his or her business. Capitalists wanted to treat their workers like any other *commodity* they bought and sold. When they bought the worker's labor power, capitalists believed that while the worker was at work he or she could be ordered to do anything the capitalist wanted. Legally, the capitalist had the *absolute* right to dismiss any worker. This meant that if a worker complained about sexual harassment, tried to organize a union, or protested against being asked to work so rapidly that his or her health was endangered, the worker could be fired. Once a capitalist hired a worker, the capitalist had the legal right to make *all the rules for working*. These rules included the location of the work to be done, the hours during which work was to be done, the types of tools and machinery the wage earner would use, and how rapidly the wage earner was to work. If the wage earner disliked these rules, she or he had three options: to stay and suffer, to quit work, or to make an individual or group protest. Each option had its costs. If a worker could not find another job, quitting work, while legally possible, was not practical. But in times of economic expansion, the wage earner who quit working for an employer she or he believed was unfair could hope to find another job. Individual or group protest, including protest by unions, was sometimes successful. When open protest failed, the employer often fired the objecting free laborer or the group (or group leaders) of free laborers.

Wage earners knew that they were in a low-power position compared to the capitalist employer. Persons in high-power positions, especially when their power is not limited by law, often use that power to benefit themselves at the expense of others. Wage earners often thought that their employers kept too much of the revenue produced by their employees' labor. The views (1915) of R. D. Scrom, a skilled ironworker, are typical of this viewpoint.

> Why should we, the producers of all wealth, be the objects of charity and pity by the hypocritical rich who never produced a dollar in their lives. . . . We being the producers of everything produced why should we not produce for our own profit and enjoyment instead of producing for a wage and the bulk of the profit going to the parasitic capitalist . . .

Like Scrom, many manual workers often considered themselves to be the only legitimate *producers* in society. They frequently concluded that the persons directing or managing a business were nonproducers who did not really work. Manual workers were envious of owners or managers who performed well-paid nonmanual work in a safe, clean, quiet, comfortable office while blue-collar workers labored in dangerous, dirty, noisy, hot, or cold work environments. Furthermore, many manual producers believed that the nonproducing manager or the business owner *was making money by "skinning" (exploiting) the true producer*.

We call this viewpoint *producerism*. It arose before the emergence of capitalism. Industrial wage earners (and small farmers) used producerism to explain the injustices they believed they suffered at the hands of large landowners, capitalist merchants, manufacturers, and bankers. Such workers objected to wages they felt were too low, to fines they felt were levied just to make more money for the employer, to the firing of workers who complained about harassment and occupational hazards, to the refusal of business owners to purchase safety equipment, and to the dismissal of workers who were exercising their rights to free speech by talking about forming a union. Many wage earners believed that they should receive the *full value* of the products they made. This demand ignored the contributions of investors, who provided capital to start businesses, and managers, whose efforts did help businesses operate.

Workers conscious of their existence as a class of producers, apart from capitalists, did not necessarily agree on how producers could improve their condition. Some wage earners favored Henry George's Single Tax on unearned capital gains on land held for speculative purposes. This tax, it was believed, would lower excise and property taxes paid by wage earners, giving them more income. The Single Tax would also force speculators to sell their land, driving down land prices, thereby encouraging more economic development, which would create jobs and raise the wages of workers. Other workers stressed the need for political reforms to reduce the influence of the wealthy on elected officials and to increase the amount of direct democracy. They believed these changes would give producers more influence over government policy (see Chapter 11, pages 229-230).

Some producerist workers wanted to eliminate capitalism and the wage system entirely, although they differed about what the best alternative might be. Some workers wanted to replace capitalist enterprises with worker-run *cooperative* businesses. In the 1880s, many cooperationists thought that governments should lend money to worker cooperatives, while other workers wanted no such aid. Workers who were syndicalists wanted physically to seize each *separate* capitalist enterprise and have the former employees run the business. Other workers favored a national democratic socialist solution: an *elected* national government would confiscate all large, privately owned businesses, which would then be owned and operated by government. These socialistic solutions aimed to eliminate the profit motive and the ownership by capitalists of productive property, substituting the collective ownership of productive property by producers.

People from all income groups in the United States, and even a few millionaires, embraced democratic socialism, especially between 1870 and 1920. The powerful moral appeal of democratic socialism as an ideology lay in its blunt criticism of the unfair use of economic, political, and legal power by capitalists. Socialists also argued that the *profit motive* and *competitive market forces* pressured capitalists to exploit their workers and led to frequent *overproduction*. This caused business depressions, which were accompanied by unemployment. Socialists contended that minor reforms would not remedy the exploitation and inefficiency (especially overproduction) of capitalism. An entirely new system was needed.

Socialists expected that once the means of production were operated on a nonprofit basis, with the national government managing overall production on a *cooperative rather than a competitive basis*, all unemployment would be eliminated. (Socialist economists claimed that capitalism required a significant number of unemployed wage earners even in nondepression periods, since this "reserve army" of the unemployed would lower wages, thereby increasing the profits of business owners.) American socialists, many of whom were devout Christians who believed that Christ and the early Christian church embraced socialistic values of community responsibility for the needy, claimed that a socialist form of government would manage industrial production to avoid wasteful overproduction, would never suppress beneficial technological innovations, and would spend the money necessary to protect the health and safety of workers. Under socialism, a democratic government would care for those who were too old or too sick to earn a living, or had been so psychologically damaged by the poverty created by capitalism that they were unable to be effective workers.*

Capitalists, of course, did not want their businesses seized either by groups of workers or by the national government. Capitalists maintained that without the influence of the profit motive and competitive market forces, efficient production and

---

*Before 1900, virtually all socialists in Europe and the United States were democratic, parliamentary socialists who expected a socialist electoral victory to usher in the age of socialism. A new strain of socialism was developed in the twentieth century, especially by the Bolshevik wing of the Russian Social Democratic Party. The Bolsheviks believed that a violent revolution would be necessary to displace capitalists from power, and that after the revolution, a small group of socialists—the vanguard of the proletariat—would have to establish a dictatorship to consolidate the gains of the revolution and prevent opponents of socialism from staging a counterrevolution. The Bolsheviks expected that this dictatorship would eventually be disbanded, but were vague about the kind of government that would succeed it. Once in power, the Bolsheviks founded the Communist party to rule in the name of the people. In most other countries, socialists split into two rival camps: Those who supported democratic socialism referred to themselves as socialists; those who supported the methods of the Bolsheviks in Russia called themselves communists.

Karl Marx and Friedrich Engels attached different meanings to the terms socialism and communism. They used socialism to denote the first phase of social transformation, in which a democratic socialist government owned the means of production and provided income security to all. People would be financially compensated in proportion to their work effort. Marx and Engels expected socialism to evolve into communism, a stage of society in which all would contribute to society in accordance with their ability and would receive from government all that they needed as individuals.

material abundance could not be attained. But when the socialist vote was on the rise in the first decade of the twentieth century, some capitalists supported moderate economic reforms (especially workers' compensation) in the hope that by agreeing to provide for the economic welfare of many injured workers they would blunt some of the socialist demand for improving the welfare of workers through comprehensive, radical changes (see pages 232-234).

At certain times during the last 100 years, *particular* groups of American blue-collar workers or farmers have favored *selective* socialism. These hard-pressed farmers, railroad workers, and coal miners—wanted a few, but *only a few,* businesses to be taken over by government. In the late 1880s, Populist farmers wanted all railroad, telephone, and telegraph companies socialized. After World War I, railroad workers favored national government ownership of the nation's railroads, while coal miners advocated nationalizing coal mines. Each of these groups of workers hoped to get higher wages and better treatment from a government employer.

Between 1890 and 1930, many urban consumers were also attracted to the approach of selective socialism. Unhappy about poor quality service and high rates charged by urban gas companies, electric companies, water companies, and subway and trolley car companies, these consumers, including many middle-class consumers, wanted particular urban service companies taken over by city government. In other cases, these consumers proposed starting city-owned (municipal) service companies. It was assumed that nonprofit, efficiently run municipal service companies would *compete* with private urban utilities, thereby driving down rates charged by the private firms and forcing the firms to improve the quality of their services.

Socialism as a political movement never captured more than six percent of the national vote (in 1912), although the Populist party's presidential candidate, running on a platform that demanded selective socialism, obtained 12 percent of the vote in 1892. After World War I, socialists in the United States helped organize many unions, and supported welfare-state programs (see

Chapter 11). During the 1930s, Congress created only one government industrial enterprise, the Tennessee Valley Authority (see page 211). Public housing programs, which started on a small scale in the 1930s and expanded between 1949 and 1975, authorized state and city governments to own and manage housing for low-income tenants. But full-blown socialism— government ownership of the main means of production—did not appeal to most Americans. They feared that government could not manage effectively, especially because they believed professional politicians would run government, and would only care about cushy jobs for themselves and their allies. Others felt it was wrong to confiscate private property. And many were concerned that in the absence of the profit motive and market competition, there would be no incentive for government-owned enterprises to operate efficiently.

IV

While most Americans were not socialists, *this does not mean that most people fully trusted free market capitalism.* As the nineteenth century advanced, many consumers and producers advocated government regulation of (1) the prices charged by private enterprise and (2) the quality of consumer products and services sold by private enterprises. Especially as the average size of the capitalist firm grew larger and larger, many Americans believed that only government regulation could protect the consumer and the producer against being ripped off by oligopoly pricing, hazardous working conditions, and unsafe or shoddy goods and services.

Between 1800 and 1860 most American businesses were relatively unregulated by government. But city governments did sometimes regulate the weights and measures used by retail sellers. Massachusetts regulated the way railroads issued stocks and bonds. In the 1829, New York State began an insurance fund to help banks protect the money of depositors. Banks that chose to join the fund had to agree to abide by regulations governing their banking practices.

Demand for more extensive, compulsory government regulation of capitalist enterprises began with the passengers and *businesses* (merchants, farmers, and manufacturers) who used railroad services. In 1869, the Illinois legislature created a state railroad rate commission, and many other states soon followed suit. These commissions regulated the absolute level of railroad rates and determined whether or not railroads were being fair in the rate discounts they gave to large shippers and to shippers in specific towns and cities. In 1887, Congress created the Interstate Commerce Commission, which would regulate the rates charged by interstate railroads (railroads that crossed state lines). In short, businesses who depended on the railroads demanded that governments regulate the rates charged by the railroads.

In the early twentieth century, consumers pressured many state governments to form public utility commissions that would regulate the rates and areas served by the transportation and communication companies. Many of the largest urban utility companies also favored state regulation because they expected (correctly) that the state public utility commissions would *protect the bigger companies against new competitors* who tried to enter the areas already served by the large companies.

Under capitalism, businesses competed with each other. Sometimes the competition was ruthless and involved violence, bribery, extortion, and conspiracies to fix prices and allocate markets. In the 1830s and 1840s, small businessmen demanded that state governments dissolve all monopolies. After the Civil War, many large corporations—monopolies or oligopolies—were created. They often used their economic power to bankrupt smaller competitors, usually by lowering prices below the cost of production. Having eliminated most of their competitors, oligopolies and monopolies charged consumers higher prices than they would have had to pay if there had been true price competition in the industry. Small and medium-size business owners generally wanted the state and national governments to file antitrust lawsuits aimed at breaking up big companies into much smaller firms that would engage in genuine price competition.

Many businesses, including some large corporations, backed the creation (1914) of a permanent regulatory body, the Federal Trade Commission (FTC), to provide protection when they were being squeezed by other businesses. Between 1915 and 1921, the FTC did a fairly good job of ensuring the equitable treatment of capitalists by other capitalists. In 1913, Congress responded to the consensus of bankers that some kind of central bank was needed to regulate the money supply. The Federal Reserve System was an example of *mixed* regulation by government officials and private sector representatives elected by the banks who joined the system. The president appointed the six members of the Federal Reserve Board, which in turn, appointed two-thirds of the governing board of each of the 12 district Federal Reserve Banks. Each district's member banks elected the other third of the Federal Reserve district bank board.

Some writers who were concerned about the economic power of the large corporations emerging under capitalism hoped that new technologies would undermine the power of the large corporation. Writing in 1903, John Graham Brooks, a Massachusetts minister who thought that huge monopolies should be socialized by government, predicted that new technologies would enable small businessmen to compete successfully with large corporations. Because it was such an efficient and inexpensive source of power, Brooks believed that electricity would enable small manufacturers to match the low production costs of large corporations. Scientific agriculture would enable the small farmer to become prosperous. Seeking to avoid the massive bureaucratization that full-scale socialism would require, Brooks looked to science and technology to

> extend the regime of private property holdings in which interest, rent, and profits in a thousand small industries may prove more fruitful to society than if they are socialized.

As the twentieth century dawned, technological advances were making the mass production of sophisticated consumer products possible. Henry Ford and a team of talented engineers took the lead in developing mass production methods to manufacture automobiles. Ford used specialized machine tools to make auto parts, and then assembled automobiles on moving conveyor belts that came to be known as assembly lines. On each assembly line, the car that was being built moved from worker to worker. Ford's engineers also installed chutes that brought to each worker the parts that had to be added to the larger section of the car that was moving on the assembly line.

This *mass production* system helped each worker to use time efficiently. No longer did each worker have to waste time walking to a supply area to get new parts. Since each worker had a single, specialized job, *worker training time was reduced*. Ford engineers expected workers to master their assembly tasks quickly and to *increase the speed* at which they performed operations on the car. This increase in efficiency also meant that workers labored at a faster pace and without any pauses. Many workers found such work exhausting. Many left assembly-line jobs for other jobs. Others stayed, and accepted the trade-off between an intense work pace and the higher-than-average wages they were paid.

Between the end of the Civil War and the Depression of the 1930s, the capitalist economy of the United States grew vigorously. Despite considerable anti-big business agitation, banking and manufacturing companies grew larger and larger between 1890 and 1930, with concentration increasing in most product categories. Large investment banks, like J.P. Morgan and Company, facilitated the merger of companies that had previously engaged in ruinous price competition.

The greater stability of large companies offered their workers more secure jobs and enabled the companies to sell their products overseas, which created more jobs in the United States. It is also likely that many technological innovations could not have been implemented by firms that lacked large amounts of capital or that did not have the ability, by virtue of their size and connections with investment banks, to borrow the funds needed for the development of new products. Conversely, in some instances large firms suppressed new technologies that competed with their products. For example, some historians believe that after World War I General Motors, which had bought all the trolley lines of Los Angeles, wanted to kill mass transit so that the automobile would become the preferred form of personal transportation. General Motors decided not to replace trolleys that ran on steel rails with more efficient and flexible electric trolley buses (which ran on rubber tires and used overhead poles to get electricity from power lines). This decision prevented mass transit from achieving the efficiencies that would have made it attractive to riders.

After 1896, the U.S. economy experienced a huge growth spurt, which lasted until 1929. (There were two exceptions to this trend: in the 1920s coal mining declined drastically and cotton and wheat farmers suffered when the prices of these crops fell sharply.) World War I established the United States as the leading international economic power. American banks became the major money lenders in the world. By the 1920s, productivity had risen so much that real wages increased enough to allow middle-income Americans and skilled blue-collar workers to buy telephones, cars, refrigerators, and washing machines. American capitalism was producing the goods.

V

But then the Great Depression hit. There were many reasons for the long Depression that began in 1929 and continued until 1941: excessive speculation on the New York Stock Exchange, encouraged by allowing investors to take out loans to buy stock without investing much of their own money; the increase in tariffs effected by most industrial nations, which choked off international trade and eliminated the jobs of those who made products sold abroad; the Federal Reserve Board's failure to realize that its monetary policies did not ease enough to help a seriously damaged economy; an income distribution that, by virtue of very low wages for most wage earners, put too little purchasing power in the hands of consumers; the lack of new consumer products in the late 1920s, which would have stimulated more investment in factories; and the decline in the ability of mature capitalist economies to generate rapid investment of savings in the production of additional goods and services. All these contributed to a collapse that left one of every four Americans without a job and another one-fourth of all Americans with intermittent employment.

When the American economy collapsed in the 1930s, many people lost faith in the ability of capitalism to recover. John Maynard Keynes, an English economist, argued that the capitalist economies of the United States and Western Europe had changed as they had matured and had reached the point where capitalist enterprises could no longer generate *enough* investment to sustain economic expansion. Too many capitalists were taking too long to raise and invest money to make new products. Put another way, Keynes' studies showed that classical economists had been mistaken when they concluded that all savings were rapidly invested.

Keynes was not a socialist. He sought a method to stimulate capitalist economies so that prosperity would return and the kind of poverty that he thought led to demands for socialism would be eliminated. *Government spending was Keynes' answer*. He argued that mature capitalist economies required a permanently *higher* level of government spending, which he believed would stimulate investment that otherwise would not be made. (This kind of spending would be called *pump priming*.) Keynes believed that government spending would create employment. The wages paid to newly employed workers would create more consumer demand. Higher consumer demand would generate more investment.

Keynes argued that keeping the capitalist economies going would often also require a *modest* amount of *deficit* spending by governments. But during a major depression, large-scale deficits could be incurred, without causing severe inflation. Keynes believed that any kind of government spending would stimulate capitalist economies, although his personal preference was for more housing for people of modest means.

Keynes was proposing a permanent role for government *fiscal stimulation* of capitalist economies. During the 1930s, *few politicians and government officials in the United States accepted Keynes' ideas.* Rather, President Roosevelt and Congress focused on reforms that *reduced overproduction by* having the national government *regulate* many sectors of the economy and used *government insurance of the risks taken by large and small capitalists* as a method of stimulating economic growth. Congress enacted programs of government regulation of the production of farm goods, coal, and oil, reducing output by setting quotas for each producer. The airline industry was regulated to avoid excess competition. The federal government facilitated the reorganization of the railroad industry to eliminate unnecessary competition. Labor relations were regulated by the 1935 National Labor Relations Act, whose author hoped that reducing the number of strikes would aid economic recovery, and that unionization would bring higher wages, which would stimulate economic growth by increasing consumer demand.

Congressional legislation in the 1930s also regulated financial institutions, many of which had recklessly invested the money of depositors and investors, causing them to lose much of their wealth. The Securities and Exchange Commission (SEC) regulated the New York Stock Exchange and the new stock exchanges that were created after World War II. Investors would now have more protection against being cheated by fraudulent stock advertisements and insider trading. The Federal Deposit Insurance Corporation (FDIC) examined bank records to protect the funds of depositors. The FDIC also insured the money deposited in banks, thereby increasing the confidence of depositors in the banking system. Both these types of financial regulation were intended by New Dealers to stabilize the financial institutions of modern capitalism. If depositors and investors had no protection against being cheated out of their money, they would not make their money available to investors. (Banks lent out part of depositors' money to businessmen and homeowners.) As the preamble to the 1934 law creating the SEC put it, government regulation was designed

> to change the practices of [stock] exchanges and the relationships between listed corporations and the investing public to fit modern conditions, for the very purpose that they may endure as essential elements of our [capitalist] economic system.

Another important technique adopted by the national government to help stabilize the economy and promote economic growth was the provision of *government insurance, especially for the risks businesses took when they borrowed money to grow.* We have already mentioned the FDIC's insurance of banks that chose to join. In 1933, the national government began insuring the mortgages of many farmers and urban homeowners. This allowed people who could not afford their payments to get new, long-term mortgages that had lower monthly payments. The Federal Housing Administration (FHA) was created in 1934 to insure the loans made by banks to home builders and renovators. In the years that followed, FHA insurance and similar federal and state programs have played critical roles in stimulating housing construction, one of the largest and most dynamic sectors of the capitalist economy in the United States.

The Tennessee Valley Authority (TVA) was the only example of a government industrial enterprise created during the 1930s. It built hydroelectric dams in seven southeastern states. The inexpensive electric power generated by TVA dams was sold to private power companies or to cooperatively owned electric companies that operated in rural areas. During World War II, the cheap and abundant electric power produced by the TVA encouraged many war industries to locate in the southeast, stimulating the economy of that region. The TVA also served consumers throughout the nation by publicizing figures detailing its actual cost of producing electricity. These figures showed that many electric power companies had been fooling state utility commissions and the Federal Power Commission by claiming that the cost of producing electricity was higher than its actual cost.

The 1935 Banking Act fully empowered the Open Market Committee* of the Federal Reserve Board to influence actively the growth rate of the money supply. It would do this by buying and selling U.S. government bonds, which either put more money into circulation or removed money from circulation. In 1935, the Federal Reserve Board was also given the authority to set the federal funds rate, the interest rate that banks charge each other for overnight loans. Banks borrowed money from each other on a short term basis when they had made so many loans that they did not have enough reserves to comply with the reserve ratio (reserves as a percentage of liabilities) that was also set by the Federal Reserve Board. Thus, when the Federal Reserve Board wanted to stimulate economic growth, it could encourage banks to loan money by lowering the federal funds rate. Cheaper interest rates on short-term bank-to-bank loans allowed banks to loan out more money, since they could borrow more cheaply to make up any shortfall in their required reserves.

The overall logic behind most of the economic reforms Congress enacted in the 1930s was that capitalist markets were not automatically self-correcting. Government action was necessary to stimulate business investment, to reduce overproduction, and to curtail the fraudulent actions and risky policies pursued by bank managers.

Yet in 1941 the essence of American capitalism was still intact. The overwhelming majority of the means of production were still *privately* owned. There had been no nationalization of existing capitalist enterprises and credit markets. Only one new national government enterprise, the Tennessee Valley Authority, had been created. But American capitalism was being stimulated by national government spending, by means of operations of the Federal Reserve's Open Market Committee, and by government insurance programs that helped small businessmen (including

---

*This committee included the now seven-member Federal Reserve Board and five members elected by the 12 district banks of the Federal Reserve System. Thus private-sector bankers had significant input into the decisions of the Open Market Committee.

farmers) and some large companies* reduce the risks they
incurred when they borrowed money for business ventures.
Many capitalist enterprises were now more highly regulated, as
the national government sought to make capitalism work more
efficiently.

World War II proved that Keynes's theories had been right.
The national government engaged in massive deficit spending.
The economy revived and prospered. There had been so much
slack in the economy and there were so few consumer goods
produced during the war that there was not any major inflation.
However, most government officials and politicians were still not
yet converted to Keynesianism. To many, Keynesianism seemed
to be socialistic. True, it did call for a higher level of spending by
government. Clearly some kind of bureaucracy would be
necessary to decide on the kinds of government spending that
would "prime the pump." But there was nothing in Keynes'
theories to suggest that governments actually would have to
produce anything. Governments could "prime the pump" by
buying goods and services from private, capitalist enterprises.

In 1900, the national government's budget had been three
percent of gross national product (GNP). From 1946 to 1962,
national government spending averaged 16.9 percent of GNP.
Defense spending rose rapidly after 1947, as the Cold War
intensified and the Korean War began (1950). Although some of
President Truman's and President Eisenhower's economic
advisors were Keynesian economists, their advice was not
responsible for the increase in government spending. In a sense,
the national government adopted Keynesian policies *without
consciously embracing Keynesian theory*. Why? As Congress
responded to international emergencies, defense spending and

---

* There were some insurance programs for large capitalists, including
insurance against losses when exporters were not paid by foreign purchasers
of their products. After World War II, the national government provided *free*
insurance to the owners of nuclear power plants against any damages that
were caused by malfunctions that exposed members of the public to radiation.
This was a huge subsidy, since private casualty insurance would have been
very expensive.

spending on scientific research that was related to military technology were viewed as essential to national security. Congress also initiated spending programs for veterans' health and education, public housing, private and public hospital construction, basic scientific and medical research, aid to colleges and universities, and interstate highway construction. (The federal government began to give states and cities money for part of the cost of road building in 1916.) Private enterprises received most of the contracts for the construction and production necessary to provide for national security, housing, roads, and research facilities. The overall capitalist economy expanded rapidly. Most of the citizen groups and business groups that lobbied for these programs and the legislators who voted for them were not aware that *the overall effect of their efforts was to make the national government "prime the pump" as Keynes had recommended.*

In 1949 and 1954, Presidents Truman and Eisenhower consciously followed one of Keynes's policy guidelines—that taxes should not be raised when a recession was occurring. (Not raising taxes led to small budget deficits.) In 1963 and 1964, the Kennedy and Johnson administrations used Keynesian theory to justify modest tax cuts to stimulate the sluggish economy. The 1964 tax cuts had the intended effect. Between 1965 and 1969, military expenditures for the Vietnam War—financed by excessive deficit spending—rose sharply, stimulating both rapid economic growth *and* significant inflation, just as Keynesian theory predicted.

In 1975, as the Vietnam War was winding down, a sharp recession hit the U.S. economy. As the economy rebounded in 1976, many American businesses realized that for the first time they were facing stiff competition from foreign manufacturers. The mid-1970s signaled the beginning of a new era for American capitalism, during which the domestic market was no longer monopolized by domestic producers. Businesses responded by trying to cut costs—labor costs, the cost of complying with environmental regulations, and the cost of making the workplace healthier and safer. The mid-1970s also marked the beginning of a new stage in production technology, the *automation* stage. Self-adjusting machinery directed by electronic components, including computer chips, was much more productive than nonautomated equipment. Consequently, *technological unemployment* became a serious problem.

Beginning in 1978, Presidents Carter and Reagan convinced Congress to reduce some types of federal price regulation (for oil, natural gas, and airlines), hoping that price competition would stimulate exploration and new services. It was believed that new business conditions made these regulations ineffective. The national government continued to use price supports to subsidize many farm crops. The Federal Reserve Board and the Open Market Committee continued to influence interest rates and the rate of growth of the money supply. The 1982 recession was deliberately planned by the Federal Reserve Board to reduce double-digit inflation.

Congress had not thought of Medicare and Medicaid, financed by general and Social Security taxes, as a Keynesian policy. But as these programs stimulated more demand for medical services, provided by health services companies and independent entrepreneurs (doctors), health care became the biggest growth industry in the U. S. economy, and government spending as a percent of GNP rose. The military buildup started in 1981 by the Reagan administration and the increase in government spending for health care raised federal government expenditures to 24 percent of GNP by 1985.

As this essay is being written, in the spring of 1995, a newly elected Congress is debating proposals to cut severely national government spending. Some supporters of these cuts are concerned about the size of the budget deficits. Some believe that the private sector is capable of stimulating the economy by itself. Others are opposed, on principle, to the expansion of national government power, which they fear is distorting the federal system in favor of national government, as opposed to state government power. Lowering taxes is also an important objective of the budget cutters, although there is a heated debate about which groups—high- or middle-income taxpayers—should receive tax cuts.

Opponents of drastic cuts in national government spending warn that it will reduce investment and therefore cut the growth rate of capitalist businesses. This is a Keynesian argument. Big cuts in national government medical and scientific research grants, most of which go to nonprofit university scientists, run the risk of ending the funding that has helped the nation's medical businesses become world leaders.

Significantly, none of the advocates of lower national government spending and deregulation are opposed to giving tremendous power to the Federal Reserve Board and its Open Market Committee, which are authorized to regulate bank reserves and to buy and sell billions of dollars of national government bonds so that the government can influence the rate of growth of the money supply, thereby providing a general framework for business prosperity. In 1995, national government spending was 21 percent of the GNP. The budget balancing plans being debated in Congress in 1995 would lower this level of spending to 18 percent of GNP, which is the average level that existed between 1955 and the early 1960s. This is a far cry from the three percent level of 1929.

Mature capitalism in the United States is different from the capitalism of the nineteenth century. Mature capitalism is more regulated and stimulated by government spending than it was 100 years ago. While many Americans are uncomfortable with the greater amount of government influence on the private sector in today's economy, it is also clear that many people, including many capitalists, do not want to return to the kind of lightly stimulated, lightly regulated market capitalism that existed a century ago.

The last chapter in this book analyzes modern liberalism, the idea that individual liberties, economic growth, and equality of opportunity cannot be maintained in any society unless government regulates especially powerful groups and individuals when they act to deprive people of their liberties and equality of opportunity. Modern liberals also believe that social stability and social justice cannot be maintained unless government acts to ensure that all children and adults attain a minimum equality of economic condition.

CHAPTER 11

Liberalism

I

This book began with a discussion of the concept of liberty. It ends with an analysis of liberalism. Note that both liberty and liberalism have the same Latin root, *liber* (to be free). Freedom from economic, religious, and social restrictions, as well as freedom to improve one's condition, have been the basic objectives of liberals. Long before the nineteenth century, when the term liberalism was first used to describe the pursuit of these goals, many men and women sought liberty. Slaves and serfs (and often servants who were bound for years at a time to masters who had virtually absolute power over them) deeply resented being unfree. They sought the liberty to choose freely where and how to make a living, marry, and sell their property. Running away and violent rebellion demanding the rights (liberties) of freemen were the main protest tactics used by unfree people.

Throughout most of recorded history, the unfree and relatively powerless free people of human societies believed that *government officials posed a special threat to the freedom and liberty of the common person.* Frequently the elite person who owned or commanded the labor of the unfree/free person was also a prominent official of *local* government. There were virtually *no limits on the exercise of governmental authority by such elite officials.* The powerless people of the world often believed that government officials made unfair, arbitrary decisions—especially in local courts—that deprived men and women of their property (through fines and confiscation), their ability to choose where and how they would make a living (by denying permission to begin a business or to use common village lands for grazing animals, hunting, and gathering wood), and their personal freedom (by forcing them to fight in foreign wars, by jailing them, and by executing them). Similarly, while powerful elites could limit monarchs' power over them, the "little people" of the world were *totally at the mercy of the authority of monarchs*. A king or queen could levy taxes without consulting the powerless, begin wars that led to high casualties, order men and women to adopt a state religion, and imprison anyone whose views were critical of the kind of society the ruler wanted to establish.

The emergence of democratic republics, in which only voters had the authority to decide which elected officials would make and execute the laws that would govern each nation, ultimately led many people to abandon much—but not all—of their historically conditioned distrust of government authority. During the last century, industrialization created a diversity of economic groups. The national economy became more complex. Economic activity became and more subject to fluctuations resulting from changes in the international supply of agricultural and manufactured goods. Hard-working farmers, industrial wage earners, and businessmen often found that despite their labors, competition and exploitation made it impossible for them to make decent livings. At different times, different economic groups within the American population turned to the democratic governments they elected and asked for some kind of aid— regulation, a cash subsidy, or the creation of a government agency to provide a service—that would help them cope with economic hardship or expand the freedom of the members of the group by protecting them against unfair treatment by others. Especially in the twentieth century, persons concerned about protecting and expanding their own liberties and those of the general public often came to view government power as a *means to enhance liberty*, rather than seeing government as the primary threat to liberty. Yet Americans never forgot their long-standing fears about the potential for the abuse of power by government.

II

During the Middle Ages, people living in towns often paid nobles and monarchs for charters that gave the residents of the towns many liberties. The most important liberties were the right of the propertied residents to elect their own town governments and the right of townspeople to engage in any kind of commercial activity they wanted. People who owned land— including large landowners—were often subject to feudal rules that limited their right to buy and sell land. By about 1700, affluent landowners succeeded in pressuring the English Parliament to remove such restraints on the freedom of a property holder. On the European continent, the French Revolution produced similar changes.

Agricultural and urban communities were the first groups to demand the right of self-government in the years after 1000 A.D. They based such demands on their memories of older, self-governing communal institutions that had been eliminated by the rise of feudalism. During peasant rebellions, peasant revolutionaries demanded the *restoration* of traditional, prefeudal village self-government. The 1525 German peasant rebellion is very important because the spread of knowledge of the Bible led the peasants to use Christian theology, and especially the works of St. Paul, to *justify the equal application of the notion of personal freedom*. Thus they wrote:

> It has been the custom hitherto for men to hold us as their own property [as serfs], which is pitiable enough, considering that Christ has delivered and redeemed us *all*, without exception, by the shedding of His precious blood, the lowly as well as the great. Accordingly, it is consistent with scripture that we should be free and wish to be so. [emphasis added]

The German peasants were not anarchists. They wanted the protection of government authority. But they wanted *self-*government, which would give them more protection against the possible abuse of power by government officials:

> We are . . . ready to yield obedience according to God's law to our elected and regular authorities in all proper things becoming to a Christian.

As time passed, those who argued for liberal policies added nonreligious arguments to religious justifications. During the English Civil War, groups of landless farmers and small farmers argued for the abolition of monarchy and the creation of a self-governing republic in which all those who were economically independent would vote. Speaking for *affluent* English merchants and landowners, John Locke argued that government should not be allowed to violate the basic liberties and freedoms of an *affluent* minority of men who were not members of the aristocracy, or had not established alliances with members of the aristocracy that dominated the executive branch of the English government (which was directly under the authority of the monarch). Locke insisted that social stability required protecting the natural rights of all *substantial property holders*. The Bill of Rights that Locke and other affluent Englishmen insisted be included in the Settlement of 1689 (see pages 8-9) was designed to *limit* the power of government to interfere with the freedoms of *substantial* property holders. In other words, seventeenth-century English liberals sought freedoms for *a minority of adult men*, not for the masses.

Locke's liberalism *allowed for the existence of a monarchy*, limited by representative institutions elected by one-fifth of the adult male population. A century later, all monarchies were being criticized by "radical" English liberals like Tom Paine and by many of the peasant and artisan groups that were active in the French Revolution. *All* citizens, they argued, should be protected against the violation of their liberties by government. Since monarchs were not elected, they were especially likely to deprive the average citizen of basic liberties. Paine, who had been born poor, attacked monarchical power as illegitimate, a violation of the basic equality of rights established by God when he created humankind. Arguing that the Bible "expressly disapproves of government by kings," Paine turned his attention to the evils of the *hereditary* principle by which kings, queens, and members of the English of Lords were selected. Here Paine's argument was not Biblical but practical: "Men who look upon themselves born to reign and others to obey soon grow insolent." Paine's antimonarchical, antiaristocratic liberalism led him to conclude that human rights could only be protected by an elected, republican form of government.

Paine's experiences with monarchical governments, which he viewed as inherently tyrannical, led him to fear the abuse of government authority. Formulating a view of government that was very similar to Thomas Jefferson's, Paine wrote in his 1776 pamphlet, *Common Sense*, that "government even in its best state is but a necessary evil, in its worst state an intolerable one." But despite this negative justification, Paine was very definite about the *need for government*:

> Wherefore, security being the true design and end of government, it unanswerably follows that whatever form thereof appears most likely to ensure it to us, with the least expense and greatest benefit, is preferable to all others.

Why did Paine believe people needed government to provide security? Because he saw people as prone to sin and antisocial behavior, including attempts to take the property of others unfairly. Paine thought that in a republic the most useful service a government could provide its citizens was a *negative* function: protecting citizens from their own "vices." As he put it, "as nothing but Heaven is impregnable to vice" people could not be expected to behave honorably and "this remissness will point out the necessity of establishing some form of government to supply the defect of moral virtue."

In the newly formed United States, small farmers, artisans, and some prosperous merchants and large landowners shared Paine's fear of excessive government power. They believed that even in a republic, with an elected government, liberty could easily be threatened by excessive government power. Hence they liked the system of checks and balances that the Constitution established for the national government and insisted that all the powers not specifically given to the national government by the Constitution be kept by the states and the sovereign voters (see Chapter 5 pages 92-93).

Thomas Jefferson and many democratic republicans had the same concerns. They embraced the ideas expressed in the phrase, "That government is best which governs least." But many people misinterpret the meaning of this slogan. Jefferson did not believe that *no* government was desirable. Like Paine, Jefferson believed that government was needed to protect property and generally to keep order. If government action was necessary, they preferred to rely on state governments, not the national government. Thus, when Jefferson concluded that public universities would help preserve republican liberties, he advocated founding a *state* university in Virginia.

As President, Jefferson would boldly negotiate (with France) the Louisiana Purchase (1803). Was this *expensive* purchase of millions of acres of land a violation of Jefferson's liberal principles? He did not think so. Jefferson expected that the acquisition of the Louisiana territory would promote social stability by giving the nation more land, land that could be bought by millions of small farmers. The political stability of the republic would be promoted by increasing the number of self-sufficient farmers. Like Aristotle, Jefferson and most other democratic republicans feared their liberal, republican society would become unstable if there were large numbers of poor, economically dependent voters. Unlike urban wage earners, tenant farmers, and agricultural laborers, Jefferson expected that self-reliant farmers would be citizens who would vote free from the intimidation of large landowners or employers. Landowning, self-employed citizens would be less likely than dependent landless agricultural laborers and factory workers to become impoverished people who would ask for poor relief or public-works jobs. By using government power boldly in one specific instance, Jefferson believed he was guaranteeing the survival of a liberal society in the future, one that would not suffer from the economic polarization that in the Roman Republic had led to the emergence of tyrants who had provided the "mob" of poor, unemployed citizens with bread and circuses, and then had used the mob to influence elections and intimidate government officials. Jefferson insisted that all citizens would be eligible to buy the land of the Louisiana Purchase. He knew that the national government would need to establish only a limited number of land offices to sell the public lands. Jefferson was using government power to benefit the general public, but in a way that minimized the extent of that power.

III

Fear of concentrated economic or political power was an essential part of the liberal tradition in the nineteenth century. Initially, liberals feared government power more than the economic power of wealthy private individual and government-licensed corporations (mainly banks, railroad companies, and canal companies). But as the size of business enterprise grew, many Americans became alarmed at the potential of the *large*, *multistate* corporation to abuse workers, exploit other businessmen, and undermine the democratic political processes of the republic.

By the 1830s, shoemakers were warning that the independent artisan, producing shoes in his home with the help of his wife and children, was threatened by the emergence of large workshops that employed shoe workers, making them dependent on the workshop owner for their living. During the next 30 years, many artisans in other trades, whose jobs were also being eliminated or simplified by new machinery, and who were forced to work in factories under the control of another person, protested that their loss of economic independence would threaten the stability of the American political republic. The artisans attacked their new employers as a "monopolizing class" who build up "their own popularity and aggrandizement, at the expense of the honest part of the community." Artisans demanded that their state legislators pass antimonopoly laws to make it difficult for businesses to grow larger. This was protective government regulation.

In 1868, Charles Francis Adams, Jr., warned that railroad corporations were a particular threat to the democratic political institutions that had chartered them:

> Modern society has created a class of artificial beings [railroad corporations] who bid fair soon to be masters of their creator. . . . These bodies . . . are already establishing despotisms [dictatorial institutions] which no spasmodic popular effort will be able to shake off.

The modern business corporation, said Adams, exercised

> power such has never in the world's history been trusted in the hands of mere private citizens, ...[power that would] ultimately succeed in *directing government itself* . . . The corporation is in its nature a threat against the popular institutions which are spreading so rapidly over the whole world. [emphasis added]

Adams was typical of many nineteenth century liberals in that he believed that the remedy that the public would seek against dangerous corporate power—increasing the power of government to regulate the corporation—would violate the Constitution's limits on government power.

> The national government, in order to deal with the corporations, must assume powers refused to it by its fundamental law, and even then is always exposed to the chance of forming an absolute central government.

Looking at the national scene in 1868, Adams was concerned about the passivity of the general public, which, he believed, did not appreciate the dangers of the large corporation. The public's passivity raised the possibility that if the central government increased its powers to regulate large corporations, the corporations would retaliate by using their money to seize control of the national government.

But by the early 1870s, antirailroad sentiment among midwestern farmers and retail store owners had risen to a fever pitch. The public in the midwestern states demanded state commissions to regulate railroad rates, both to make them lower and to end the railroads' practice of favoring some towns and cities over others with special low rates. These businessmen, who felt their own businesses were threatened by the kinds of rates set by the railroads, viewed government regulation of railroad rates as the only possible solution to their economic problems.

Meanwhile, factory and mine workers began to organize in unions. Their unions sent spokesmen to state legislatures to lobby for safety legislation and state safety inspection of mines and factories. These industrial workers also asked their elected legislators to pass laws shortening the work week and requiring that wages be paid every two weeks instead of once a month. Workers demanded that legislators pass laws to eliminate the common law rules state court judges had developed that made it almost impossible for a worker injured as a result of her or his employer's carelessness to collect damages.

In short, by the 1880s, groups of producers in rural and urban settings were calling on their democratically elected governments to regulate the practices of businesses. This development marked the beginning of a new trend in the history of liberalism. Groups of people who believed they were being treated unfairly by large, powerful economic institutions *sought protection for their liberties through government regulation.* In an age of big business, they believed that only the power of government could protect them against maltreatment. This does not mean that these groups were not concerned about the possibility that expanded government power could be used to infringe upon their liberties. Rather, *they had concluded that liberal ends*—protection of their basic rights to produce, to be paid for their work, and to be as free as possible from workplace injuries—*could only be attained by relying on government power.*

In the 1880s, many farmers formed cooperatives to make farm equipment and to market the crops farmers raised. But when these cooperatives failed, generally for lack of enough operating funds, the farmers concluded that a government takeover of essential businesses—especially the railroads—was the only way that they could be freed from the burden of what they regarded as the exploitative charges. In 1892, hard-pressed farmers in the South and in Kansas, Nebraska, Minnesota, North Dakota, and South Dakota formed the Populist party. The Populists proposed *national* government *ownership* of the nation's railroad, telephone, and telegraph systems. Populist farmers in the South also proposed a system of national government banks, the sub-treasury system, that would lend money at below-market interest rates to farmers. The sub-treasury banks would be providing loans that commercial banks refused to give to small farmers. The Populists also demanded a steeply graduated income tax, which they hoped would confiscate most of the wealth of rich individuals and corporations, who the Populists believed had built their fortunes by exploiting the typical farmer or industrial worker.

Looking to expand the power of the national government to help farmers reduce the cost of borrowing money for their businesses and to lower the cost of transporting products to market and of transporting farm machinery from factory to farm, the Populists, unlike Charles Francis Adams, did not worry about a passive public. The Populists knew that they were part of an aroused group of farmers, a group that blamed their plight on the profiteering of the nation's large banking, manufacturing, and transportation corporations. Because the Populists believed that the public could be, and was, aroused over the economic practices of corporations and the way big business used its money to attack "the Republic and endanger liberty," they had no hesitation in expanding the power of government to solve the problems of many citizens. In an 1892 statement that presented the case for modern liberalism—using the power of government to solve social and economic problems—Populist writers confidently called on government to promote the freedom and liberty of citizens:

> We believe that the power of government—*in other words of the people*—should be expanded. . . . as rapidly and as far as the good sense of an intelligent people and the teachings of experience shall justify, to the end that oppression, injustice and poverty shall eventually cease in the land.[emphasis added]

This statement represented a basic reversal of the type of methods used to achieve liberal goals. Rather than preserving freedom and liberty by asking for limits on the power of government, the Populists believed that *having government provide important services to the public increased the ability of the average person to make a living and to exercise her* or his *basic liberties.*

Like Jefferson and early nineteenth-century democratic republicans, the Populists believed that a person without economic independence was likely to lose his or her liberties. Twentieth-century liberals would argue that in an age of large-scale business—whether manufacturing, retailing, service, or transportation—most people would be employees working for others and would not be self-employed farmers and artisans. As Governor George W. Clarke of Iowa explained in his 1913 inaugural address,

> The individual employee of the great railway system was as nothing. . . . the truth is that the general government . . . must add . . . [its] strength to the weakness of the individual or classes of individuals, especially if unorganized, so that they may become equal to the combination with they must deal . . . There must be regulation and control in the interest of the public welfare.

The Populists and twentieth-century liberals were proud of their republican tradition of government based on the consent of the people. Abraham Lincoln had described this system in the Gettysburg Address as "government of the people, by the people, and for the people." The Populists used the same logic: the "power of government" was the power "of the people." If elections were fairly run, an aroused public would elect government officials who would respond to the needs of the public. Since the Populists believed the public was aroused, they focused on demanding changes in the way elections were held so that the will of the aroused public would exert more influence on elected officials.

Populist farmers and less radical farmers, unionized workers (both liberals and socialists), and early twentieth-century middle-class liberals backed three reforms designed to make elections reflect *more directly* the views of the voting public: direct election of U.S. senators (instead of election by the state legislatures, where the Populists believed business influence was dominant); direct legislation—the initiative and the referendum—to give majorities a way of passing laws when corporate interests dominated a legislature; and the Australian ballot, which included the candidates of all parties. (The existing ballot system required a voter to request the ballot of the party for whose candidates they intended to vote. This lack of privacy meant that an average citizen's political leanings would be known to the economically powerful, who could threaten voters who were voting against their wishes.)

The populist movement's demands mark an important turning point in the history of liberalism in the United States. *Like earlier liberals, the Populists were concerned about liberty and freedom. But the Populists had concluded that the rise of the modern corporation created immense power that constituted an unprecedented threat to the liberty and economic welfare of the general public. The Populists believed that the only way to protect the public against the threats posed by big business was by expanding the power of government through a program of selective socialism and tax reform.*

During the first two decades of the twentieth century, many rural and urban residents began to call for various types of government regulation: special commissions to force big businesses to pay their fair share of taxes; public health regulations to prevent the spread of contagious diseases; mandatory medical examinations of school children; government inspection (state and national) of milk and meat products;

government requirements to label the contents of legal drugs; government approval of chemical additives that preserved and colored food; state regulation of electricity, natural gas, and telephone prices; and minimum wage and maximum hour laws for women. *Regulation* of the prices of some businesses and of the quality of the products sold to consumers *was often backed by the businesses* that depended on the services of the firms to be regulated (as in the case of railroad regulation). *But some businesses actually sought to be regulated by government.*

Businesses that favored some type of government regulation of their activities included the major meat-packing companies, who in 1906 asked for national government inspection to identify and condemn canned meat that was contaminated by excessive bacteria: otherwise, European governments would ban U.S. meat exports. (The meat packers fought proposals by consumer advocates in the United States to extend such inspection to meat sold at home. But having conceded that regulation was necessary to the sales of meat exports, they could not logically maintain that it should not be applied to meat sold to the American public.) The largest U.S. manufacturers of medicines backed the 1906 Pure Food and Drug Act because they hoped that strict labeling requirements would discredit the products sold by quack medicine producers. In many states, large electricity and telephone companies favored the creation of state public utility commissions that would regulate the rates of the companies because the regulatory legislation also ordered the public utility commissions to refuse to allow competition with the existing distribution systems of the electrical and telephone companies.*

---

*The justification for giving monopoly status to the electrical and telephone companies was that these technologies should be monopolies. Economists believed that electrical and telephone services were *natural monopolies* and that the consumer would get lower prices if no competition was allowed with these companies, since the high costs of putting up transmission lines would lead to price wars between competitors, with both losing money, one probably failing, and the survivor then raising rates dramatically to recover its losses.

Western farmers and businessmen, living in states with small populations and limited tax bases, lobbied Congress to finance irrigation projects. The 1902 Reclamation Act responded to these pressures by allocating money from federal land sales to fund these projects (see page 197). At about the same time, President Theodore Roosevelt, supported by some lumber companies and railroads, lobbied Congress to expand the authority of the Department of the Interior to conserve recreation areas and natural resources by creating national parks and by *regulating the rate at which natural resources* (lumber and metals) *were removed* from lands owned by the national government. (Remember, each time in the nineteenth century that the United States had acquired new territory by means of treaty or warfare, the national government owned this land. When the a territory became a state, the national government retained ownership of any national land that had not been sold to a buyer. A large amount of land, much of it rich in timber and mineral resources, fell into this category.)

Between 1900 and 1920, several hundred small and medium-sized city governments started municipal enterprises to replace private utilities that produced electricity, distributed natural gas, delivered water, and operated electric streetcar transportation. Enthusiasm for municipal ownership was generated by consumers' extreme dissatisfaction with the poor quality of the services provided by private companies and the belief that these firms overcharged the public. Consumer campaigns to have city governments take over privately-owned electric streetcar lines in big cities came close to success, but failed in New York and Cleveland. In New York City in 1905, William Randolph Hearst, the multimillionaire owner of a national chain of newspapers, ran a losing race for mayor on a platform stressing municipal ownership of the city's subways. In Chicago in 1907, the newly elected mayor favored municipal ownership of the city's trolley cars. To block government ownership, the trolley car companies agreed to let the city government's engineers supervise the repair of streetcars, and to give the city 55 percent of any profits that exceeded a five percent return on invested capital.

Significantly, most of the voters who backed *municipal* ownership were not willing to extend the principle of government ownership to manufacturing, mining, and interstate transportation companies. This shows the reluctance of the liberals of this era to back government enterprise that was not controlled by *local* government. While such liberals favored increasing the *regulatory* authority of the national government, they feared giving it the power to produce goods and services (outside of delivering the mail and providing for the defense of the nation). While many European nations, which lacked the strong liberal traditions of the United States, had government-owned railroads and mines, support for such an expansion of national government authority was lacking in the United States.

In the period between 1909 and 1917, all the nation's industrial states passed workers' compensation laws. These laws, which provided income-replacement benefits to workers injured on the job, represented the beginning of an important element of twentieth-century liberalism, the *welfare-state* principle. Using the power of state governments to provide for the *income security* of injured workers was seen as an action that gave injured workers and their families the help they needed to (a) avoid starving while they were recovering from injuries and could not earn money and (b) be freed of the mental anxiety of worrying about their loss of income while they were recovering from injuries. Workers' compensation payments helped the families of workers who were permanently disabled or who died in accidents avoid becoming dependent on charity. Because injured workers were legally entitled to these benefits, workers' compensation increased the freedom that workers and their families enjoyed, since compensation payments helped them avoid the psychological stigma attached to private charity and public relief.

Many middle-class liberals viewed the expansion of government powers to remove injustices and to make the economy operate more efficiently as a way to blunt the appeal of socialist ideology. Theodore Roosevelt warned that unless the national government was given effective power to regulate railroad rates, the demand for a government takeover of the railroads would increase. Willard Clark Fisher, a professor of economics at Wesleyan University, believed that workers living in a political democracy deserved *industrial* democracy, by which he meant the right to organize labor unions. He warned in 1905 that

> the only alternative [to unions] tending to produce industrial democracy is socialism. If labor is thwarted in its non-political organization, it is only reasonable that it should turn to political measures, which is simply and purely socialism.

Similarly, supporters of factory safety and sanitation legislation argued that if the work environment was healthier, workers would be less likely to want to join unions and vote for socialist candidates for public office. And advocates of workers' compensation—including many large and medium-sized businesses—warned that if the unfair commonlaw doctrines that protected negligent employers (see pages 79-80) were not replaced with assurances that most injured workers would receive compensation for medical expenses and lost income, workers would lose respect for the legal system of capitalism and would become more susceptible to the influence of socialist doctrine.

IV

During World War I, the national government assumed vast powers: it set delivery policy for the railroads, regulated the prices of coal and oil, *guaranteed* high prices to cotton farmers, assumed responsibility for ordering employers to engage in collective bargaining with workers so that workers would not strike and interrupt war production, and launched an unprecedented campaign to root out disloyal people. At the start of World War I, private sector entrepreneurs had refused to coordinate their business activities to give priority to the production of the guns, ammunition, ships, trucks, clothing, and food necessary to military victory. When the national government stepped in, most Americans accepted this expansion of power, because it seemed to be the only way to win the war; but most Americans did not want these expanded government powers continued when peace returned. By 1920, two years after the war had ended, Congress had allowed all these powers to lapse.

However, the fact that the national government had successfully mobilized the country to win World War I had a lasting impact on the thinking of most liberals and convinced many others that the assumption of new regulatory powers by the national government could be beneficial. When an economic crisis hit the nation, beginning with the stock market crash in 1929 and continuing until the nation had a 25 percent unemployment rate in 1933, an unprecedented number of impoverished people backed liberal policies that used the power of the national government to (a) aid the unemployed, (b) help those with diminished income save their homes and farms, (c) regulate the banking system, (d) regulate different industries to try to reduce overcompetition, (e) provide loans to farmers and manufacturers to help them finance more exports, thereby creating jobs in the United States, and (f) institute a permanent social safety net (welfare state) that prevented many people from falling below the subsistence level.

During the New Deal years (1933–1945), the national government's authority was greatly expanded. President Franklin D. Roosevelt, a relatively small group of Democrats, and several Republicans from western states were fully committed modern liberals, favoring a *wide variety of government programs* to revive the economy and advance the social security of the general public. Other elected Democrats *selectively* supported new liberal programs that would help *their constituents* with their particular economic difficulties. By 1945, because of the demands of many different groups within the nation, the national government and most state governments had added a variety of regulatory functions, had created programs to loan money to individuals (to buy homes) and businesses (for expansion), had initiated a variety of new government services, and had put in place programs that committed federal tax dollars to fund price supports for farmers, college education for veterans, and food stamps for the poor (which farmers favored since food stamps increased purchases of the products they produced).

During the 1930s, Congress created unprecedented, nationally-financed public works programs that provided jobs to millions of unemployed people. In 1935, Congress enacted the Social Security Act, a complex income-maintenance program that reflected the strength of the tradition of federalism in the United States. Only two parts of this law created programs exclusively administered by the national government: the old age pension system and benefits for the blind, disabled, and mentally ill. The law required each state to make employers fund an unemployment insurance system, but each state determined the level of benefits and rules for eligibility for its unemployed workers. Each state also had total freedom to decide on the level of income-maintenance benefits it would give to mothers with dependent children; the national government would simply reimburse the states for about half the cost of these benefits. All these programs are examples of the welfare state idea, which holds that government should use public jobs, food stamps, and cash benefits to establish a safety net that prevents people's standard of living from falling below the subsistence level. The 1938 Fair Labor Standards Act created a national minimum wage, which not only helped increase the welfare of some low-income workers, but also stimulated economic growth by putting more purchasing power in the hands of low-income consumers, who were likely to spend their higher wages immediately.

The rapid expansion of the powers of the national government during the years of the Depression reflected the popularity of the basic principle of modern liberalism—to enhance the independence and welfare of individuals or groups by turning to government to solve problems that individuals or groups could not solve by themselves. The 1936 Democratic party platform endorsed this principle. It pledged to use the power of government "to regulate commerce, protect public health and safety and *safeguard economic security* [emphasis added]." The platform also defended the 1935 National Labor Relations Act (NLRA) as a proper use of government power to enable powerless individual workers to exercise their "*right* to collective bargaining and self organization free from the interference of employers [emphasis added]." Without such government protection, workers did not stand much chance of success in confrontations with large, powerful corporate employers.*

President Franklin D. Roosevelt proudly embraced the term "liberal." In his 1936 campaign kick-off speech, Roosevelt argued that in 1933 Americans had been suffering terribly, and that there had been so many unjust economic practices in the United States that the nation had faced a "crisis made to order for all those who would overthrow our form of government." Roosevelt believed that economic reform was the only way to avoid revolution:

> We were against revolution. Therefore, we waged war against those conditions which make revolutions—against the inequalities and resentments which breed them . . . Americans were made to realize that wrongs could be set right within their [existing economic and political] institutions. We proved that democracy can work . . .

But some Americans were troubled by the sum total of New Deal reforms. They feared that increasing demands for new government programs would lead to full-fledged socialism, in which the government took over the ownership and management of all productive resources. Yet in the United States there were few people who favored full-blown socialism. Even the strongest liberals favored only a *few* types of government enterprise: providing public flood control and electric power projects where

---

*The NLRA protected the civil liberties of workers by making it a violation of federal law for any employer to discriminate against employees because they engaged in union activities. If found in violation of the NLRA, employers can be ordered to reinstate (with backpay) those employees fired, and "make whole" those who had been demoted or otherwise discriminated against.

private investors were unwilling to risk their funds; taking over bankrupt passenger railroads; or operating a national health insurance system on a nonprofit basis. Liberals typically argued that government regulation and cash grants to businesses, students, the disabled, and the poor, were the best way to eliminate the economic injustices and insecurities *that would push people to turn to socialism to solve their problems.*

On January 6, 1941, with World War II underway, President Roosevelt delivered his annual address to Congress. He described four freedoms that he thought the people of the world needed: freedom of speech and expression, freedom of religion, freedom from fear of war, and

> freedom from want—which, translated into world terms, means economic understandings which will secure to every nation a healthy peacetime life for its inhabitants . . .

This speech shows that modern liberals have not abandoned the concerns of past liberals about preserving *vital civil liberties*. But modern liberals insist that economic freedom and security can only be achieved by means of regulation to protect the consumer, cash subsidies to encourage essential industries and scientific research, some kind of regulation of the overall economy, and government-mandated income-maintenance programs.

The critics of modern liberalism, who were to be found in both major political parties, feared that government power would not stop expanding in the post-World War II years. Almost all southern senators and representatives opposed new liberal programs in the years after World War II, because they feared that any program that increased the authority of the national government would encourage the use of that power to end racial discrimination in the South. Yet the demand for government aid for particular groups within the nation was so great that even Senator Robert E. Taft, Jr. (known as "Mr. Republican" to his contemporaries), who after 1945 had opposed every new liberal program proposal, concluded in 1948 that the national government should fund public housing construction. (Public housing would be administered by city and state governments, with the national government providing funds to cover the difference between the rents charged to tenants and the cost of operating the housing and paying off the loans that had been taken out to finance the construction of the housing.) Taft knew that there was a huge shortage of low-cost housing in the nation, and that private sector building contractors were *not building housing that could be afforded by low-income workers because the builders could not make a profit on it*. Thus Taft backed a liberal program, using the taxing power of the national government to provide *decent, affordable* low-income housing whose construction was beyond the financial capabilities of state and local governments and was not being undertaken by capitalist entrepreneurs.

In the years after World War II, many militant liberals, who had previously focused their reform efforts on economic inequalities, also began to concern themselves with the rights of suppressed social castes (especially people of color). During the 1950s, African Americans exercised (despite much violent opposition from whites) their rights of freedom of speech and assembly to protest racial discrimination. The modern civil rights movement, led by people of color, but joined by many middle-class whites and many white labor union activists, used public, nonviolent demonstrations, which sometimes violated local laws against parading without a permit, to pressure local economic elites and government authorities to end racial discrimination. The civil rights movement included Hispanic Americans living in the East, the Midwest, the Southwest, and California. Ultimately, it developed enough moral influence and political clout to convince Congress to pass the Civil Rights Act (1964) and the Voting Rights Act (1965). The inclusion of women in the Civil Rights Act of 1964, and the emergence in 1966 and thereafter of an active women's movement, created new pressures to give women equal opportunity to men. Administered by national government officials in the Department of Justice, and supported by the courts, civil rights laws pressured local government to allow all people of color to vote (a goal achieved by 1975) and influenced many employers (including governments at all levels) to end racial and gender discrimination in hiring and promotion. The expansion of the civil rights of minorities and women was consistent with the historic goal of liberalism: to expand the liberties of the individual.

During the 1960s, the Vietnam War divided many liberals and liberal organizations (especially labor unions). The rise of black nationalism led to bitter divisions between white liberals who had supported the civil rights movement and African-American activists. The increasing appeal of Islam to many African-American liberal activists stimulated a rise in anti-Semitism, because followers of Islam were critical of Israel's policies toward its Islamic neighbors. Jewish liberals who strongly supported Israel castigated African Americans who voiced anti-Israel, anti-Jewish views. By the 1970s, the Democratic party, which had been the home of most activist liberals, was greatly weakened by these developments and by the backlash of southern whites and many white union members against Democrats who supported civil rights legislation.

However, while many Americans became hostile to liberalism directed at removing caste-based inequalities, they remained convinced that government action was necessary to solve particular economic problems they encountered. In 1995, there was hardly an elected official who did not believe that government power should not be used to promote the economic well-being and advance the freedom and liberties of *some* groups or the entire nation. For example, many Americans want to have the government regulate abortion, claiming that it violates the rights of the unborn. Many opponents of government-insured loans to college students favor continuing to supplement the income of farmers by providing cash payments to farmers when the prices of crops grown fall below specified levels. Congressional proponents of cuts in income-maintenance programs for the poor nevertheless favor the maintenance of a huge standing army, whose size would have terrified the politicians of Jefferson's age, since they feared that a large standing army might seize control of the government. Polls show that most Americans favor government regulations that reduce water and air pollution. The speaker of the House of Representatives in 1995 was opposed to using government power to regulate (and reduce) the pollution of the environment by private enterprises and by government military installations. But he recognized the national government's obligation to create the conditions that lead to economic growth, specifically by having the Federal Reserve Board regulate the nation's money supply.

Compared to Americans of the past two centuries, most twentieth-century Americans, and especially post-New Deal Americans, have increasingly relied on government to achieve liberal ends. But this does not mean that all Americans agree on either the particular liberal ends that should be enhanced by government programs or the particular programs and groups of citizens that should benefit from government interventions. There is tremendous *competition* among different groups in our society that want to benefit from government action.

Viewed historically, and looking underneath the anti-government rhetoric increasingly used by most politicians, the current political debate about the role of government in the United States has become a debate about the *kind of liberalism* people want. People debate the kinds of government programs that are desirable, the types of freedoms and liberties which should receive protection from government interference, and the overall size of government needed to encourage the preservation of freedoms and liberties. In a democracy, the government is under strong pressure to respond to the needs of different blocs within the voting public. While public opinion polls show that most Americans worry about the extent of national and state government power, a reflection of an old human fear of concentrated authority, the polls also show that *virtually each individual, group, or subgroup of Americans strongly endorses specific government programs that give those individuals or groups assistance in coping with the problems that are of concern to them.*

In our twentieth-century democratic republic, it seems that citizens have a love-hate relationship with their government. They want government to be much more active than did most eighteenth- and nineteenth-century Americans. But like the citizens of the past, people today are uncomfortable with their reliance on government power and are fearful that it can be abused in ways that limit the fundamental liberties that they hold dear. *There is no way out of the paradox.* If people believe that they *have to* rely on governmental institutions for protection, they always will run the risk that the power that protects can also turn against the individual or the group. However, in a *democracy*, blocs of voters have a peaceful way to defend themselves against government abuses of civil liberties or to eliminate government expenditures that large numbers of voters do not favor. Voters can use the ballot to remove elected officials from office when they support policies the voters dislike. This is a right that is still not enjoyed by the majority of the people in the world.